# Recovery
# Run

Writing this book was a tough call, not just for me but for a ton of people because none of this was a solo venture. It covered some of the most painful periods of my life and that spilled into my daily existence because I was reliving it as I was writing it.

I received constant affirmation from the awesome running community I am proud to be a part of especially Running the World, our amazing Facebook community. Their love, support and lunacy have been incredible. The group is more than a running club to us, it is our family complete with rebellious kids and inappropriate uncles (Chris P Rice). We love you all.

I also want to thank Leanne Davies and Run Mummy Run who offered endless support and as I bored them to death with tales of gastro intestinal horrors and the trials of finding co-ordinating running socks. An unstoppably supportive group of women, they are a force to be reckoned with and I love being a part of their tribe. Macmillan Cancer Support who have had such a radical and positive effect on my life these past years. I owe you my sanity (what's left of it). Mark Anderson who freely gave his time and expertise organising my jumble of Facebook posts and rambling blogs into something that was vaguely readable whilst ignoring (at my behest) my hideous grammar and punctuation. Joni Thrush for being my injury sounding board and voice of reason.

Finally and predictably I need to thank Marc and Cleo. I could attempt to describe what they mean to me but I think the book does it better. During writing this book they made all the right listening sounds, laughed in the right places and told me where the shit bits were. They are the harshest of critics and most enthusiastic of cheerleaders. In short, they are the story of my life, my greatest achievement, my swansong.

Xxx


P.S. Apologies to Chris Martin and Coldplay, I'm sure you're all very lovely people.

# In case you were wondering…

# Recovery Run
## Nicky Lopez

Nearly seven years ago I was diagnosed with cancer, more specifically Non-Hodgkin's Lymphoma. It wasn't a colossal surprise, I'd been unwell for a while and lost masses of weight, misdiagnosed with swine flu in early July by mid-August it was clear there was a serious problem. I didn't actually know what Non-Hodgkin's Lymphoma was; nobody mentioned the word cancer on my diagnosis so I thought I'd had a lucky dodge. It was when the words prognosis and chemotherapy were mentioned that reality began to bite, and it took a real chunk. With an initially optimistic outlook and the prospect of just six months chemo I was hopeful by the following summer I'd be in the clear. By the following year I was unresponsive to treatment with an aggressively spreading cancer and rapidly running out of options, my prognosis changed from positive to bleak and with that my universe tilted and changed forever. That was then.

I'm here and standing on the brink of my first six months cancer free. After over six years of increasingly gruelling and progressively experimental chemotherapies, radiotherapy, antibody treatment and lots of surgery, cancer has left the building. Or if not, it's in a state of hibernation and one that I hope will last a long time. And yes, I'm a changed person. Physically I look a few years older than I should, my signature bald head has been replaced with a middle aged frump of a mop, I look like a mid-nineties David Hasselhoff tribute act only with smaller tits and no tan. I'm all but deaf in my left ear and I have only around 20% vision in my right eye after a couple of rogue tumours at the base of my brain several years ago.

And despite what people may think I'm a little more fragile than I once was, I feel a little more deeply, cry a little more readily, stress a little more easily. That which doesn't kill you may make you stronger in parts but it also makes you graphically aware of your own mortality and it also makes you feel a bit knackered too.

But yeah, there have been more positive changes, cancer was as much my saviour as it was my nemesis. It handed me back my life after teaching me how to live it to the full, not everyone gets that opportunity and I'm grateful for it. Anyone who has been close to death and has had to climb back out on the other side will tell you that the world looks a lot different afterwards, colours are a little sharper, everything feels more...sort of...I was trying to think of a word for it but that's the best way to explain it, everything feels more, I feel more, I feel everything more.

Life has changed in a way that my head hasn't learnt to make sense of yet so it's a learning story, assimilating old things in new ways. Running has helped me with this, I began to run seven years ago today, a few short months prior to my diagnosis. It was something I had forgotten about when I was writing this book, I'd probably washed it from my memory in the ludicrous amounts of wine and vodka we'd gunned down immediately afterwards.

When I say I began running, what I should say is that this was the first time in my adult life it had become a necessity to own a pair of trainers. It was hardly a run. My friend and then work colleague Naomi and I had rather inexplicably decided to do a duathlon that the school we worked in had organised. Inexplicable because the pair of us had no interest or experience in fitness but rather had the well-earned reputation of being hard drinking party girls. Both single mums at the time (bizarrely we both ended up with two unconnected Geordies who lived within minutes of each other) our days were spent lunching at the pub then knocking back horrific quantities of booze at the weekend. I'd come into education after a long stint working as a flight attendant and the party lifestyle was pretty ingrained. We didn't give a shit about being healthy or fit, in our mid-thirties why would we? We were practically immortal.

Not wanting to do things the conventional way we decided to do the run three legged and the bike ride on a tandem. It was hilarious; pant wettingly funny from start to finish. We staggered, giggled and gooned our way around the course. To be fair Naomi was in better shape than me, I sat on the easier, rear seat of the bike and waved regally to the hysterical kids while Naomi tried to haul our considerable arses round the school playing fields. She swore at me quite a lot that day. When we ran we would stop at frequent intervals to piss ourselves laughing but the truth is that I couldn't run 200m without stopping. I was a physical wreck and in August that year I would realise that something needed to change if I was to survive.
So I became a runner.

And running has taught me to survive, it has taught me so much about strength; not just physical power but about my own capacity for mental fortitude. Through running and now writing about running I am learning to make sense of the chaos that I have been through. We've been through a lot, me and this body, we've done three London Marathons, five Great North Runs and a whole lot of other escapades amidst a shitload of treatment and an offensive amount of painkillers. It's a long and complicated journey, an unfamiliar route that I haven't yet learnt how to navigate. Along the way I found the greatest co-pilot and purser though and I'm thinking that the skies look bright and the conditions are clearing as we speak.

Cabin crew, prepare for take-off.

# 1

# A Sloth, A Storm and A Superhero

**Friday 1st January 2016**

New Year.

Same me.

Fine.

Keep it up.

That was my resolution this morning when I saw the bazillion January 1st 'New Me!' Facebook posts and adverts about planned body makeovers and transformations.

To be honest I was bloody knackered at the time and in the throes of a massive cheese hangover. Marc and I had laughed as I'd said it, slugging down coffee and thanking the universe today was a rest day. New Year's Eve had been a sofa and dairy produce fest. I know what you're thinking, these crazy bastards know how to party. In our defence it had been quite a year, one which my slightly vodka and chemo addled mind will trundle back over in due course. This morning was all about relaxing and eating. A long run yesterday to exorcise the ghosts of a bitch of a run two days before had left me feeling pleasantly knackered and cheerfully disposed to refuel in an irresponsible manner.

We'd wanted to finish our running year on a high and a beautiful sunny New Year's Eve morning and ten comfortably (as comfortable as various levels of ass pain along with sweating like a bitch and a constant desire to stop for an hour and a half can ever be) chatty miles had done the job to a turn. So it was with a fair bit of ironic self-satisfaction I sat watching the gym membership commercials whilst simultaneously smashing as many pâté based products into my face as I could handle without chundering. It did bring back to me though a question that has run through my head for ages. Why is physical activity so tied up with self-loathing?

I had a long internal discussion last year on this subject (internal because I seriously doubt anyone else could follow my interminable line of drivel), about why the coach in our head is such a bastard and of what benefit that truly is. I know for some people the tough talk really works and I can totally get that, we all need an arse kicking at times but calling myself out mid run was starting to piss me off. I was a bitch to myself and I'm not entirely sure I deserved it. I'm not reinventing the wheel here, it's a commonly held truth that approaching an activity with joy and positivity is going to reap a whole better outcome than shouting the shit out of yourself.

So there I sat, full of liquid meat and grump getting cheesed off seeing girls making posts about their old self and how they were going to beat her because they knew her weaknesses, how they were going to pound the streets shouting litanies of self-abuse into their own ears while they sweated, hurt and made their fat cry. It sounded flipping horrendous and not the least bit likely to entice me away from a cake.

And it's not just the girls, there was post after post of guys talking themselves down about their lazy, fat selves and how they were going to turn their weak, useless, emasculating bodies into mountains of glistening muscle via a series of crash diets and relentless torture. And I wondered what I've wondered so often. How about enjoying movement just for the sake of it? Is that even a thing? Isn't that how it's meant to work? By all means smash your PBs but you don't need to smash your own spirit in the process. Get ripped but don't tear yourself to shreds getting there.

So here it is, I'm going to try a different way, a kinder way. To the voice in my ear that says I'm weak and lazy I'm going to dare myself to say "fuck you". Don't give me a hard time, show me a good time and I might just get somewhere.

After I've had some more of this delicious cheese…

**Saturday 2nd January 2016**

"Crikey you've come a long way!"

That's what the bloke said to us as we passed him for a second time along the beach this morning.

And we have.

I doubt he knows that six years ago before I even owned a pair of running shoes, I was told I had cancer. That at some point over those six years I'd be told that my treatment wasn't working and that it should stop. He wouldn't realise that I not only did I buy the running

8

shoes but also that I ran a 5k in them. Then a 10k. Then a half marathon. Then a marathon. Then some more. But more importantly he didn't realise that I would meet the man now running beside me and how he would change my outlook on life and running forever. That he would teach me how to love the run. But more on that later...

We headed out today still blurry headed with cheese and alcohol. We'd checked the weather studiously, some would say obsessively. It's become an insane habit we both share, I'd say the Met Office app gets the vast proportion of its hits from us two. I'd like to think it was based on judging the best route but in reality it's all about the swag, we're the vainest pair of arseholes in existence. It's probably one of our most real crisis from day to day. What the hell will we wear? In a frenzy of early day's enthusiasm we bought it all, now have a running wardrobe that would clothe a moderately sized nation. In short, Nike own our asses. So you can imagine how chuffed we were to see a cool, wind and precipitation free two hour window. I chose a bright turquoise ensemble which I reckon could be clearly seen from the international space station. Funny from a woman who generally dresses in a palette that consists of black, navy and grey that I should feel the need to be at my most visible when I am sweating bullets, gasping for breath and often lurching wildly at lampposts.

Off we went and from the outset Marc wasn't feeling it. As we tend to run a lot together these days we're very tuned in to how the other is doing simply from the sound of their breath or the tilt of their body. It's a weird kind of closeness that I don't think everyone would understand, I knew before he said it that he was finding it tough. It's not an easy thing to see, to watch the person you love struggle both mentally and physically and there's fuck all you can do about it because the reason it happens is as indeterminable as it is to solve. It's just a runner's thing. I know this because Marc has had to do it with me on countless occasions, in fact just last week I had the seven miler from hell which took me through eighteen different levels of self-loathing and despair.

But today it was his turn and the worst thing is that like most things he does it so much better than I do. Whilst I moan, cough, cry and curse he just lowers his head a little and goes a bit quiet. He pushes on in a solid, stoic manner probably contemplating my violent murder as I jabber inanely in an attempt to entertain or distract. Despite my suggestions to shorten the distance, to slow the pace he just keeps on keeping on. And I've learnt a lot from him about this. In the past six years he's had his share of shit. He had to deal with the sudden death of his beloved mum Audrey to whom he was a full time carer. She was both a stroke and Multiple Sclerosis patient and so I think he in turn had learnt how to deal with pain and suffering with grace and acceptance. He turned his life around by taking an NHS care assistant job and working hard to move onto Emergency Services which also involved a move from his home town in the North East down to us here in the North West. And amidst that he met and fell in love with a girl with a pretty bleak prognosis. And in return she fell in love with him too.

So on we ran, it was warmer and sunnier than we'd expected (damn you and your lies you Met Office bastards) and the heat was adding miles into our legs. At the five mile turning point I was aware we were heading straight into the sun without a breath of wind. Oh bollocks, this did not bode well. We were however saved...sort of. We ran back through Hightown towards the coastal path that would lead us back home and as we did clouds began to gather and the wind began to rise. Now historically I bloody hate the wind, it gives me concrete legs, glue feet and an inability to breathe without sounding like Mutley from Wacky Races but today I was so grateful for it.

But Christ, it was cold, it was ass shittingly freezing. My hands seized up and my bald head tangibly shrunk even more than its already freakishly small size (pinhead and proud). But I knew it wouldn't just soothe Marc, it would also ignite the fighter in him, the indomitable Geordie spirit. And it did. This man doesn't feel the cold, like most Geordies he's bizarrely impervious to it and sees coats as some kind of insult to his masculinity. His already substantial mental toughness became pure grit and he steeled himself through the remaining miles even stopping for a lark about and photos at mile seven.

I guess running has taught us both as much about life as life has taught about running. Play the long game, accept there'll be a little pain along the way and never, never, ever give up. You'd be surprised how far it can take you.

## 3rd January 2016

Rest day today and it's been a bit of an arse of a day.

It's a very real truth that the days you can't run are definitely the days you need it most. Cleo, our hilariously sarcastic and generally amazing 14 year old has had a rough old time of it lately. I can tell you that nothing in the world stresses me more. Seeing that I have a minor heart condition and the strain of the day has left me with an aching jaw there was no way I could risk a run. We're now cuddled on the sofa, the three of us, having cried, laughed and put the world to rights. It's good to kick off the trainers, regroup and reflect. Outside the rain is pounding the pavements in our absence and the wind is doing its best to rattle us. It won't win, it never does. We learnt this on a recent run and these were my ramblings at the time…

## 12th November 2015, Liverpool

I like to think of every run as a learning experience, chance to grow, an opportunity to develop both as a runner and as a human being. With that in mind I'd like to share with you a couple of things Marc and I learnt during our 8 mile run this evening...

1. When trying to exorcise the demons of a previously horrific run it's probably best not attempting to do so in the arse end of a hurricane on an exposed beach in the dark.

2. A massive tailwind on the way out is never a good thing.

3. Horizontal rain in 60mph gusts hurts…badly.

4. Running towards a military firing range checkpoint in the dark wearing a Captain America t shirt, tights and a very bright head torch can be misread as a challenge to our nation's security.

5. That said, when same guy in Captain America t shirt takes the brunt of the storm full force in the face to shelter you, you know you're onto a good thing.

6. Storms have names. If you'd have been behind us tonight you'd have been mistaken in believing this one was called 'For Fuck's Sake' or 'You Absolute Bastard'.

7. Black caps can be difficult to chase after on a dark coastal path when you're fighting to stay upright and said cap is moving four times your speed in the opposite direction.

8. Headlamps are awesome.

9. Dads are awesome. Especially ones that pick you up in a warm car from a very cold beach.

10. Storm Abigail might be a badass but she's no match for the collective idiocy of Team Dopez.

All in all a hilariously bonkers experience which was epic, incredibly tough and immense fun.

## Monday 4th January 2016

Marc went back to work today and so it was a solo run for me. After weeks of post work and holiday runs together I felt strangely apprehensive about going by myself. But the truth is that as much as we love running together we equally savour running alone. There's something alluring about a solo run, the freedom of going where you want for as far as you choose and stopping when you like. And there's also the whole 'me time' thing; those still, meditative moments when your thoughts are quietened and you just 'be'. The idea of such mindful, soul nourishing runs have always appealed to me. In a life which is often noisy and chaotic I treasure the steady order of a run alone where I'm responsible for nothing or no one but myself.

It was a dull January morning; Cleo was cocooned in bed desperately clinging to the final few days of post-Christmas slobbery amidst the spectre of the impending return to school. I like to spend as much time as I can with her during holidays, our busy lives don't always allow for undisturbed mum attention. I'm aware the days of her enjoying it are dwindling as Build a Bears are replaced with Mac Cosmetics and ribbons and tutus make way for an ever increasingly terrifying range of what appears to be fetish wear and piercings. So it made sense to hit the road while she was still hitting the sack. After two clothes changes (my dad ever at loggerheads with the Met Office had me convinced the sun was 'cracking the flags' outside) I trotted off towards the beach.

Marc says he can usually tell within the first few hundred metres what sort of run it will be. For me it takes a couple of miles, I'm a mistrusting commitment phobe when it comes to running. Despite feeling great and finding a comfortable, steady pace almost straight away I still harboured portents of doom. I don't know why but I get nervous before every single run, I convince myself that every other run for the previous six years has been a fluke, a lucky break and today is the day that I'll be found out. Maybe today is the day I'll discover I'm not really a proper runner.

Today was not that day.

I started out towards the beach enjoying the coolness of the air and the chance to whack on my bizarre running playlist. This afforded me the rare opportunity to scream lyrics from artists as diverse as NWA and Public Enemy to S Club 7 and Chesney Hawkes into the faces of people I have never met whilst grinning maniacally and sweating profusely. Indeed, I imagine the workmen who were treated to my screamo version of Let It Go were enthralled by my vocal talent as much as my athletic prowess.

Turning onto the beach I'd already decided, this was going to be a peach of a run. And it was. It was one of those life affirming, thank the universe, who gives a crap about my mahoosive camel toe types of run. I laughed, I sang, I even outstretched my arms and gave thanks at one point. Yes, I had to run around a roundabout twice to make up some distance to the hilarity of the locals. Yes my mother rang mid-way asking me something vitally important about a hinge and a taekwondo class and yes I slid about 100 yards on a rogue dog turd flailing my arms like a sweaty, Lycra clad windmill but who cares? I felt brilliant.

I came home and collapsed onto the sofa with chocolate cake and coffee knowing that not all runs are like this but some runs are and that's just fine by me. I was even more chuffed when Marc got in from his own solo run having had a great one too.

I guess sometimes it's important to go against your own judgement and take a little leap of faith accepting that it may be that you can actually do it, it is actually going to be OK.

In running we trust.

## Tuesday 5th January 2016

A so called rest day today. What it actually comprised of was Cleo and I rampaging through a 'Designer Outlet Village' swearing at price tags and eating deep fried things covered in sugar. I did consider getting a run in at the end of it all as I had bought some swaggy new shorts but it is January and I am not insane. Besides, it wasn't a run day and the fact that I'd even considered running was enough.

It was a far cry from the days when I would do anything to avoid a run, in fact it felt like a chore at best and oftentimes a punishment. The simple fact was, I just didn't enjoy it. I would hear the legends of 'runner's high' and tales of awesome adventures involving happy, glowing faces and it was a stark contrast to my tough, sometimes painful, sweaty trials. For sure I revelled in the post run self-righteous smug fest and the feeling of having some control over my body but the actual process of running, the physical act felt uncomfortable and bastard hard. As a languages teacher I have discovered that it isn't enough to teach someone a subject, you have to teach them to love it and that's the bugger. How do you get a person to enjoy something that is difficult, repetitive and sometimes a bit boring? It's kind of the same with running, anyone can show you how to do it, how to master the correct posture, teach you about cadence and breathing and all sorts of other mechanics. But how do you teach someone to enjoy something that particularly at the start can be so tough, so demanding and frequently defeating? Marc has been the most awesome coach in teaching me the impossible, how to love the run.

Often when I'm running I have some pretty big thoughts (I'm going to save the ones about giant magnets for air travel and rubberised safety stairs for another time) and I tend to record them when I get in, not so much for posterity but more as a kind of sadistic ammunition with which to bore people to death. I read a lot of posts about how to get through long runs, tough runs, up hills etc. and most often it comes down to the mental game, the motivation, the conversation that we have with ourselves that can make or break a run. Now in the past few months I've become a very different runner, I'm faster (from around 10.30 minute miles to 8.30-45) more efficient, more positive and altogether happier. Whereas once I used to dread inclines, these days I take on hills, hell I actively seek them out. My average run has gone from 5 miles to 8 miles and now 10 and instead of just enduring them, I enjoy them. Lately I look forward to running as often as I can.
So what changed?

Well OK, I lost a little weight which has probably contributed to my pace. But what else? It occurred to me that the only other thing that has changed is my attitude. Many times when I've been running with Marc in the past he's commented on how upsetting it is when I'm hard on myself. I apologised for taking walk breaks or slowing down, cried during races when I found it tough going and generally made the whole experience a negative one for both of us. I mean who wants to see their loved one in floods of tears or gritting their teeth? But after three years of running together his coaching and patience has finally paid off and he has taught me the most elusive of things, to enjoy the run. How did he do this?

Simple, by being nice.

So often we confuse hard talk with motivation and the voice in our head is a harsh one with little mercy. The mantras that I've used in the past have been at best tough and at worst bordering on self-abuse. I have called myself a little bitch, said that I have to defeat myself and shouted at myself. I've been my own biggest critic for way too long. Sound familiar? Whilst I'm all for pushing limits and testing boundaries I'm not completely convinced that the whole 'unless you puke, faint or die' thing is for me. It doesn't sound like much fun and if it's not fun then why the hell am I going to do it again?

These days the voice in my head is an altogether nicer one, a kinder one. It reminds me of how far I've come and how much further I can go. When I slow down or take a walk break it tells me that I don't need to apologise, it tells me to say something positive like 'I'm finding it tough going but I'm determined to get there' or 'this is the best way for me to enjoy this run and that's the most important thing'. When I'm running fast and going well it applauds me and tells me to remember this and be proud. When I see a hill approaching I smile and I take all the time I need because I can do hills in my own time, in my own way. And the funny thing is? I don't stop as much, I don't slow down and hills are now fun (this is a lie but you see what I'm getting at).It's basic psychology I guess, we do it with our kids. If we make things fun for them then they learn, they have enthusiasm, if we treat it as a chore then they won't want to do it. The same applies to me with running, I don't want to hear a sergeant major screeching in my ear, that's not how I chill out and running is my chill time. I want a goddamn cheerleader!

15

So next time you go for a run and you're finding it tough, have a word with yourself, but make it a kind word. If you want to stop then stop, it's OK. If you need to walk a little then do it, it's OK. When you see a hill then have a go at it, but at your own pace. If you want to walk a bit then that's fine but you make damn sure you run down the other side because you earned it, even if you have to stop at the bottom! I know it's not for everyone, some people thrive on the tough talk, but for me I'm liking the new voice in my head.

She seems to think I can do anything.

**Wednesday 6th January 2016 Epiphany**
Knowing that the weather was going to be a bit poo tomorrow I was determined to get a last of the holidays run in today. I'm back into the workshop tomorrow and school on Friday. I've absolutely loved the freedom of daytime running and it's turned into a happy routine. I have a leisurely breakfast of sourdough toast with peanut butter and a mug of Redbush tea along with my meds. I then assess the weather with my usual dose of Met Office app mistrust (although I mistrust the doorstep test even more), get dressed and head off.

Today I was mindful that this would be the last run of its kind for a while so I wanted to really relish it. The gods were not only on my side but I'm pretty convinced they are also runners. The weather was bloody awesome. A squeaky clean sky with a crisp, bright sun, there was a suggestion of a cool breeze that would temper the effort of a brisk ten miles. As I reached the beach I was in full West End mode belting out random song lyrics and handing out Hollywood grins, Christ knows what I must have looked like. The truth is I don't really know most of the lyrics and tend to just guess at them so I have no idea what I'm really saying. I caught myself today screeching 'Let it go and I'll rise like a bread that's done' which I suspect may not be the correct words. A little later I caught myself saying 'She's just a girl and she's on fire, living a catastrophe but she knows she can fry her feet' which whilst lyrically inaccurate was yet ironically true.

Anyway, I was fantasising what my days would be like if I didn't have to go to work. The fantasy was borne out of a wonderful exercise/relaxation day that Marc and I had spent together when I finished chemo. I was imagining that I would have long, joyful runs in the morning followed by a soothing swim and hydrotherapy session. After that I would have a light lunch and then return to an intense gym workout and another jacuzzi finishing with a final steam session. I would prepare a delicious healthy meal and then retire before midnight ready for another day of the same joyful routine. Then I reflected on the reality which would involve enormous weight gain, a deep tan, a lifetime of hangovers and probable blocked arteries.

Because the truth is that working, like exercise keeps me on the straight and narrow. Because my 'me time' is so rare it's also so treasured. Because I work hard it resolves me to play hard, to keep myself healthy, to eat right and to be the best version of myself I can be. Left to my own devices I would eat too much and sleep too little, I would exercise less and indulge more and in doing so I would lose so much. The fact that I fight and struggle so hard to fit my runs in makes me savour every second of them. In short, work makes me love my life just that little bit more.

So as I came to the end of my awesome, happy, hard, sunny, glorious ten miles today I didn't feel resentful or sorrowful leaving the sunny road behind but rather hopeful and resolved to enjoy every second of the one that lies outstretched before me.

Here's to making it count.

# 2
# Trainers, Tights and Trumps

**Thursday 7th January 2016**

As predicted the weather sucks today, it sucks in a way that no matter what was depending on it short of human life I would not go for a run. In fact even then it would still effect a huge moral conundrum. It's cold, it's mega windy and it's raining. It's the kind of rain that hurts a little bit and the gusty type of wind that stops you in your tracks every few minutes. I think nature likes to knock runners down a peg or two sometimes and remind them that even though they are indeed a vastly superior race oozing liquid awesome from every overworked pore that they are also innately and fallibly human. Nature is a badass bitch who lifts heavy and she wants you to know it sometimes.

It was this that got me to thinking about the sartorial mine field that is running kit. Yeah I know it's been done to death, the dos and don'ts and the common rookie errors but I tell you I still make them all the time. The reason is this...I'm a vain assed showboater. I care enormously about how I look when I run, which seems to be a total faux pas in the running world. For some hideously inexplicable reason there is an attitude amongst some runners (and I emphasise the word some because I'm guessing the vast majority couldn't give a shit) that how you look is directly related to how much effort you put in. Theories such as if you still have make-up on your face after a run you haven't tried hard enough are bandied about along with the more terrifying notion that you actually shouldn't wear make-up at all to run in. It seems that serious runners should eschew all notions of vanity and devote themselves and their appearance solely to the run.

You may have heard the phrase 'all the gear and no idea' insinuating that if you're utilising gadgets (albeit highly sophisticated ones that have been painstakingly designed to improve the experience) then you're don't really know how to run properly.

What a crock of bollocks.

Most running gear (with the possible exception of my Stella McCartney parachute jacket) for runners is highly technical and there to ameliorate the process of running. From smooth anti chafing materials through to ergonomically designed phone holders. And yes, you can take your bloody phone with you and still call yourself a runner, not everyone is disposed to disappear incommunicado for several hours a day. It's fine, take the call, you're still a runner.

I also take issue with the increasingly judgmental section of runners who feel that taking a photo, or God forbid a selfie, mid run is a hanging offence that assigns you for life to the ranks of the rookies, the amateurs. I've been running for six years and throughout it all I have assiduously recorded my experiences via photography. I've taken photos of incredible sunsets, wildlife I would never have witnessed had I not been running and yes, hundreds of selfies of me and Marc. The thing is that I have always been acutely aware of memory making. I guess having a six year reminder of the fragility of your own mortality makes a person want to take photos, want to record moments and to capture memories. One day when I can't run I'll look at these shots with wistful joy and recall the happiest days of my life. When we're gone Cleo will show them to her children and hopefully she'll feel warmly proud of the two idiots gooning and goofing and she will see our smiling faces and know what fullness and wonder we had in our lives. She will see us as we want to be seen, how we would like to be remembered, at our most alive and having awesome fun. That's a pretty good legacy I reckon. And besides, it breaks up the run and gives us pause to lark about, which is always good.

As far as being a rookie is concerned I will say this with conviction. No matter how long you've been running at some point you're going to have runs that make you feel like you're at square one. There will be days when a mile feels like a mountain and your legs will feel like they belong to a different body. This is one of the beautiful ironies of running, we're all rookies and every run teaches you something different. The greatest runners embrace this ongoing education of their feet and are open to continual growth. They reach high and stay humble.

I digress (I do this) as I was previously banging on about running gear. I was thinking yesterday about how the right gear can make or break a run, especially in bad weather. I had been wearing my current favourite ensemble, a pink and grey hyperwarm top and tights and I was congratulating myself how I'd pitched it just right for the weather which is a rarity for me. I tend to get super-hot after about a mile and so despite hating being cold I usually have to wear a little less than the weather would suggest I should to accommodate this.

Yesterday everything just felt comfy and right and I love it when that happens. My tights didn't dig into my waist giving me a muffin top and my top was just the right weight so as to not have me cursing the cool or sweating like a nun at a Chippendales gig. I wear a Buff mostly which is a seamless tube of material you can utilise in multiple mystical ways ranging from the practical to the frankly ridiculous. It's a great piece of kit and I highly recommend it. I wear mine generally as a hat and then pull it over my head as a loose cowl as I inevitably get too hot. At times I've used it as a headband to keep errant earphones in, a wristband to soak up sweat, even as a protective buffer when my Camelbak rubbed my neck on a long run. In truth though I almost always end up using it as a snot rag to stem the mucousy tide of my ever dripping nose. Yes, I'm a very hot chick. I should also note that the word buff in Liverpool (which I am assured also applies in most other parts of the country) means naked. You can imagine that I have had to give some further explanation when I have mentioned to people how much I enjoy running in the Buff.

I felt great in my outfit but it wasn't just the easy practicality of it that made me feel good, I looked good in it too. I think there's a great deal to be said for feeling that you look attractive when you're running. I'm totally all for women (and men) who focus entirely on comfort and what feels best, that goes without saying and if a woman feels empowered by going natural and not wearing make-up on a run then high five on that one too. But for me, the often self-conscious, extremely clumsy and slightly eccentric runner I like to feel that I might, for just that brief moment in my day, appear to the rest of the world to have my shit together. The right running outfit can do that for me and whilst I spend more on my running gear than I do on my 'normal' clothes it's not a necessity to break the bank. Most high street stores have sporty ranges now which boast the same kind of technology that the high end sports market promote. The clothes are designed to help you run not only in comfort but also in style encouraging you to feel good about yourself whilst you display your awesome to the rest of the world. That for me at least, has to be a cool thing

I don't often get it right though, I had the suck ass runs from hell before Christmas and clothing did play a part. Here's how they went...

### 5th November 2015, Liverpool

So, the story of my run today.

Well in summary it was an utter bap ache. If it were footwear it would be Crocs with socks, if it were food it would be a dog shit with a side order of cat vomit. As I started I knew I had made a sartorial faux pas in choosing long tights and a t shirt, I had seriously misjudged the temperature of the gloomy looking day. It was bloody roasting, I mean practically sub-tropical. I was sweating profusely within ten minutes and my face was burning. Did I say I love Autumn? Scrub that, it sucks.

Three miles in my legs started aching and the wind started blowing; not a light, seasonal, refreshing breeze of course, more like a hairdryer going full tilt in my face. I was also developing an increasingly urgent desire to poo. By now I was randomly dropping F bombs loudly along the beach. At my five mile turning point I decided I had two choices, suicide or prayer. I foolishly opted for the latter and petitioned every deity who might listen; God, Allah, Buddha, The Universe (even Zeus got a mention) to get me back with my sanity and bowels intact. I managed to drag my crazy, flailing limbs another two miles before shouting "For Fuck's Sake!" at the sea, much to the delight of the small, elderly rambling group who appeared from behind the shrubbery.

I decided things could get no worse, I was at rock bottom, things could only improve from this cataclysmic juncture.

I was wrong. For the next two miles my usually inanimate key which was safely stowed in the handy inner pocket of my Skins decided to come alive and attempt to unlock my right buttock.

At nine miles I sat down on a wall by the local leisure centre and stared at the sky with bitter resentment, at this point a cyclist randomly cycled straight into the wall and knocked me off. Fuck. My. Life. I'd like to dedicate the last half mile to Conchita Wurst who rather confusingly appeared on my playlist like a bearded angel, willing me home with gentle words of encouragement.

All in all it was a less than heroic ten miles.

Time for vodka.

## 26th December 2015, Liverpool

So in an effort to work off the frankly offensive amount of lard that we consumed yesterday we decided to get ourselves out for a run this morning. Despite being wet it's still weirdly warm so that brought on the usual Team Dopez wardrobe dilemma. We spent a good half hour fannying about with tops, jackets, hats and caps before a firm decision had been reached. Finally, in typical nonsensical fashion we had selected nigh on matching outfits so we headed out looking like two proper arses.

We decided that we would do a nice, easy ten miles (and by 'easy' we mean pace, not distance, ten miles is never easy). It was good to be out in the air but wow the streets were wet! Huge puddles spanned the pavements and the gutters were fast flowing rivers, we have only a tiny fraction of the flooding that our neighbours a little further north in Lancashire and Cumbria currently have to deal with and our hearts go out to them.

So puddle dodging it was and this gave rise to the decision to head to the beach with the promise of clear pathways without the three foot trench of leaf sludge that borders our every pavement making crossing the road involve a Nureyev type ballet leap to avoid sinking forever into mulch. It seemed breezy but a warm breeze so despite eyeing every waving tree suspiciously I felt this was the best plan. As we turned right on the beach the wind seemed to drop and this made me very uneasy. Where had it gone? In true panto style a voice in my head shouted "IT'S BEHIND YOUUUU!!!" And by God it was. Now as you may know I've developed a prodigious fear of the outbound tailwind on a run, it only spells glue footed misery for the return leg. And this felt like one hell of a tailwind. Whoop. Anyway, we enjoyed it while it lasted feeling the benefit of the lift it gave us. We watched the tide crashing against the shore and panted happy hellos to festive morning walkers.

Then we turned round.

It is at this point that I would like to thank Stella McCartney. Having elected this morning to wear a beautiful Adidas running jacket she designed I had been marvelling about how loose, soft and comfortable it felt. What I didn't realise was that on facing the wind said jacket would actually turn into a parachute. This instrument of insanity then dragged me in the reverse direction with the force of a herd of wild horses.

Stella McCartney I'll wager is not a runner, nor takes advice of runners when devising running gear. Either that or she sees running as a new form of extreme sport which involves the possibility of being swept out to sea through the air. Or maybe she's a sociopath. Anyway it was a mind bogglingly difficult, ridiculous and hilarious experience battling through nearly two miles to reach the safety of the sheltered roads. Once there it was reasonably plain sailing to get home and we finished with smiles on our faces and some life left in our legs.

**Friday 8th January 2016**

I tend to be a little on the anally retentive side. I like routine, I like order, I like planning. It's not sexy but then neither are unwashed, sweaty running tights or empty vodka bottles. Having a stick up my ass keeps me sane. So when Marc suggested an unplanned run after work tonight I was trapped somewhere between delight and hysteria. I also happened to be standing over a box of Celebrations when I got his text so immediately committed myself to it by shoving three miniature Twix in my cavernous cake hole. There was now no turning back.

The thing is I really needed it and he knew it. We've been having a really stressful time at home lately and it's frayed my nerves to distraction. It was Friday and I didn't want to carry this feeling into the weekend. A run can de-stress you in the most amazing way, it can give you thinking time whilst clearing your mind, it can solve a problem or diminish it. In the song 'Let It Go' there's a lyric 'It's funny how some distance makes everything seem small and the fears that once controlled me can't get to me at all'.
True story.

But still I had my doubts. I hadn't assiduously planned my outfit, I hadn't pored over the Met Office app for an unreasonable amount of time, I hadn't unnecessarily recharged my Garmin, eaten appropriately or planned a route and distance. It would be spontaneous, it would be a bit wild. This is not how I do things, but there was much Twix to atone for so off we went. It was thankfully really dark and really cold so the outfit was a no brainer, thin vest, a cosy top and tights. I couldn't find my usual thongs so I opted for commando style, as my tights were well fitting and opaque.

As we stormed off into the night we uttered one phrase repeatedly... 'Holy Shit!' Because it was cold, it was bollock shrinking, ass clenchingly cold. I pulled my sleeves over my fists and felt my feet turn to blocks of solid ice. In a weird way I was glad though, the shocking blasts of frozen breath going through my body were so consuming they forced my mind into a state of suspended animation insisting it focused on nothing but breathing and running.

There comes a point in our beach route where we reach a roundabout and the road splits to opposite pavements, Marc traditionally takes one and I the other. I don't know why we do this, we just always have, we say goodbye to each other at the diverge and then hello as it rejoins. It's become somewhat symbolic of our relationship, the individuality and independence we both value so much along with our togetherness. Over the years when one of us has been having a tough time or a hard run the other has stayed with them on their side of the path. Sometimes one of us will whisper a thank you but it's mostly a silent thing, an unspoken gesture of support.

Tonight Marc ran on my side of the path and I remained in this trance like state for a while until I heard his voice breaking my icy coma telling me I was going too fast. This is a familiar warning sign to me, a siren that I'm running on emotion and stress, I gathered myself and regulated my pace returning my mind back to the road and looking up to see a diamond scattered blanket above my head. Suddenly I was reminded of my place on this earth, the gift and value of my life and how much I needed to trust the universe that things would work out.

The vast beauty of the thick, black, studded sky gave me some perspective about the magnitude of my own worries and I decided in that one moment that for tonight at least I should place them aside and just breathe. It was also at that exact same moment of epiphany that I developed what I can only politely refer to as 'front bottom wind'. A litany of staccato trumps raining forth from my foof like some sort of genital machine gun.

# Recovery Run
## Nicky Lopez

I have no explanation for this whatsoever other than the lack of underwear. Without going into too much physical detail I don't think things are particularly flappy down south, OK I've been through childbirth and yes, it's seen an age appropriate amount of action but nothing, nothing could have prepared me for the seal clapping that had begun to accompany my every stride. I began to do a series of increasingly frantic pelvic floor crunches which caused me to swerve and lurch across the path much to Marc's bemusement. I should also mention at this point that the insane tie that adorned my top had started whipping me repeatedly in the face as if to accompany the whoopsie drumkit I already had going on. Then as quickly as it arrived it left with a final, seemingly endless raspberry blow.

The rest of the run was gentle, peaceful, and steady and 8 miles of everything I needed it to be. I think life is an amazing thing. During your most difficult moments you can find profound beauty and amidst all this there are moments of ridiculous, nonsensical idiocy. Every second we're alive is an unplanned run, in all its chaotic, disordered wonder. And secretly, I wouldn't want it any other way. Foof farts and all.

# 3

# The Rookie

**Saturday 9th January 2016**

I wanted to return for a moment or ten to the whole rookie thing. When Marc and I were running last night we saw lots of runners out and about, no weird thing, it was early evening and the weather was cold but still. We saw the guy who runs in shorts in all conditions defying icicles on his nuts and nipples that could cut glass. We saw the marathon girl, a slip of a lass with a lean, awe inspiring strength. She streaks past us like a diamond hard flash with the speed and agility of a pro 5k runner, but we know she's run miles and miles with the same intense power and unwavering smile. We see the usual cheery kinsfolk, runners with whom we identify in terms of both demographic and ability; fast enough to hold our own but slow enough to suggest our Friday nights are spent not so much in the company of athletes at the track but rather with vodka and chips. We give each other knowing nods and panting hellos as we do on each other's recovery runs (aka hangover days).

I love runners, even the arsey ones who think they invented the bloody split short. Runners seem to have a clarity of thought, an awareness of the gift of health and an appreciation of the outdoors unlike anyone else. And of course they should. What kind of person participates in a sport that can bring you to your knees as often as it lifts you from them? Who would push their body to the edge of their comfort zone in the bleakest of conditions in the flimsiest of clothing oftentimes in total solitude and call it fun?

I think it's because of this beautiful lunacy that we get each other, we huddle in dark corners of the Internet in our sweaty masses and share tales of PBs and bodily functions that would simultaneously bore and disgust the average person. But it is a wonderfully contradictory activity. We run for meditation, for solitude, for peace and to breathe in the wonder of nature and then collect in our thousands to race along a central motorway through an inner city. We run for company, camaraderie and togetherness in silent groups where the sound of footfall and breath is our only communication.

And runners are funny, in a way that only runners get. They understand the priceless hilarity of the one sock run and can laugh about sports massages that verge on GBH, bleeding nipples and ice baths. Runners think torture is hysterical. But above all most runners I know are kind and endlessly supportive. You want to see the best in humanity? Watch a runner struggling at a race. Other runners will cheer, pat on the back, hold hands and sacrifice their own race to walk beside them. You think the world is a cold, uncaring place? Watch a runner fall in a marathon and see at least twenty people forfeit about sixteen plus weeks of intense, often agonising training to stop and look after them. Because it could be one of us, and no man gets left behind.

And when I say runners, I mean all runners. From the guy in the all-weather shorts and the marathon girl to the several new runners we saw out last night. Their inexperience betrayed by their too fast pace and heavy clothes, the look on their faces which is between painful hopelessness and ambitious excitement. And we admired them, we were inspired by them. Because we know only too well how hard those first few runs are, what colossal obstacles they will conquer both in their minds and with their bodies. Some of them will quit and that's fine, it's not for everyone. But the fact that they're out there, sweating, fighting in the cold makes them a little bit heroic.

And we know their pain, all runners do, not just because we remember how they feel but also because we feel it too sometimes. Like I said, in running everyone is a rookie and every now and then you feel like a first timer no matter how long you've been doing it. Running teaches you humility whilst giving you an enormous dose of fighting spirit.

The jury is out as to whether a positive attitude can have any effect in the fight against cancer but I tell you from my own experience that running taught me how to deal with the tough times of cancer in a way that nothing else in the world could have. As for making me any smarter? I'll share with you my thoughts from a recent pre-Christmas run and you can judge for yourself…

**17th November 2015, Liverpool**

So for tonight's run I decided to use all the wisdom I'd learnt from the lessons of my previous storm run. You know the one about not trying to get over a tough run by going out in biblical weather, the one about not trusting a strong tailwind, the one about not running on the beach in insane wind, the one about not being a total idiot? You remember the ones?

Cool.

So, I was having a good think about those lessons tonight during my seven mile run. I approached my turning point on the beach at a scorching pace benefitting from a prodigious tailwind I reflected on the fact that I am, in fact, a complete tool. Because what you really need to do after two nightmare runs is to pick the windiest night of the year to go for a run on the most exposed coastal path you can think of. Why would I do something so insane?

Like I said, I'm a tool.

But despite being a tool I learnt something new, something about me. I'm persistent, dogged, determined. Some would say bullheaded. I realised why I keep going back, why I keep throwing myself into the fire like some wheezing, Lycra clad moth repeatedly hitting a lightbulb.

I hate to lose.

It's not like I enjoy pain, God knows I'm no stranger to it in life, so if anything I should avoid it. And I love easy runs. I love happy, carefree runs where everything just clicks into place. And don't get me wrong, I'm no hero. When it's not going my way I'll whine like a bitch and cry and curse and use language that would get me arrested. But the runs I get the most from seem to be the tough ones. I guess I wear them like a badge of honour, like I've slayed the dragon, exorcised the demons. These are the runs that prove to me that I can take the hits and still keep going. And in a way I suppose I see it as a reflection of my life, if I can do that I can do this. Like my motto 'fall down seven times, stand up eight'.

So it looks like I'm going to remain a tool, still going to bang my head against the wall, still going to chase the storms. There will be days it won't hurt, it won't be tough and my feet will fly. But for all the days in between I choose to throw myself into the fire.

Because that's where the Phoenix will rise from the ashes.

## Sunday 10th January 2016

This time last year Marc and I got engaged. We had planned to do it before Christmas but treatment had been so intense it had left me unwell and confused and it just didn't seem the right time.

While we were running today Marc said that I hadn't yet talked about my illness properly in this book and wondered why. I told him that despite being a total gob on legs for most of the time, in this instance I was struggling to find the words. But it's a massive part of my journey, it led me to running and in turn led me to him and to the life we have today so no matter how much I try, I can't ignore its existence or its legacy.

In August 2009 I was diagnosed with cancer, more accurately Non-Hodgkin's Lymphoma. I had been unwell for a while, lost a lot of weight and I knew something was amiss so it wasn't an enormous surprise. Initially I was scheduled for 6 months of chemo and given hope that all would be well. Two years later I was still in treatment and still not responding. A couple of friends were doing Race for Life and so I thought I'd try it too. It seemed like the thing to do and on reflection I think it was the first time I had accepted that I actually might have cancer, those adverts might be about me.

I bought some cheap trainers and convinced myself that I was about seven times fitter than the reality. I streaked through the door towards the park knowing that 3 miles was a doddle. I was thin, I was lean, I had this. What I really had was a bad case of cancer denial and a smoker's cough. About 4 minutes in I stopped to cough up my respiratory system, then I started again. Then I stopped again. And so it went for 3.1 miles taking around 55 minutes not including breaks. It was like a bizarre extended fartlek session involving short sprints followed by desperate, wheezy standstills.

For some reason I completely overlooked the whole couch to 5k program thing and decided to go for gold. The next day I felt fine, the following day like I'd been attacked. I didn't run again until race day. On the day itself I plodded through the run in the same stop/start fashion and crossed the finish line without grace or style. But I'd done it. And I was proud.

# Recovery Run
## Nicky Lopez

Quite what then possessed me to enter the Great North Run that year I'll never know. But I did and a little later I'll tell you about it. After that I was hooked, not so much on running but on racing. Despite my treatment being gruelling I became addicted to the feeling of achievement, the massive rush of empowerment a finish line would give me. I joined a Facebook running group called Running the World and adored the camaraderie of other runners. I also got chatting to the friendly, if bloody cheeky admin, Marc. After a while we accepted the inevitable, we fit each other in the weirdest and best way and we became a couple.

Marc lived in Newcastle and I in Liverpool but we were determined to make it work. We never once considered it wouldn't. My health on the other hand was erratic, with each new treatment regime we had great hope then devastation. After one operation my hearing and sight were both damaged. Then I developed a heart problem. At times my fingernails fell off, my teeth were taken out, my body was bruised, my spirit shattered.

But we kept running. We ran through it all. Through triumph and disappointment, pain and heartache we ran race after race. Three London Marathons, five Great North Runs, hundreds and hundreds of miles. Cancer accompanied me on my runs but it never conquered them or me and for that I will forever be grateful.

But back to today...
Today I really didn't want to run. Most weekends we do a long run and given that our weekday runs tend to be 10 milers we try to do the half marathon distance over the weekend. It's a happy distance for us and keeps us from having to change our schedule to train for events. Plus it allows us to eat more food and being honest that's usually our primary motivation.

But today I didn't want to run. Cleo's ass o'clock Saturday morning skating lesson had been rescheduled to today and so we were up in the small, dark hours freezing our baps off in an ice rink miles from civilisation for several hours. By the time we got home at 10am I was cold and shattered, I just wanted to go back to bed. Every inch of me wanted to get into bed. Even Cleo told me to get into bed. Marc usefully commented that there would be no shame in slacking off or quitting while he ran and though others may not understand he would still support me in my decision.

Knob.

So despite my better judgement I got kitted up in my comfy greys and braced myself. Holy butt crack it was cold, I praised myself for wearing my comfy jacket (usually reserved for sub-zero runs) and cursed the deities for their lack of compassion. It was windy and I hate wind. When I say 'hate' I mean I absolutely sodding despise the bloody stuff, I really do. It seems to seep into me and find every last corner of weakness. It makes my breath laboured and unnatural and my body fight against its force. It feeds off my energy and saps my soul. I can wrap up from the cold, I can even rejoice in the rain but I cannot hide from the wind.

We decided to run the canal route to protect us from the brunt of the icy blows. It would also present the driest run for us given the recent biblical rains. The path towards Liverpool is heavily urbanised and is lined for a large part by factories, warehouses and one particularly aromatic recycling plant that causes us to gag every time we pass it. This is particularly welcome with a hangover and has led in the past to a mid-run dry heave workout. We're a classy couple. Within two minutes of running I had plopped into an ankle deep cavern of a puddle sploshing muddy crap halfway up my legs. I then realised why I only wear my comfy grey jacket on sub-zero runs. It is essentially a duvet and I was now effectively cooking under it.

Parts of the path were spanned with deep puddles so we ran in 'not double file' as Marc calls it. Today Marc led the way, he sensed my tiredness (perhaps from the profanities I'd spewed for the first ten minutes we were out) and wanted to set a happy, comfortable pace. Pacing is a great forte of Marc's; where I struggle to find that sweet, steady rhythm he finds it in seconds, his footfall like a soothing metronome hitting the path with a consistent accuracy. It was strangely comforting to follow, to allow my feet to mirror his knowing that they would be moving at just the right speed to keep me comfortable (and from dying on my arse).

Through the sharp winter sun I followed and I started to feel a peace that gentle, continuous motion can bring. The miles ticked over and the tired legs loosened. Just as I sensed that Marc had committed to the 13.1 distance he stopped, we were 5.25 miles in and he said it was time to turn for home and call it a ten. I was so happy I could have cried. I was pushing myself towards a distance that today would have hurt solely to prove a meaningless point to myself. I suddenly realised how tired I was and how hard the extra 3.1 miles would have proven. Ten was enough. I had nothing to prove.

We happily trotted home while I reflected on how at some point in my journey running had stopped being something I do and had become something that I am. My days are not defined by running but I do believe that they are crowned by it.And this guy who leads me on when I'm tired, who protects me from the elements and knows exactly when to stop even when I don't, well he's pretty damn fabulous too.

And a year to the day we decided to spend the rest of our lives together; amidst a bleak, industrial landscape he gave me a view well worth chasing.

**Monday 11th January 2016**

I couldn't run today. As I've mentioned before Cleo has had a heap of emotional shit going on and it had to be handled this morning. I really wish she ran. Not because of the health benefits, she's a tall willowy length of awesome that can eat eight meals a day and still find room for supper. I just think she's born to run.

I imagine her striding out, her infinite legs covering mile after mile with effortless grace. She would, no doubt, be destroying her multitudinous brain cells with the vile, horrific European dance music she subjects her ears to played at a bizarrely quiet level. While other kids blare out their music at full tilt Cleo prefers a mid-level, inoffensive hum. If she planned a rave it would take place in a library. She would run though, just because she could and her cares would spill behind her in a river and she would leave them so far away.

But she's 14 and she doesn't yet know that the street will love her more than the sofa and her phone is no match for the endless CinemaScope of sea and sky that waits patiently to meet her. She doesn't know that it would make her feel invincible in a world where it is so easy to feel powerless.

Because that's what running can do, it can squeeze the pain from your heart and pour it into your legs in a tidal wave of relief.

# Recovery Run
## Nicky Lopez

Running gives us the opportunity to be our most heroic self, a larger than life version of our usual mundane reality. Running allows us to see ourselves as the incredible, intensely amazing creation that we are. To put it plainly, running makes us believe that anything is possible, including the best of ourselves.

And running can be your shrink, it can put your head into a place that years of therapy would struggle to achieve. In my darkest times over the last few years running has been my beacon, my sweaty, painful ray of hope. When I was at my most unwell and unable to get out of bed I would dream of the road. In the days that medication controlled my thoughts I would comfortably drift to a path by an unknown ocean where my legs would take me over hills and through dunes, my breathing clear and strong, my eyes forever focused on the horizon. When I despaired I would recall finish lines I had crossed just days after the rigours of chemo and my hope would be renewed. When my dear friend Caroline took flight to a different horizon I ran with her by my side, sometimes flooded with sadness other times with gratitude that my feet were still touching the earth. There are days I swear she cycles past me with her engulfing smile and glittering eyes as if she's rejoicing in my survival and daring me to live bolder, brighter. During the harshness and the happiness of recent memory I have shared it all with a run. Like a drunk washes the day down with a shot I have made the road my drug, my addiction and my escape. Here are some thoughts from a recent adventure...

**27th October 2015, Newcastle**
Ten miles today from Whitley Bay to the Fish Quay and back again and it really was a game of two halves for me. From the outset I found the run tough, the wind was blowing strongly into our faces and I couldn't find a breathing pattern. It was considerably cooler too this morning, the smell of winter is definitely beginning to hang in the air. It was just one of those days where nothing feels quite right, nothing feels smooth. My hat was annoying (I actually stashed it behind a wall 2 miles in), my top was too hot.

I guess the fact that I'm pretty stressed and anxious at the moment had the greatest bearing on my run. Along with the forceful weather I struggled with my inner demons, overthinking, overanalysing and clawing for solutions. The run had turned into a battle in both ways, every breath was gasping, my legs were heavy and sore, every uphill a struggle and I felt disjointed and chaotic. Marc is a strong runner so when he tells me to slow down it's because I am running incredibly erratically.

Approaching 4 miles I was ready to go home, sometimes you're just not feeling it. We stopped briefly at the bolted rampart to Tynemouth Lighthouse. It was closed off to the public because of the strong winds and poor visibility. As we turned to run towards the quay I regrouped. I realised that I was doing the run a great disservice. This is a route that I adore, that I long to run when I'm not able. I was pounding out my problems on it and using it as an emotional punchbag and whilst that's fine for some runs it's just not good enough for this one. This route is my happy place, where each turn has its own smell and its own taste. This is the route with the monolithic hills that I actually enjoy because they make me feel strong and more importantly, blessed.

Suddenly my mind was clear, I wasn't here to find answers or to exorcise demons. I was here to run, to let go, to give in to the blissful, simple automaticity that only running can bring. And once I'd accepted that my breathing became relaxed and rhythmic, my legs loosened, the winds were behind me and the roads all ran downhill. Before I knew it my heart was singing.

And when I had finished the funniest thing happened, my worries didn't seem so overwhelming anymore. Maybe the vastness of the North Sea had given me a little perspective, maybe I realised I'm stronger than I sometimes think, maybe I just needed to loosen my grip a little. Who knows?
I guess there's a lot of truth in the phrase 'How you handle the uphill battle determines everything'.

## Tuesday 12th January 2016

I had planned to run today, in fact I'd committed myself to it. When I say 'committed myself' what I mean is that at work I wilfully ate a shitload of lasagne, garlic bread, biscuit and chocolate based on the notion that I would be running ten miles later on this evening. The problem is that I went for a post lard arse lunchtime walk to assess the weather down at the beach and discovered rain like bullets and 50mph winds. There was no way I could brave another headwind horror so I tossed the idea. I arrived home half a stone heavier to find our race bibs for this weekend's Cancer Research Winter Run 10k.

I'm not used to running 10k, it's a distance we don't frequently run. The last time was in the Mo Run in November. Now I have a history of entering races when I've had a few drinks, everything seems feasible, everything seems awesome. I rarely contemplate the associated travel and accommodation costs involved which can be nothing short of monstrous. Especially if you travel with Cleo. Because we feel the need to compensate her for tolerating our endless running talk, shopping trips for her that end up in Nike, early mornings and early nights (although they rarely happen) we make sure an away day race experience is a good one for her. This usually involves the kind of hotels that are more accustomed to Creme de la Mer than Ralgex. This run was on home turf though so we knew that the CleoBeast would be slumbering until midday at least by which time (barring any hideous catastrophe) we'd be back home.

I do love race days, I love the giddy nerves leading up and the jokey camaraderie of the event. I love the whole carnival atmosphere of mass participation events, it's one of the things that make running such fun. Race day is the equivalent of going to a huge party and the awesome thing about being a runner is that you get to choose when, where and how many parties you go to.

I've never been competitive on race day either, neither of us have. I guess we're in a happy, lucky position of just loving to run. If I get a PB then that's awesome but on the whole it's not my motivation, my general impetus is to have fun and remember the day. Our philosophy has always been that the hard work is done on the training days and race day is the victory lap. They're the opportunity to celebrate your own awesomeness and feel a bit like a rock star. The fact that they're such unique runs makes them stand alone in terms of experience and I really hope I can give you a glimpse of the incredible times that we have had along the way.

# Recovery Run
## Nicky Lopez

**21st November 2015 Mo Run, Croxteth Park, Liverpool**

Given that my last couple of runs have been incredibly tough because of the weather I wasn't exactly looking forward to this morning's run. Minus three degrees, 40mph gusts and an exposed country park made the prospect of Liverpool Mo Run about as much fun as poo on toast. I'd also had chemo on Thursday so the bowels didn't bode well either.

I'm a shallow soul though and the chance to try out my swaggy gilet (birthday gift from the mister) was tempting me massively. It takes a damn cold day to get me into a jacket and this looked to be it. So off we went fuelled with a breakfast of champions (McDonalds breakfast wrap, I'm sure it's what Mo has and what all good oncologists recommend) and headed off into the watery winter sun.

We'd opted for the 10k and I was glad, I always find the first 3 miles of the run the hardest so I'm not fond of a 5k. After hitting the toilets (hello again Ronald McDonald) five minutes before the run I was raring to go on a number of levels. It was eye wateringly cold and so I was happy to get a bit of a sweat on. This it seemed wasn't going to be a problem - the aeroloft was warm, I mean 15 tog duvet warm. I'm not complaining at all, it totally did the job but a degree warmer and I would have ripped it from my body and stamped it into the dirt.

Oh yes, by the way, there was dirt and lots of it. Part of the run was pretty boggy and although in my mind I leapt through it like a sure footed gazelle in reality I was, as usual, a graceless buffoon. The comedy moustache and eyebrows I had welded to my bonce with glue were now getting on my bangers and it was only the fact that in removing them I would have also ripped off half my face that kept me from tearing them to shreds. I also missed my sunglasses, I now have around 30 more wrinkles from squinting.

I normally run halves, I like halves; halves are predictable and reliable. Halves are the Nan of running. Halves are steady, ploddy and solid. They're long enough to find your stride and short enough not to sacrifice your sanity or bowel movements to the distance. 10ks are weird. You have to run faster than you normally would for what seems like a lifetime. You can't settle into a rhythm and you feel a bit uncomfortable for the whole thing. Give me a comfy, meditative, slow 13.1 any day.

Marc asked me at 5 miles if I was enjoying it, 'Yes!' I cried unconvincingly whilst my left lung tried to escape via my throat and my legs (and butt) turned to lava. Drama Queen? Moi? Never! For the last mile Marc was bouncing along whilst I was playing the 'STOP versus NO' game in my head. We got there though and we finished in 51.48 which I was just fine with.

In short it was a fun way to spend a morning, loads of lovely people, a great location and a good dollop of larks. We ripped off our taches and guzzled coffee and sweets in the car like the greedy plebs we are and ended up consuming around 4 times the calories we'd burnt. Another reason why I love halves.

**Thursday 14th January 2016**

I have a complicated relationship with thumb loops. I'm strangely, inexplicably drawn to them, they seem to be number one on the criteria list when I'm choosing a long sleeved top and I'm not really sure why. I can see their attraction, the long, knuckle covering sheath of fabric that negates the need for cumbersome gloves. But they present a major difficulty. Cold thumbs. Thumb loops are essentially an ancient form of torture reserved for cold weather runners. They fool you into the notion that they provide superior comfort and warmth but in reality they basically freeze your thumb to the point of snapping. There is an upside, because of the position they ice your digits into, everyone you pass thinks you're having a super awesome run. Thumb loops are liars, they suggest one thing and deliver quite the opposite whilst turning you into an amazing, living commercial for them. Sneaky bastards.

This was largely what I was reflecting on during the first few miles of a half marathon run this morning along the Leeds Liverpool Canal. I'd like to mention at this point that if you're reading this and you're not from the UK then you won't have a buggery clue as to where I'm referring and for that I apologise. (If there exists a benevolent and slightly deranged overseas benefactor who would fund a series of pointless and possibly catastrophic runs over there then I'm definitely your girl.) However if you do live in the UK, particularly England then I would urge you to find your nearest canal and run it.

Canal running is awesome, it offers the meditative solitude of running next to water along with structured, flat paths and ever changing landscapes. There are countless opportunities for shelter from the elements and the wildlife is rich and diverse. Most people, including myself, live their whole lives without discovering their proximity to a canal. Despite being blessed enough to spend time in two of the most magnificent coasts in the world (ok I'm biased but seriously, the North East and North West English coasts are sublime) I still head to the canal and love my time there.

For much of the remainder of my run I was contemplating why I get so nervous, so stressed before I run. I used to wonder if I was the only person who was like this but I'm assured I'm not. Prior to absolutely every single run I develop the most paralysing nerves. All of a sudden every good run I've ever done before has been chance, a lucky break. I doubt myself in the worst way and I've no idea why. In my head I know I've turned many corners in my running and especially in the last 12 months so it baffles me why my stomach lurches before even the most innocuous of training runs.

I guess that because every run is so distinct, so unique in its nature it adds to every run a certain unpredictability. And I think this is one of those beautiful contradictions that I love about running, despite my need for order and routine I also adore that no matter how many times you tread the same path or cover the same distance the experience is always different, even if in just small ways. Today's run was an opportunity to get some miles in without having to cope with the near drowning the weather has been doling out.

It was a shiny, sunny morning and despite my friends at the Met Office predicting a foreboding tailwind we gobbed down enough peanut butter to effect a no way out scenario. Ok, so it was cold enough to freeze our nips off. My face was frozen into an inane grin and my thumbs were rigidly stuck upwards in my bright turquoise top giving me the appearance of a particularly stoned children's TV presenter. I felt good though, we took it gently and despite the bitter cold, the sun also had some welly in it. In time our mad, joker like faces thawed and we started to feel rather warm. Before we knew it we were baking. We hadn't thought to bring sunglasses and so we were treated to a discombobulating, strobing rave as we passed every set of railings.

But still it was pretty lovely, we chatted and fell silent in turn as the miles ticked along. Even the arsey, scouse geese who usually give us

# Recovery Run
## Nicky Lopez

a total bollocking seemed cheery today and they flapped and giggled as the two goons in Lycra trotted past. As we reached Liverpool centre and turned back towards the canal we lost the sun and simultaneously entered the Large Hadron Collider that is the Dock Road. Even on the best of days it's like being trapped in a wind tunnel but today it practically knocked us horizontal. The strength of the gust was hilariously comedic though and so we didn't seem to care as much as usual, we laughed at it, right in the face of it until we reached the Narnia like entrance of the towpath.

As we ran through the colourful graffiti the sun poured through the industrial, multi levelled beauty of the locks and it was otherworldly. We seemed to sail on effortlessly for the next couple of miles in a smooth, comfortable groove. Marc ran on ahead and acted as a heroic human windbreak. Yes there was a prodigious headwind but as the strong sun was at our backs we were kind of glad of it, besides it was nothing compared with what we've learned to handle on the coastline.

In the last couple of miles I said how the remaining part of the run had reminded me of marathon training, the icy, sunny days and pushing in the final steps for home. It felt easier now though, there was no struggle, no fight, no 'at any cost' feelings coursing through me. Marc reckons it's because we've run so much now our bodies have adapted, they're used to distance and time. I know that's a part of it but I'm sure it's more. I'm inclined to think that we've weathered so many storms, faced so many hurricanes that we no longer fear the elements in the way we did. In the same way that we know the power of the forces of nature we also know our own. And instead of fighting those forces we move with them and through them.

The force is strong in us two.

# 4

# Love and the Snot Rocket

**Friday 15th January 2016**

Every year for the past three I have begun marathon training from scratch. Having found the worst of my treatment to be through the winter, running has taken a back seat to survival. And so with each January I've started right from the beginning. Thankfully the tried and trusted Marathon Rookie programme we use kicks off pretty gently with 5ks but last year these proved to be some of my most testing and confidence killing runs.

I can palpably recall the pain and frustration I felt fighting the blasting wind down the more scenic eastern route of the canal, at some points during my first few runs there were tears and an enormous feeling of doubt. How the hell was I ever going to make it through a marathon if I couldn't get through 3 miles? The magnitude of the mileage was terrifying me and for the first time in my running life I considered giving it all up. I was tired, overweight, very unwell and had no inclination whatsoever to run. Running had become a painful, depressing battle that shook me to the core and left me spent for days.

I'd say that I had fallen out of love with it but in truth I don't think I had ever really fallen in love in the first place. Running up until now had been a way to test and prove myself, it was a barometer with which I could measure how much pressure I could take but it wasn't something I could say I truly enjoyed.

Yes, I enjoyed the events and of course I loved the friendships I had developed with fellow runners but in honesty I didn't feel like one of them, I was an honorary runner but not a real one, even running with Marc- amazing, supportive, encouraging, wonderful Marc I always had the skin crawling fear that I was holding him back. Inside my mind I knew what a great runner he was, what he was capable of when he set his legs free and ran untethered by the responsibility of a sluggish partner.

# Recovery Run
## Nicky Lopez

I apologised relentlessly during our increasingly longer training runs and berated myself for my lack of stamina and ability. And then something happened...

Somewhere along the way Marc introduced a gentle but effective tough love strategy. I've mentioned it before but it deserves reiterating as it was a defining moment not only in my running but also in my life. He convinced me that the apologies and talking down to myself were not only upsetting to him but also creating a self-fulfilling prophecy. I was setting myself up for failure. In slow degrees I learnt to find the positives in tough runs. Marc was exceptionally patient encouraging me to slow down to a pace that felt not just comfortable but easy. We stopped when we wanted, frequently at first and then when we needed which became less and less often. Long runs became happy adventures that I would plan for and feel almost excited about. When I was OK I would breathe deeply and appreciate it vocalising my enjoyment, when it was tough I would accept it wasn't easy and be proud of what I had achieved.

And it worked. From those small seeds of positivity grew a tiny shoot of hope about running that didn't really fully bloom until September 13th 2015, but nonetheless a change had taken place, I had started to love the run.

It had long been my goal to get to a level of fitness where I could feel comfortable regularly running a decent distance, maybe a half marathon without it hurting me or being a massive undertaking that I would need to prepare weeks or months in advance for. My first goal was to be able to frequently run a 10k after work. Over the course of last summer I achieved this largely due to consistent running (the perfect weather helped a heap) and a mega diet my consultant had put me on causing me to lose a shitload of weight. I swapped my structured shoes for a faster, lighter pair and so following Marc's example I began to increase my distances. My usual midweek runs of five miles and 10k became seven and eight miles with a weekend run of ten or eleven.

By September my short weekday run was eight miles and my regular was ten. At weekends we started to try to run half marathons and now we do this as often as we can. Once my pace became unimportant it magically seemed to become significantly faster. Now Marc and I run at a very similar speed and although it shouldn't really matter it's a great feeling to run with him on equal calibre, I feel proud and I know he does too. To be fair he always did.

It's a great place to be in and now as we are talking about increasing our weekend runs to 14 or 15 miles I am truly in love with running. The secret to it all was inside my head and by allowing myself to enjoy instead of endure; with the help of Marc I unlocked my heart to the possibility that I could find it hard and happy at the same time. The happy runs are life enriching making me feel empowered and alive, the hard runs are tests and lessons that strengthen me.

And there are tough runs of course, don't be fooled. When I talk about running a half marathon comfortably I should qualify that, 13.1 miles is never comfortable, it's always a big deal. Bearing in mind the pretty gorgeous half we ran yesterday I'll contrast that with one we ran in Newcastle just after Christmas. It's a great reminder of how you can be tested to the limits and yet have the most brilliant time if you approach it with the right attitude.

## 28th December 2015 Newcastle, 8am this morning...

Marc: Get up

Me: No

Marc: WHY ARE WE EVEN DOING THIS?

Me: BECAUSE WE'RE IDIOTS!

And so we got up and headed out for a cheeky bank holiday half marathon. Marc had done an awesome job mapping out a route for us. It not only took into account the wind direction (I've had enough of headwinds) and four different types of landscape but he'd also structured it so the first six miles were practically downhill. And a beautiful route it was too.

Taking us along the historic waggonways along which coal from the pits used to be transported to the port. The weather was mild and clear and everywhere was still and calm. Marc unlocked secrets about the local history along the way making the paths and trails come even more alive to me. He'd really played a blinder with this route. On reaching the quay we turned and ran towards Tynemouth then onto the coast I love to run. The sea looked wild and majestic and it felt like a privilege to be out there, sharing in the magnificence of the ocean.

# Recovery Run
## Nicky Lopez

At Whitley Bay we waved goodbye to the salty spectacle and headed towards West Monkseaton. It was at this point I realised that Marc was in fact an agent of Satan sent to destroy me and my very spirit. For reasons which he cannot say (mostly because he keeps convulsing with laughter) Marc had decided to map the final three and a half miles of the run taking in every single bloody hill in North Tyneside. I shit you not.

By the time we had reached 12 miles I was near hysterical with madness and altitude sickness. I had begun to measure the desperate, agonising distance in lampposts, grasping crazily for them spluttering and wheezing. Our friends drove past and tooted their horn, what to them may have looked like an enthusiastic double armed wave was in reality a tragic and hopeless attempt to throw myself under the wheels of their car. I didn't even have the energy to do that.

When we finally finished I was babbling maniacally about killing Marc in several different ways whilst he laughed demonically with red face and glinting eyes. I have never felt such a crushing hatred for a person in my life as I did for that split second.

On the flip side, it was an ace adventure with my northern soulmate in one of my favourite places on the planet. And revenge is a run best served cold...

**Saturday 16th January 2016**
So, when I said about runs being best served cold I may have been tempting fate. Today was a bollock freezer of gargantuan proportions. Having both had a long ass week in work we were just too knackered last night to attempt a run, we curled under a blanket on the sofa with Cleo and hibernated for the evening with deliciously filthy steak and chips. Although we both like to keep an eye on our weight we also appreciate the importance of a greedy bastard night now and again.
And we are proper greedy bastards.

So we were left with little choice but to get out for a leg stretcher after Cleo's bum clenchingly early ice skating session this fine Saturday morning. I say fine when what I really mean is Arctic. Put it this way, when we left the relative warmth of the sub-zero ice rink we had to add several layers of clothing to get to the car which was approximately 20 metres away. Yes I may be a soft southern Jessie

(Marc considers anywhere downwards of Durham to be 'the south') but I'm telling you, it was cold on another level this morning. And I was tired; so, so tired.

Because of our work commitments and the ritualistic torture that is figure skating spectating we generally average around 4.5 hours sleep on Friday nights making Saturday runs a horrifying prospect. On the way home I fell asleep several times in a madly attractive open mouthed, drooly state leaving me with the breath of an old shoe and the imprint of a seat belt on my face. To the core of my soul I absolutely did not want to run. But run we did.

It was tough, the cold seeped into every gap in my clothing and despite wearing my gloves my fingers hurt acutely. The pavement had become a second, more brutal ice rink than we were used to and my lightweight running shoes magically transformed into instruments of terror hell bent on landing me on my now frozen arse. My toes felt severed and my legs were moving in a bizarre mechanical manner like a drunken android that must have looked nothing short of insane to the many dog walkers about. Breathing was uncomfortable at best and my leaking nose pained with a raw sting.

But nature has a great balancing act and what she took from us in comfort she gave back to us in beauty. Frosted trees dripping with icicle garlands and grass frozen stiff into a spiky gorgeousness, even the tarmac had become studded with crystals. The air was clean and sharp and as we hit the beach we knew we had made the right decision. It was hard though, our legs were tired and stiff and the coastal path seemed an endless streak of white before us.

We had decided that 8 miles would be more than enough today, we have the Cancer Research UK 10k Winter Run in the morning so we didn't want to overdo things. What happened next may turn out to be a defining moment in both my relationship with Marc and indeed my life itself. Either way when I reflect on it now I'm still unsure whether to crease up laughing or puke in degraded disgust.

As we approached the halfway point past the Plinth of Awesome (a strange free standing sculpture on the coastal path that we named ourselves and depending on what kind of run we are having is also known as the Plinth of Arse) I was remarking to myself what an absence of wind there was (yes, it's becoming an obsession) which is unusual for this very exposed part of the coast. Thinking no more of it we reached the gate that leads off to the rifle range and so turned and headed for home.

It was at this stage that the unthinkable happened. In a moment of combined heroism and unintentional terrorism Marc ran on ahead of me to protect me from the sudden, formidable gust that bellowed across the dunes. For reasons I doubt neither of us will ever fully understand he also determined this to be the optimum moment to blow a snot rocket.

And not just any snot rocket.

This was clearly one he had been building up to, it was a culmination of several months of manflu and other less life threatening sniffles. As snot rockets go this one was a beast, a veritable monster of mucous, a baron of bogies, a king of catarrh that Marc had been carefully cultivating to be released with ultimate power and impact. The next few moments were a mixture of confusion and carnage. The fierce gust that Marc had chivalrously intended to protect me from had also given the snot rocket maximum velocity straight into my face. It took me a moment to fully comprehend what had taken place but as I looked at my spattered top and felt an icy thickness glob down my left eye and spread across my cheek there was the dreadful truth. I had been slimed.

At first we just stared at each other for an infinite time not knowing quite how to react. Feelings of vile disgust, trauma, embarrassment and absolute cataclysmic hilarity mingled together in a cacophony of emotion. Marc was both mortified and paralysed with mirth at the same time. In the end we reverted to our default mode of childish guffaws and eye wetting giggles. Marc made several attempts to apologise but each time we dissolved into cackles. I can't say that we handled the whole thing in a mature and sensible fashion; I will say that as it happened the shrieks could be heard for many miles and the profane screams that followed will ring in the hearts and ears of the rambling club for a long time to come. It definitely added a whole new dimension to the run that served as an unexpected and rather sticky distraction.

The rest of the run passed in a state of hilarity and shock and the utter ridiculous foulness of it all carried us home safely. We waved at fellow runners and intermittently pissed ourselves laughing. Running has taught me amongst other things how to man up, it's given me gumption and I can confidently say it's spilled over into my non running life. I am definitely tougher, more resilient and braver because of running as it's in making those bone numbing first steps out of the door when you're dog tired and hungover that mental stamina is built.

It's also taught me not to take myself so damn seriously; you can bet that life will put you back in your place in a billion nonsensical ways. So you develop a can do attitude, a why the hell not approach to life.

During my hardest runs I tell myself that I am learning to be strong, and it's true. If ever there was a sport that can bring out the badass in you its running. If you've ever run in tit freezing cold or biblical driving rain you'll know what I mean. There's something ridiculously funny about the sheer madness of it. While the rest of the world at large give you looks that range from admiration through to 'what the actual fuck are you doing?' deep inside you know you're doing something a little bit awesome, a little bit edgy. I believe it's in those moments that you find your inner superhero. Speaking of which...

### Sunday 18th May 2014, Great Manchester Run, Manchester

My first Great Manchester Run in the May of 2013 had been an unexpectedly brilliant day, it was the next proper race I had taken part in after my inauguaral Great North Run and because I had entered alone I was far from genuinely excited in fact I was extremely nervous. What had possesed me to go to a race on my own I'll never know.

As it wasn't far from home my family had offered to come with me and I was so glad of the company, as it was an early morning start I would take the train there and they would follow on with Cleo in the car. Somewhere along the way I found out that one of my oldest friends, Helen Bradley was also running, she had moved to Manchester many years ago and because of my constant flitting around we had rarely seen each other in about ten years so we had arranged to meet and start the race together.

It was a fab day, Manchester is a wonderful city and the race was, as usual with the Great Run series, brilliantly organised and well attended. My 10k finish time wasn't blisteringly good but I had enjoyed the experience so much it didn't matter. The post-race party in the

Spinningfields area of the city was fabulous fun with live bands, pop up bars and runners sprawled out on grassy verges enjoying the sunny, festival atmosphere.

When I met Marc a few months later I knew it was a race he'd enjoy so we both signed up. What we hadn't accounted for was that by the beginning of May 2014 I had become very unwell again and so began a four week radiotherapy regime. Before I began the treatment I was extremely positive in my expectations, I had taken lots of advice and spoken to a number of people who had been through similar; everyone agreed that compared to what I had been through this would be relatively low impact and I would tolerate the treatment very well. In terms of fitness, well... we had just run the goddamn London Marathon. We were on super form and brimming with enthusiasm. It was a race however that nearly ended very badly for me.

We had started out on a gorgeously warm, sunny Sunday morning for the short train ride from Liverpool to Manchester, the train teeming with chattering runners all bearing their race numbers on a multitude of brightly coloured charity vests and T shirts. One of the things I love most about the race day experience is being witness to such amazing stories as to what brings people to the race. Oftentimes I am moved to tears reading the back of a vest bearing a story about a lost or sick loved one and I am always inspired by how such sadness can be turned into something so positive. And it's not just about death and disease, many people have their own wonderful journeys of transformation whether it be weight loss, confidence or adversity. Most people at a mass participation race come with a story to tell.

As we left the train at Oxford Road and turned the corner towards McDonalds we laughed at the crowds of runners wolfing down breakfast muffins and milkshakes, it would have been rude not to join them. We destroyed our food and made use of the comparatively civilised on site facilities before heading to the start line.

The Great Manchester Run is organised into waves in the same way as the Great North Run but in Manchester each wave starts separately giving the huge number of runners in the narrow streets the convenience of their own designated start time. A common feature of the Great Run series is the insanely energetic mass warm up routine that takes place at the start of their races. Let's be clear here, I'm no killjoy and I like to think I know how to have a good time but contorting my body into a a series of increasingly complicated and frenetic poses and stretches whilst clapping and waving my arms like an ecstasy spiked raver is not my idea of good pre run prep.

I'd taken part in this organised lunacy only once before my first Great Manchester Run and I was so exhausted by the end of the routine I could have done with a lie down in a darkened room not a ten kilometre race. I'm not an expert and I may be going out on a limb here but I'm pretty damn sure that on the start line you don't see Mo Farah or Jo Pavey doing a demonic line dancing workout.

This time I was prepared, I had warned Marc of the impending aerobics set and he took my sage advice to opt out. As the runners whooped and cheered, lunging and star jumping we stood calmly by, gently smiling with an air of smugness that we weren't making ourselves look foolish. What he hadn't realised (but were later informed via many, many, many video clips) was that the event was being streamed on live TV to the nation and as around 30,000 good sports all crouched to the floor in unison, two green vested, self-satisfied dickheads could be clearly seen bang in the centre of the street standing motionless like King and Queen Buzzkill.

After the madness had subsided we stood in the golden sun waiting for the gun to herald the start of the race, it had begun beating strongly, uncomfortably strongly. Being northerners we automatically assume that any race around our hometowns that doesn't take place in July (and even mostly when it does) is going to be accompanied by swathes of cloud, icy gusts and perhaps a little snow. Not once did it enter our heads that it would be warm let alone hot. It was Manchester for fucks sake, there is no sun in Manchester, just drizzle and trams. It would seem that we had chosen to run in vests and I with a bald head on the hottest day Manchester had seen in years. The race hadn't yet begun and I was already burnt, I also felt unusually tired and unwell.

Radiotherapy, I've discovered like most forms of medicine has different effects on different people. The vast majority of people handle it far better than chemo and find it reasonably tolerable. I am not one of those people. Radiotherapy for me was exhausting. I guess I was tired to begin with, I had trained for a marathon then run one and I was working and going to hospital every weekday. I was burning the candle at both ends and eventually I was going to get burnt and somewhere outside Old Trafford on that day I was nearly cremated.

As we started the run I already felt odd, my head felt light and a little dizzy and I was hot but I also felt shaky and shivery. If I'd have had any sense at all I would have told Marc and I know he would have instantly made me stop but I had no sense whatsoever, just bluster and a misplaced cockiness that I was invincible. As we went on I knew that there was something seriously wrong, my eyes wouldn't focus and I was struggling to run in a straight line.

At mile four I confessed to Marc that I wasn't feeling my best but I didn't tell him to what extent. He was desperately concerned to get me some water but we had passed the only water station a while back where I had already taken a full drink. We were at one of the only points in the run where the support thins out so there were no passers-by to help. I slumped on the side of the road in hazy despair whilst Marc held my hand and tried to reassure me. The sun was beating on the back of my head and making me feel worse, there was no other choice but to keep moving. We had around a mile and a half left to the finish line and I became stupidly determined to reach it. Marc argued with me to the point of shouting at me to stop but I was deliriously hellbent.

I had made finishing the race become symbolic in some idiotic way and although I can't make sense of it now in my head at the time it all mattered so very much. I leant on Marc and he practically dragged the pair of us over the finish line that day. There was no pride, no elation just bitter tears. I felt totally defeated and Marc was angry with both me and himself for having allowed such a dangerous situation to play out. Sitting in Spinningfields later that day with my family I realised how lucky I had been to not go home in an ambulance or worse, I was extremely dehydrated and suffering from exhaustion.

Tough times followed with my health and I didn't run again until August that year. I had learnt a lesson though, I was not invincible, very far from it. I was extremely human complete with all the frailty and vulnerability that comes with humanity. And from that moment on I have appreciated my life a little more keenly, listened to my body a little harder and held onto Marc and Cleo much more tightly.

## Sunday 17th January 2016, Cancer Research UK Winter Run, Liverpool

This morning we rose in the dark again to run, with one question in my mind (well, apart from 'where are my pants?' which is my all time, number one request to the Gods) and that question was this...

What the buggery fuck are we doing this for?

It's cold, it's dark, it's fricking snowing out there. We're middle aged, I have a slightly sore knee, we're not going to win, we haven't had a sleep in for nearly three years, nobody cares if we get fat, we're going to die anyway so it may as well be in the warmth eating cake.

These very real facts played over in our minds as we fell over each other in the dark pouring our creaky (yet still age defyingly hot) bodies into tiny pieces of Lycra and gossamer like jackets that despite having the consistency of a gnats wing promised resistance against the most arctic of conditions. We solemnly ate breakfast, staring at each other with bitter resentment, inwardly blaming the other as the orchestrator of this wintery insanity. We knew it was time to reassess our lives, to look at our priorities and so made a decision...

Let's do this shit.

We pulled into the car park on the grimmest of mornings and gazed at the gloomy sky. Now don't get me wrong, Liverpool is an awesome city, it's my home town and I am incessantly vocal about my love of and my pride in it but a cold, grey Sunday doesn't do it any favours. On a sunny day the imposing waterfront buildings (known locally as the Three Graces) rise majestically from the river topped by the proud, majestic Liver Birds. The water shimmers as the ferries chug alongside enormous cruise liners and every bar spills out with a buzz. However, on a dark winter's day, like most northern cities, it's grim. The buildings were more gloomy than graceful and the streets were wet and sombre. It's as if the whole town had been painted in grey scale then dropped in a puddle. Even the flurry of snow that started to fall looked decidedly dank.

But we're not a town to be kept down.

As we approached the Arena where the race began we could hear a Scouse voice bellowing hellos and exchanging friendly jibes with the lines of bin bag clad runners. The atmosphere within the Arena was jolly and there was a warm conviviality like we were all members of the same secret lunatics club. The race warm up cleverly began inside the building before we were ushered to the start line with a mercifully scant two minutes to go. As the horn blew we crossed the start line with a blast of snow and a frosty sigh of relief.

The route itself was pretty unremarkable passing through a largely industrial area of town. There were some small but steady inclines and some welcome downhills. The main issue with the race was with my lunatic attire. In an effort to keep out the dastardly chill I had worn three layers of reasonably heavy duty clothing. This from a girl who typically overheats in a vest and running jacket it was an act of total idiocy. I also wore a Buff. And a fleece hat. To complement this Michelin Man style ensemble I had accessorised with Marc's fleecy running gloves. These gloves are legendary in our family as being so uncomfortably warm that no one can stomach wearing them for more than a short while. They are mystically turbo charged thermal. They are also massive and I have hands that go beyond dainty to be freakishly tiny. It was my opinion today that what these gloves really needed was a super-size hand warmer in each of them.

Within the first mile I was actually dying, sweat was gushing from every pore and my face was scarlet. In frantic increments I started trying to tear whatever accessible gear I could from me like some sort of lumbering sweaty striptease but I appeared to have seventy thousand thumb loops anchoring the entire outfit like cement to my hands. The only thing I could successfully remove was the now blisteringly hot hand warmers which had effectively melted my palms into the massive fingered gloves. I flung them across the street in panic and desperation and watched a passerby look in aghast suspicion at the steaming package I had thrown at their feet.

The rest of the run was tough but manageable. I was struck by the dedication of the other runners, being a Cancer Research race it had a totally different feel. A lot of people were there to do more than run, they were there in honour of someone, dedicating their efforts, all their hours of training to a loved one. And it was quietly moving to be amongst. I was reminded once again how running can be so much more than a sport, today for many it was an expression of love and a tribute. I kept this feeling with me through the remaining miles and it inspired me, I felt proud to be a runner.

Marc acted as an amazing pacer running a few steps ahead of me and in doing so not only motivated my speed but also created a clear path amongst a relatively busy field of entrants. Fellow runners were friendly and there was a fun ski themed water station at the halfway point. Marc was concerned at one stage that I wasn't enjoying it and I can understand why. In a half I tend to be chatty and often jokey but I'm not a natural 10k runner, I never know when I should pace myself and when I can really let rip. I guess it's a lack of experience.

On reflection I could have run faster today, I know Marc was having a great run and had heaps left in the tank. But I was scared of over committing myself and having to slow dramatically or even stop. I was feeling pretty steady until mile four when I started to flag a bit but Marc kept the pace up and was awesomely encouraging as always.

The last mile along the waterfront into a headwind is a feature of most races in Liverpool and a particularly mind bendingly demented one at that. It's as though race organisers have mistaken Otterspool Prom for Venice Beach and feel that participants will run their final mile in summery, carefree bliss along a sun blessed strip. The reality is that you're likely to find yourself dicing with death (or a broken ankle) along a narrow walkway of crazily laid cobbles and unexpected bollards where even in the height of summer chances are you'll be taking a force five gale and driving drizzle straight into your face. Santa Monica we are not.

I started to really tire in the last mile but a very well timed One Direction song (History) and pretty romantic moment just before the six mile point put the wind in my sails and a fire in my heart. We raced triumphantly into the Arena where the finish line was (stroke of genius I'd say and great for spectators as well as cold, tired runners) and crossed the finish line in 51.15. We ran straight into the arms of countless polar bears whom we hugged and high fived as we slurped down the complimentary coconut water. It was as bizarre and surreal as it sounds and yet it was also utterly brilliant and unique and made the whole event all the more memorable.

After chatting to a few friends we had ran into we jogged back off to the car and ate our entire body weight in fried pork products then collapsed into warm beds gazing at our super awesome medals. 10k as I've said before is not my distance, it's too long to run flat out and too short to get into a decent rhythm but it's manageable and we always have fun doing them.

And I did have a good time, I finished nice and fresh with lots of energy and feeling good and that's got to be a bonus. It was a great morning with lots of fun and a great group of fellow runners. And as for being frozen? The cold never bothered us anyway.

### Tuesday 19th January 2016

I may live to regret saying this but I like night time running, there's something very special about it. Of course there are drawbacks. There's the safety aspect (although I'm a very particular demographic being a tall, sweaty, out of tune bald chick in hi viz-it's a specialist market) and whilst I don't believe the world is populated with sex crazed psychopath, nevertheless it's always a consideration.

There's also the practical aspect. Perfectly flat, well-lit pavements pose a very real threat to a clumsy knob like me so dark, uneven paths are a veritable death trap. As well as all this it's hard to get out there when you've had a long day at work, it's cold outside and warm inside and all you really want to do is eat pie and be not quite drunk enough to warrant a hangover tomorrow.

But there are massive, incredible attractions too and if you can run safely, ideally with a tough Geordie (other regions are available) bloke with a powerful head torch, then I highly recommend it. Running in the dark is an entirely unique experience and it can transform an over familiar route into an epic adventure.

Tonight was no exception.

It was a cold, still night; the kind where a mist hangs in the blackness and coats your face with a chilly lick. We decided to run our usual coastal 10 mile route, both of us had over indulged in chocolate and filth today so in order to remain beautiful we needed to settle accounts with our lardy arses. I knew from the start I was feeling good. Whilst my 10k pace at the weekend wasn't blistering it was by no means gentle either so I was really enjoying winding it down a big notch.

I always run more slowly in the dark, maybe it's because I'm more cautious but I think it's also because I find the whole thing more meditative and so I tend to relax. This time I'd pitched my outfit right too, some highly reflective compression tights, a compression base layer and one of my trusty Gore jackets. I felt comfortable both in temperature and movement unlike the insane overdressing of the weekend.

I know a run is going well when I stop playing the numbers game. Everyone has coping strategies for difficult runs and mine is chunking, it's basically a way of creating mini goals within a run. I do a warm up, a work out, a cool down and a victory lap. So a chunked ten mile run would become 3/3/3/1, a half marathon might be 4/4/4/1 or similar.

It's a good strategy as it not only distracts you but also forces you to focus on your form. When I ran my last London Marathon I chunked it 8/8/8/2.2 and it helped me massively. It can turn an insurmountable distance into three manageable training runs and you can work brief breaks into them giving an even greater incentive.

Anyway, I know I'm having a decent trot when I don't need to do this and tonight was just that. My Garmin firmly beneath my sleeve so I couldn't see the pace or obsess about distance I was happy to just allow the miles to tick over. As we turned at the rifle range we laughed about some of the bonkers weather we'd ran in lately and how lucky we were to be out on such a still night.

And we, as runners, are so blessed.

I've mentioned before about how runners just seem more tuned into nature and their surroundings and this is true but why? I think it's because we have opportunity. As we ran along the path tonight we could see very little because of the headlamp but the smell of ozone and sea salt was intense, it filled our lungs and made us feel a billion times more alive than we had in the sleepy sitting room we had abandoned.

The tide was in, less than a few metres from us and we paced ourselves to the rhythmic melody of the waves. Marc whom we had renamed 'The Human Lighthouse' switched off the lamp and the skyline suddenly illuminated with the luminous glow of the city and the countless dots of light across the lazily folding water. It was this sight that stopped us in our tracks, it was honestly breathtaking. We stood for a while, not speaking, breathing in the shimmery mist and watching the water hit the shore in a foamy ribbon as the occasional ship slid across the horizon and disappeared into the icy night. I'm not sure how long we stayed there but I do know that very few people passed save the odd cyclist streaking down the pathway in a blur of LED or the die-hard dog walker with his steaming, panting companion.

And this is what I mean about running, this is why it's different than any other sport, this is why I bang on about it. Running presents you with experiences, it gifts you with opportunities to witness how truly spellbinding the world can be. In our day to day it's easy to get distracted by life, so lost in the melee that we miss the moments. Running hands us gobsmacking instances of utter wondrousness on a cracker, with chutney.

And you don't have to live in an exceptionally beautiful part of the world to find it, I've been blown away by the sunlight hitting an oil splat on a dock land pavement or a swan floating along a canal in one of the toughest, most urban parts of the city. Most runners I know can find a poetry in the place where they run. I think part of the reason is because it so keenly focuses the mind, giving you a sharper clarity of both thought and vision; it teaches us to see more, notice more and drink in the simple grace of our planet. Running allows us to see the world on the biggest screen in the best cinema and it's all for free.

So we stood there quietly, appreciating the privilege of opportunity and gratefully acknowledging that despite some challenges in our lives we are also frequently blessed with moments of awe. We felt lucky, humbled and weirdly emotionally charged. Marc put his arms around me and as he did I felt a tear prick in the corner of my eyes followed immediately by a blazing whack to my left eyebrow as the headlamp made contact with my skull. It was then I received an important physics lesson. Shouting 'fuck' loudly on a deserted beach causes it to echo tremendously thus resonating across the entire coastline with the intense volume of a tornado jet reaching sonic boom. Way to gift wrap a memory Lopez.

I can't be held entirely responsible for the destruction of such a tender moment though. As I held my hands to my eye in profane and dizzy confusion Marc turned away from me for what I thought was one last, lingering glance at the ocean. What he was in fact doing was urinating, with gusto. The Human Lighthouse had become the Human

Fire Engine. There was nothing else to do, I sealed the deal with a particularly high pitched fart, we sniggered conspiratorially and then legged it.

The final couple of miles of the run returned to the peaceful contemplation that they had been at the outset. The 100 Iron Men that span Crosby beach cut strong but lonely figures half submerged in the frosty depths, half staring out to the dark endless horizons before them. The miles ticked by and my legs moved without thought or design. There was a dull ache in my calves but the reassuring kind that you get with distance running and simply learn to live with. I noticed how the absence of light made this path that I know so well feel so different. In the day I am aware of impending inclines, I focus on them as I approach them. I can see the summits of hills as I begin the climb and I keep my eyes on distant objects to haul myself to the top. In the darkness for some reason I noticed the uphills less and the downhills more. Could it be that my eyes are deceiving me in the light, tricking my mind into believing that a mere bump is a hill and what looks comfortably flat is actually a wonderful downward section? Without the deception of vision maybe the road becomes exactly what it is and I am less apprehensive and more accepting. Like a child squeezing their eyes closed to block out an imaginary monster, maybe I sometimes need to shut out my fears to gain some perspective and rely on a little blind faith.

For my whole life I thought the demons lived in the night time, lurking in the darkness. Running has shown me that for the large part they exist only in the recesses of my own head and their defeat is in my own hands or rather in my own feet because with every mile I cover they diminish.

We talked over all sorts of stuff, both nonsense and importance. We had a brief ridiculous exchange about whether soldiers wear hi viz and a longer, more solemn discussion about grieving the loss of a pet. We chatted over our days and left the stresses and dramas of it on the road. The random nature of conversation was our minds way of emptying and relaxing, dumping its load onto the pathways to leave a blank page ready to be written with another day.

Sometimes when you think that nothing is really happening it's actually the time that great change is taking place. It's only when you look back on it and reflect that you can see it. It was a run of no consequence and yet of real significance. We had encountered nothing unusual yet experienced something dramatically wonderful. It was an extraordinarily ordinary adventure.

Maybe that's why I like running in the night time.

# 5

# Growing Up

**Thursday 21st January 2016**

A solo run this morning as Marc was off having fun driving ambulances and eating tangerines. It was the first time I've been down the western canal route on my own, it runs through some fairly tasty areas of Liverpool but I'm very familiar with it as we often run it together. I can say that as I'm a Scouse girl, born and bred and I'm incredibly proud of my city. Besides, it was blowing a gale and as we live right by the coast it's the only place we can get some shelter owing to the large often disused warehouses that border it. My fears were allayed as I met with nothing but friendly dog walkers and some workmen on the bridge. They probably had more cause to fear the steaming tall bald chick in Lycra wheezing towards them with a constantly streaming nose. And yes, I was belting out tunes. Today's most notable track was a particularly moving rendition of Starships by Nicki Minaj. Not safe for work by the way but it kind of suited the surroundings.

Anyhow it was a lovely run, yes it was tough on the way out as it was very windy but it was manageably hard. It's funny for me to think of how much mental toughness I've garnered over the last few years; of course my illness and its accompanying harsh treatment has played its part in that growth in strength of spirit. When I was first diagnosed I was scared and defeated, I just wasn't the kind of person who could take this shit on. I was acutely aware of my legendary lack of stamina and my mental weakness. I don't think it was until I gave up smoking in February 2012 that I began to believe I might have found some inner strength, an ability to tough it out when things got hard.

In my early running days I would stop at every corner, my long legs saved my times from looking like a slow walk but ultimately I had no resolve, no desire to dig in. If it hurt I stopped, if I was tired I stopped. In my head I remember thinking that it was fine, I had cancer so no one was going to expect any more of me, people would still admire me regardless of how long it took me to get there. And I guess in the early days many of my runs were about validation, I wanted people to admire what I was doing as it made me feel strong and important.

Of course there were days when I just couldn't do it, I remember several runs that were so heartbreakingly difficult I would dissolve into self-flagellating pools of tears. One such event was my second London Marathon which I think was a seminal moment in my running life.

I've avoided writing about this one as it stirs up old memories and emotions that I don't always like to be reminded of. In fact much of it I'd forcibly forgotten about and I had to trawl through Facebook to find photos that might kickstart my memory. Training began as always with me starting from scratch, I had barely moved since my third Great North Run in 2013. It had been my first GNR with Marc and a great day but treatment had started to lay waste to my body. We'd euphorically committed ourselves to another London Marathon immediately after the first and were bubbling with excitement. Then winter came and with it some ridiculously cold weather.

After the first couple of longish runs my doctor insisted I keep out of the extreme temperatures so I hit the treadmill and it was torturous. Back then I wasn't a gym goer so didn't have a membership to a swanky club and was unwilling to pay out for the privilege of not using it. Instead I gratefully used the school gym conveniently situated at the top of our road. Of course there was no air-con or TV just a small room facing a brick wall. I thumped out miles in that room, I can remember the smell of it still. But I was grateful of it; midweek training runs were so much more manageable and who knew that you ran so much faster on a treadmill than on the streets? I even did one of my long runs on it, around 14 miles of sweaty boredom but it beat potential pneumonia as my health was rapidly declining.

But it wasn't all bad, when the weather wasn't being a knob we had some amazing runs. My friend, Naomi joined me on her bike for the weekend runs that Marc couldn't get to. His mum was also poorly at the time and so his runs were often done in Newcastle. We would run on the same day, often at the same times and think of each other as we ran. It sounds cheesy but with 200 miles between us we really needed the mutual support. It was always weirdly comforting when we found we'd run at exactly the same pace in the same time without realising.

Then tragically Marc's beloved dog Sam passed away, he was naturally devastated. Being so far apart, connected only by text messages and phone calls made it all the more difficult. The death of a pet is always a huge loss but given that Sam had been Marc's constant companion since he had returned home to care for his mum after his dad's death made it all the more gaping. I think at that point his runs were therapeutic, cathartic and very difficult.

But we did have some runs together and they were generally wonderful. I remember an almost idyllic 9 miles through the paths of Hightown and back onto the beach. It was runs like that I adored, the sun shone and we took our time. I had invested in a Camelbak and it revolutionised the long run for me. Nowadays I can run a half marathon without the need for a drink but back then I would get a dry mouth from around 8 miles. I would fill my Camelbak with gallons of blue Powerade and take numerous gels with me, I loved the planning and the anticipation of it all. Every long run felt like a new and epic adventure but they did seem to be getting tougher. I would miss the occasional midweek run, then maybe a long run if I'd had chemo. After all I had done the distance before, I knew what to expect. But there was an issue, for the first time in my life I had an injury and it was getting worse.

When I say the first time in my life that is something of a misnomer, I should rather say it was the first time I couldn't ignore the same injury I'd been ignoring for the past two years. Over the course of that time I had developed a hip condition that would range from a twinge to searing agony depending on how far I ran. I had a couple of sporadic physio sessions but there was never enough time to see it all through. As my mileage increased so did the pain which began working its way down my leg and into my foot.

When Marc and I did our final long run one intensely beautiful March Sunday morning it all seemed OK. We headed off down the bypass excitedly knowing that our destination was Ainsdale and then back, it seemed unthinkably far to go on foot. I can recall heart bursting happiness about having made it this far despite so much difficulty, so much hardship. It seemed that the Gods were shining on us and it would all be OK.

What I didn't realise then was that all the runs I had done on the treadmill were in kilometres that I had mistaken for miles, no wonder I was so fucking good. I was woefully underprepared and so foolishly overconfident.

The 20 mile run itself was beautiful, a crisp, sunny day the return journey took us through pine woods and trails as well as beach and and villages. It was a stunning route and I promise myself every year to repeat it. From seven miles in though my hip had started to make itself known, by 13 miles my entire leg hurt and by 15 my foot had cramped in the instep so much that I had to sit down by a post office and cry.

In hindsight I knew the severity of the injury, I prepared for runs with painkillers, anti inflammatories and even took ibuprofen gel with me to rub on my hip at breaks. The whole of my right side screamed with pain and it was agonising. Despite being one of the most beautiful and joyful runs I can recall it also broke me, physically and in my spirit. Thank God it was taper time. Marc returned home and I resolved to rest up until marathon day.And then the unthinkable happened.

On the night of 7th April, just 6 days before race day, Marc's beloved mum, Audrey died. It was shockingly unexpected. Yes she had been unwell and in hospital but we had never entertained the thought of anything but a full recovery for this strong willed, brave woman. It was beyond comprehension as we both sat in the hospital ward in total disbelief.

Suddenly I felt about 11 years old, I wanted somebody to sort it all out, to make it all better but no one could. We were the grown-ups now. It was physically painful to look at Marc visibly shell shocked and utterly bereft, I kept repeatedly apologising to him. I was so sorry it had happened and if I could have bargained him out of the darkness with my soul that night I would have paid with it gladly. He stopped eating, he didn't sleep. He functioned but he wasn't present in his own body, his mind had gone somewhere else. The next day we had a momentary conversation about the upcoming London Marathon weekend merely to confirm that I would make all the necessary cancellation arrangements which I duly did.

But in the day or two that followed after I had cancelled a doubt had crept into my mind. Would he regret this? Would I regret this? I felt horrifically selfish for even thinking it but the thought kept coming back, we had worked so hard, been through so much.

On the Friday I asked Marc what he thought, should we do it? I did more than ask, I definitely pushed the point, by now I was convinced that he was doing the wrong thing. In all he had been through over the past few years, his journey from being overweight into fitness, the death of his father, his mother's illness, his beloved dog, Sam's death. Through all of this he had ran. It was what he did, who he was. If ever anything could reach into him and find his soul it was this, it was a marathon.

And so that day he posted this in Running the World...

'After a couple of days of soul searching and reflection, and despite the incredible amount of pain, grief and sorrow I feel right now, I have decided Nicky and I will be on the start line at the London Marathon this weekend after all. Why? Because it's not just about me and what I'm feeling. It's also about Nicky and the extraordinary determination and stoicism she has shown over the past year despite huge challenges. It's about our friends and family and everyone on here and beyond who has shown us kind words and support. It's about everyone who has generously donated to Macmillan on our behalf. But most of all, it's about my mum.

A couple of days before she died I held her hand and told her I wouldn't leave her in hospital to go to London and she just said 'oh get yourself away, I'll be fine'. That was one of the last conversations I had with her. Mum never gave up and despite all the horrible health problems life threw at her she took it all and kept moving forward with a cheery disposition. Despite her frail health, she was the toughest person I ever knew and the biggest inspiration in my life. So on Sunday we run, and she runs with us, free from the pain and disability of MS. Because life is all about moving forward, one step at a time and keeping your head up no matter what. Mum taught me that.'

## April 13th 2014, London Marathon, Greenwich

At the starting line my throat felt dry, it had been a strange morning. Although you couldn't help be swept along in the atmosphere of it all I was also acutely aware of the deep tide of sadness that had engulfed Marc. The sun was shining strongly, too strongly for a mid-April day and everyone looked like they were on holiday. The race itself was an odd one in that Marc and I had two completely different experiences. I've felt bad since saying I didn't enjoy the day as it was such a meaningful and significant run for Marc. Of course I enjoyed it, how could anyone not enjoy the London Marathon, it is a joyous day even in the most extreme of circumstances. But in truth I found it to be one of the most painful runs of my life and one that devastated my confidence.

I think part of that feeling was because I had so wanted to be there for Marc, to support him and guide him through. The reality was in the end that he as good as carried me for the last 13 miles.

I think it was at 6 miles in I knew that it wasn't my day, if it had been any other run I would have chucked it there and then. At 10k I was completely spent and I knew it was going to cost me enormously.

It was stiflingly hot that day and I was constantly thirsty, Marc was a man on a mission, running in memory of his mum he was totally focused. I think in many ways his focus was as much to manage his emotions as anything else. But it was cathartic for him too and it had given him opportunity to reflect, to cry openly and to accept the support of thousands of kind strangers. For that reason alone the race was worth it.

I know Marc very much carried Audrey with him and it spurred him on. I felt horrifically selfish, I moaned and cried and despaired. At the halfway point I remember my feeling of panic, I was destroyed already.

I'd also like to mention at this stage why you should always try your outfit on before race day and why you should have a practise run in it. Well of course you should, that's like the first rule of running I hear you say! Well I have never been terribly good with rules and on that day it came back to bite me on the ass. Or at least that's how it felt.

It was, as mentioned, a scorcher but I had recently become a devotee of compression wear, probably largely due to the ridiculous

Recovery Run
Nicky Lopez

injury I'd been ignoring. I felt that it had mystical qualities that squashed my calf muscles in such a way as to stop them jiggling and therefore reduce pain. I should tell you that I still hold firm to this belief and cannot be shaken. The problem was that the hot weather did not lend itself to long compression tights and neither did my vanity. A photograph taken from our first London Marathon had become somewhat iconic but all I could see on it were mega thighs, I had resolved the next time I would look amazing.

So I decided it had to be shorts, and not just any shorts, I wanted bright pink hot pants. In order to combine these with compression I had to wear long socks and so I bought neon pink ones to match. Obviously I would need to wear matching shoes but the shoes I had been wearing for training, my trusty Nike Pegasus, were white and this wouldn't work. Cue mega pink running shoes. Only these were lightweight, minimal running shoes as opposed to the ones I'd been wearing. That wouldn't hurt though right?

Actually it did hurt, it hurt a lot. Firstly my feet were wrecked. After ten miles I felt like I was running barefoot on Lego, soon after my hip began to cry and my entire right leg started burning. Of course I looked amazing though? Well not exactly. Having not given the shorts a run through I hadn't considered that I seem to have a cavernous propensity for camel toeage. The upshot was that my thong disappeared somewhere into my womb and began to tear apart my reproductive system. Then my shorts decided to follow, pretty soon I was wearing a pair of gym knickers, only you couldn't really see them.

I had fake tanned before the event (of course, I bet Mo would too) but hadn't thought to apply sun lotion. By the halfway point my legs had burnt to the same neon pink as my socks and shorts (which had become moulded to the exact shape of my genitalia.) The resulting effect was that I was naked. Naked and pink. Naked, pink and in intense pain. My butt was consuming my outfit in slow, steady munches and try as I might to liberate my underwear it had become terminally lodged.

I can honestly say I don't remember too much of the run itself, the trauma, lack of sleep and proper meals had all conspired to render us ill prepared as had my unwitting lack of training. It hurt so badly. Marc was incredible, he put his own pain aside and quite literally

64

dragged us through. There were times he got cross and I needed it, I had given up on the race and I had given up on myself. This was a step too far, one race too many, who was I trying to kid? I spent much of the final miles walking through the crowds.

The photos from the day show so clearly the pain and emotion on our faces but also the massive support that Marc gave me. Still one of my all-time favourite photos is where I am smiling and Marc has his arm around me, it was at that moment that he had made a particularly vulgar joke about my foof hoof and I broke into giggles. Even in the most intense grief (and what I realised after, his own great physical pain) he still knew how to lift me and bring me home.

The part of the race that I remember most was what that made it totally worthwhile and irreplaceable in my memory. As we came along the Mall in relative agony Marc began fumbling in his running belt. He produced a folded up photograph of his mum that he had been carrying with him. As he took my hand to cross the finish line he held the photo to his heart. When Audrey was laid to rest the following week Marc had placed the photo with her. On it he had written 'you were with me every step of the way'.

That day he taught me what true strength was and the way I looked at him had altered forever and he in turn had changed me instantly and irreversibly.

Today on the canal my attitude was different and I think that spills from my experiences but also into my new ones as well. I learnt to be tough by going through tough times both on and off the road. Today every time I felt like flagging I remembered the days when I felt genuinely too ill or pained to carry on as well as the days I just didn't have the mental grit to hang on in there. I made this run a tribute to those days. In Marc's words 'it was hard but I was harder'.

Turning at the halfway point the tailwind lifted my legs and made me grin for the vast proportion of the remainder of the run. I stopped briefly to marvel at a cormorant on the edge of the water. As this was in a very cheeky part of town I was reluctant to hang around for too long lest my feet get nicked or something. But it was so cool to see something so naturally beautiful somewhere so man made and urban. Like I said before, no matter where you live there's beauty to be found whether it be a slightly off track seabird, a long forgotten historic bridge or a wall full of awesomely, brilliantly painted graffiti that I couldn't photograph in case I got shot.

Ten miles of cold, epic fun that I'll look forward to doing in the dark with the Geordie next week.

I'm off to buy a bulletproof vest and some knuckle dusters.

# 6

# Sweetness and Light

**Saturday 23rd January 2016**

Sometimes you have shit runs, ones where nothing goes right and you can tell from the outset. From a slight kink in your knickers, a misjudged too warm top or a slippery pair of shades to an untrustworthy sphincter, a painful chafe or banging headache. Some runs just start off crap and descend into utter bollocks. Sometimes you run and it's acceptable, tolerable, uneventful, that's the best and worst you can say of it. Not every run you're going to have is going to be a hills are alive moment comparable only to the birth of a child or a marriage proposal. And neither should it be, running is as much about experience and growth as it is about joy and enrichment and as with everything in life you need a bit of shade to highlight the golden bits.

However, when you have a wonderful run it is a gift, it has the power to turn an arse of a week into an insignificance. It can take your sad, tired eyes and flip them around in their sockets until you see the world refreshed and hopeful. Today was such a run for me.

After a very busy, very stressful week at home we were desperate to get out of town. We threw our bags in the car and headed east, the three of us gobbling burgers on the way. When we arrived in Newcastle I wiped the days make-up away and with it came the larger proportion of my eyebrows and eyelashes. It shouldn't have been a big deal, it's happened many, many times before but since finishing chemo a few weeks ago I'd sort of forgotten about things like this. My eyebrows had recovered a little recently due to a new regime and I was beginning to regain a semblance of the face I once had (albeit with a few years drawn onto it).

I guess, on reflection, that it was a timely reminder to chill the hell out. I've been working very hard and worrying harder lately and I've ignored the reality that chemo is still not entirely out of my life. But last night it seemed like a big deal, it felt like a setback. I needed to do something to redress the balance, I needed to show myself that this kind of crap doesn't mean anything, that I still had it all under control.

# Recovery Run
## Nicky Lopez

And so we ran.

Marc, or 'Pathfinder' as he likes to be called (he can be a proper dick sometimes) was in charge of the route again. To be fair it is generally his job, he understands the land, the weather and direction of the wind much better than I. My usual process is considerably more haphazard, if it's windy I go to the canal and that's about as technical as I get. We decided to do a half marathon.

I like the stretched out atmosphere of a half. It's long enough to relax into it and feel significant without being so long that you feel destroyed for the rest of the day. It's a distance that requires respect, it can take up to six months training to take it on but it's a lot easier to maintain than a marathon and it's also a considerably smaller time sacrifice. I like the steadiness of it, there's no running at breakneck speeds which suits me just fine.

The route was perfect, it was challenging but not horrifically so and this made us drop the pace even more. Marc had really thought this one out; knowing that a familiar route would cause my mind to wander and dwell on stuff he had chosen a much more 'off the beaten track' way to go knowing that it would provide distraction and diversion from the strain we'd been under. And it really did.

The weather had calmed and it was the first day in ages I hadn't shuddered and swore as we set out. The first few miles from Seaton Sluice gripped the cliff edge and took us across the trails over muddy tracks and gravelly paths bringing us parallel to gaze down on the dramatically gorgeous St Mary's Lighthouse. From there we rode the roller coaster that is Whitley Bay to Tynemouth, a series of bulbous ups and sprinting downs along the mind blowingly incredible North Eastern coast of England. Past the fishing boats and chip smell of pretty Cullercoats to the sweeping Tynemouth Longsands up to the imposing ruins of the Priory that sit proudly at the top of a formidable hill (seven lampposts of wheezing terror) we ran into a steady headwind which we'd long since made our peace with.

The gentler weather had made everyone seem strangely grateful and peaceful and passers-by smiled encouragingly at us. I had worn my 'One Woman Army' Under Armour t shirt mainly because I liked the pink lettering but Marc had said I deserved to wear it, I'd earned it. I felt strong and in control again and I swear I felt that something bad had left my body, set me free. We laughed about the phenomena that is being run drunk, the way you lose your ability to think straight and speak with heavily slurred words. We genuinely sounded like we were rat arsed as we laughed, trumped and blamed it on ducks and tried to calculate half of 13 which was by that point an impossible yet somehow ridiculously funny task. We also noted how much we hate pedestrians (they walk in groups of seven across sidewalks and get offended if you politely-despite sounding shitfaced-ask them to move), extendible dog leads (death traps to all runners) and kids on scooters (why do they seem to synchronise with your exact pace then stop dead in front of you?) All of this was done sounding like we'd spent the best part of the morning getting hammered.

We turned just before the Fish Quay and happily trotted back to enjoy a tailwind and some joyful downhill sections. At 8 miles I had a tiny crisis of confidence as my calf stiffened a little as it often does. I told myself I'd been through more and tougher than this and to enjoy it because there were many days not so long ago that 2016 itself didn't seem a possibility for me. And so we chose to rejoice, to love the run.

The temperature slipped considerably and despite the fucking inexplicable headwind we battled at Whitley Bay (What the actual fuck? Does it seek me out? Is it trying to destroy me?) we felt perfectly comfortable. We kept the pace down knowing the trail section we had coming in the last three miles and it felt happy, I'd never say easy because I don't think a half can ever honestly be described as that. It felt good though.

As we headed through the muddy trails across the grasslands I felt almost sad that we were coming to the end of the run, it had been triumphant in its atmosphere. We had however parked the car at our favourite fish and chip shop on the whole planet so the incentive to finish overwhelmingly beat the desire to continue. The spirit may be strong but the stomach is mighty.

Within a mile from finishing Marc took a sudden left turn away from the track and I duly followed what I thought to be a clever short cut. What it turned out to be was a hill of Himalayan like proportion that rose up from the path and glared over me like a fat, grey monster who had eaten all my bloody chips. Giving Marc a look of aghast confusion followed by an exclamation of 'For Fuck's Sake!' we scaled the heights, stretching out calves and running on tiptoes. My temperature rose and my face pinked but I never once considered dropping. At the top Marc said he was convinced I was a one woman army to take on that hill at that point in a half marathon.

But he's wrong, I'm not. I am more than a sum of my sometimes useless and malfunctioning parts. I am a history of trial and triumph made only possible by a relentless cheering squad and a tough Geordie lad who has carried me up every hill and some mountains that others thought insurmountable. And this army marches on its stomach. Which is now very full of fish, chips, peas and curry.

**Sunday 24th January 2016**
Today as we travelled back to Liverpool from Newcastle I was thinking about what stage we would be at in our London Marathon training. It got me to thinking about the tough, tough winter training we had endured leading up to our first London Marathon back in 2013 and the incredibly epic adventure the day turned out to be.

**26th April 2013, London Marathon, Greenwich**
The first time I stood at the start line for London Marathon I was proud. It was just a week after the Boston Marathon bombings and every runner wore a black ribbon on their shirt. A minute silence was held and the atmosphere through Greenwich Park was static intensity, I have never experienced anything like it. Standing there on a blindingly sunny Sunday morning with shaking legs and hopeful heart listening to only birdsong amongst thirty odd thousand runners was indelibly profound. And there was a sense of defiance in the air, a feeling that we would not be felled by terrorism, stilted by violence, quietened by oppression. We would run together.

I think in hindsight that set the tone for the whole run as it was an epic triumph for the pair of us. Never had we felt so humbled by the unwavering, sometimes deafening support from the also defiantly deep crowds that lined the streets of London that day. It had been a bad winter and most of our training had been done in the worst conditions, we were rarely out of gloves and hats and regularly had to wear snowchains on our running shoes. It had toughened us though and given us a feeling of badass invincibility, we could take on anything after that.

The day itself was the first that the temperatures had risen to double figures in a long while and the sun shone on us as if it were also standing with us all as brothers in arms. I have never heard my name shouted so loudly without alcohol and a breakage of some sort being involved before, it was earth shattering. Every corner, every stretch I ran there would be a roar as my shining, hairless scalp glistened in the brightness and my limbs heavily creosoted in copious fake tan for the occasion glowed against my green Macmillan vest. Marc got more than his fair share of screeches and roars too, one girl who shouted out 'you look far too good to have run that far Marc' doesn't realise how close she came to getting a Kirkby Kiss (Liverpool slang for a head butt) that day had I not been delirious with adoration.

Marc at this point was experiencing a quite different type of runners high. He had rather prematurely consumed one of his Lucozade Elite gels and promptly and without warning become bizarrely and psychotically addicted to them. As we passed gel stations he grabbed them by the handful ordering me to do the same, he would then rip open two of them at a time with his teeth and demonically slurp them down shouting incoherently in my face about how good they were. I looked with horror at this Macmillan green beast before me, off his face on caffeine and sugar with pale orange goo dribbling off his chin. He started riding an imaginary horse and swinging a lasso while Rhinestone Cowboy played loudly from a nearby pub. At one point he stepped on a Lucozade bottle and the entire thing exploded across the road to his manic hilarity, he was so far gone his veins were running liquid energy.

That's not to say I didn't have my own moments of madness; mass hysteria can do funny things to you. Around the point where we passed Cutty Sark I could hear an old familiar tune playing in the distance, the crowd at this juncture of the course is famously large and vocal. Buoyed up by the roars and the music I took it upon myself to pick up the pace a little, well at least that's how it felt. What actually happened was that I started sprinting at full tilt through the ten to eleven minute mile runners (which was ambitiously pacy for me at the time) with Marc desperately trying to catch me. He started shouting my name as I notched up an eight minute mile, eventually he caught me and madly asked me what the hell I thought I was doing. I stopped dead, hands on hips and looked him straight in the eye and berated him loudly with these words "FOR CHRIST'S SAKE MARC, IT WAS WHAM!"

George and Andrew have got a lot to answer for.

It didn't stop there though, at mile 21 I gave the now almost demented Marc a jolt into sobriety. We were running along the embankment having emerged from the inexplicably titled 'Tunnel of Yes', a short underpass designed to uplift runners at the most difficult stretch blaring upbeat music and featuring flashing motivational slogans. It will however forever be known to us as the 'Tunnel of Piss' owing to the fact that if you give any blokes a large, darkened area they will automatically want to urinate in it. As we came out of the wee stinking dungeon of positivity I realised I still had 5 miles left to run.

This in itself wasn't a horrific thought except that I had quickly converted it into time and that meant nearly an hour more running.

No way.

No way.

No fucking way.

There was no physical possibility after running for 21 miles could I continue for another hour. It was then that I decided I was having a heart attack.

As Marc was emerging from his 2 hour Lucozade bad trip he started getting his second wind, no doubt fuelled by the gargantuan quantities of glucose and caffeine raging around his system. As he wide eyed, smilingly started quoting inspirational phrases lifted from Nike adverts at me I calmly advised him I was having a heart attack. That sharply wiped the grin off the bastard sugar junky.

To be fair, my feet had become wet with blood where my toenails had stripped away a few weeks before. During chemo I kept falling prey to the same skin infection and my nails on both my fingers and toes had become casualties. I usually strapped them up but today I couldn't and the pain was becoming unbearable. It was no good, the agony had sent my heart into shock and I had suffered a massive coronary. After a few minutes of manic chaos and panic, stopping and wiggling my toes for a minute and taking a drink I reassessed the extent of the damage. I decided that I wasn't arresting and was in fact being a bit of a pussy.

The next few miles were punctuated with walk breaks taking in the overwhelming love and encouragement from the simply unbelievable people of London. I have never felt so proud to be not just British but a citizen of the world as I did that day. How despite the very real threat of terrorism in the nation's capital the public had not only braved a massive event but actually come out in force. They turned up in their tens of thousands with their unstoppable devotion to lift the spirits of the runners. And lift us they did, higher than 26.2 miles could ever bring us down.

Fuelled by the charged atmosphere we resolved to run down Birdcage Walk and onto the Mall; it was there I had stood a year previously considering if this would ever be possible. I had dreams of turning at the Victoria Memorial and seeing the Palace in its full glory so we were determined to hit that ground running. Turning at Big Ben and down onto Birdcage Walk we were overtaken with emotion and both began to cry pretty openly, it was a release as much as anything, an acknowledgment of all it had taken us to get here. We were excited to turn onto the Mall and run towards Cleo and my mum who we knew would be waiting in the Grandstands.

The trouble was that Birdcage Walk is much longer than it seems on the telly and after running half of it at a much rocketier pace than you really should, you find yourself pretty screwed over. I began to stagger and veer pretty wildly. As we turned the corner I started to hallucinate, my eyes were fixed upon a tiger running perpendicular across the runners while a group of black suited policemen threw themselves at him and wrestled him to the ground. Only it wasn't a hallucination, it was real. Well it wasn't a real tiger but a bloke dressed as one who'd decided to jump the barriers and make a break for the finish line.

And that's how we completely missed Buckingham Palace. Still we hobbled down the flag lined Mall, to yet more screams. I was blindly scanning the Grandstands until I suddenly saw them, my Mum and Cleo in Macmillan t shirts waving madly. I frantically staggered towards them. Mum with a look of dire concern on her face said 'you don't look very well at all' at which I burst out crying. I hugged Cleo in a fireball of emotion, I couldn't find any words, but in her inimitable style Cleo managed to save the day with this little pearl... 'Mum, my foot is a bit sore'

Seriously.

How she's still breathing today is largely due to my fear of incarceration.

We laughed hysterically, hugged them again and set off on our final lap. Feet now on fire we saw the sign above our heads...

385 YARDS TO GO!

Awesome! Now what the fuck is a yard?

We had trained in miles, sometimes kilometres but never yards. It may as well have said

385 QUICHES TO GO!

It probably would have made more sense to be honest. In my lunatic state I became convinced that a yard was the same distance as my arm so spent the final victory strides of my marathon with my right arm stretched in front of me staring wildly at it while I tried to work out how many of them I had left to run. We crossed the line hand in hand and our hearts exploded. We stood at the other side of the finish line wrapped up in each other for what was probably an inconvenient amount of time until we heard the shout of someone from the gantry behind us. It was a photographer perched high above the finish line calling us for a photo that would be used in future London Marathon magazines. We turned towards him and raised our hands as he snapped us. The hand signal we made?

Victory.

# 7

# Education

**Monday 25th January 2016**

As we returned from our run today we saw some kids from the local school running around the block. They were grimacing in shorts and t shirts through the miserable wintry drizzle and strong winds and they looked thoroughly pissed off. It took me back to my own school games lessons and I practically shuddered at the thought of cross country. It's so odd that a sport which actively terrified me as a young girl has become the cornerstone of my life.

If you ask many people what their experience of running was in schools you won't be surprised to hear it was dire. Save from a handful of cross country enthusiasts or the lucky few who were blessed with a great teacher the rest of us dragged our puffed out bodies, aching with a stitch across gale blown fields in nothing more than tiny shorts and a cotton top. This was often accompanied by a fierce teacher of undetermined sexuality barking orders to stop dawdling and go faster. It's hardly mind blowing news that many people grow up harbouring extremely negative attitudes towards running. After all, it's cold, it's painful and I can't do it without stopping which is also embarrassing. Running is a sport which sets you up for failure then delivers it on wet field.

Even more powerful than this is the notion of running as punishment. If you were out of line, naughty, cheeky or simply underachieving (damn you and your non Olympian genes) then you would be sentenced to a lap of the field. A fate worse than death. Running was a sport that we were expected to master from the outset, a tall order given that we did not receive a singular strategy to help us improve. It was an instant exam without lessons or guidelines, how could we ever be expected to pass? No one showed us how walking a little would improve our stamina and make the experience more enjoyable. Because running wasn't supposed to be enjoyed rather endured. No one told me that one day it would get easier, that one day it would even be fun. No one told me that running might one day help to save me from death and rescue my life.

I observed a student teacher last week give a sports lesson to a group of Year One and Two children. With great ingenuity and a huge dash of fun he put the kids through their paces explaining in accessible terms the importance of stretching and using an arsenal of games and activities to encourage them to move around. At one point the alpha males of the group were stretching way beyond their limits to show their athleticism, the student drew their attention to the smallest, quietest boy in the class who was stretching beautifully and used him as an example to the class. It was a stroke of genius lifting the confidence of the weaker boy and educating the alpha boys. He created a positive accepting atmosphere and it encouraged me that there are clever, dedicated sports teachers out there and up and coming to entrust our kids to.

I wish the 13 year old me with long legs and a desperate desire to be good at sport could see me now. I wish she had been next to me today during a happy eleven mile run along the Leeds Liverpool canal to the place we call Narnia and back. It's not that I was crap at sport, I wasn't, I just didn't excel. I'd scrape a place onto school teams or just make it in the athletic squad. I didn't set the world on fire but I didn't crash and burn either. But I never saw distance running as anything but torture inflicted on us in cruel weather by anoraked adults with hot coffees.

I think that terribly awkward young woman with crazy hair and dubious musical taste would have politely laughed if she was told she would choose to run in the worst of conditions just for the hell of it. In dayglo Lycra. With flat shoes.

As it stood it was a good run, a tough one but a good one. Storm Jonas is snapping at our heels bringing with him high winds and fat rain so we knew today would be the day to get out. But as usual I was tired. Dog tired. I was the kind of tired where you feel a little bit sick with it, my head spun as I lay on the bed and my heart rate was elevated. But sleep wouldn't come. I squirmed about for a good half hour occasionally squinting in nervous disgust at the window and the dancing trees outside. Our bedroom windows are uniquely fitted in such a way as to accentuate every breath of wind that whispers past to the max. A breeze sounds like a hurricane, a gust like Armageddon. It does nothing to tempt you outside on a cold day.

After some tea and peanut butter sourdough I began to feel moderately less like a butt pimple and re-examined the possibility of getting out.

And I knew we had to.

So into the gales we ran, it was thankfully warm making the gust an almost welcome assailant cooling down our overdressed torsos. I swear we're developing Stockholm Syndrome with the wind, we're growing unnaturally attached to it and find more and more reasons to be amongst it. Along the canal towards town we battled the invisible wall, passing the bloke who always mistakes me for a dude with his cheery 'morning lads!' We happened upon a group of birds all flexing their feathery muscles in the watery sun and I was fascinated by how four different species could coexist so harmoniously amidst their inner city back drop. At risk of sounding like a Miss World contestant (I could totally win that shit) I wondered if we as humans could take notice of how peaceably we could occupy the same surroundings, maybe we just needed to stop flapping so much.

Onwards past Bootle strand, through Kirkdale where we encountered police frogmen searching the waters for clues as to a recent murder. I thought back to the birds and it felt sadly poignant. As we approached our five mile turn at Boundary Bridge the breeze became fierce. It's here that the gusts bounce around and create a bizarre microclimate of confused winds and tempestuous waters. I was just easing to turn when Marc suggested we push on an extra half mile. It seemed manageable so we continued to the locks and their riotously colourful graffiti.

At this stage I was happy to turn, my legs were a little tired but my body was tireder still. I had that panting, vaguely hysterical breathing pattern that comes with total knackeredness. The kind where you feel like you've been crying for an hour and can't regain your normal rhythm. After a brief bugger around we kicked for home, the tailwind propelled us forwards and I felt easier, less troubled. Four miles from home we came past the police divers and said a happy hello to the officer. He commented that we weren't the brightest runners he'd seen today. I'm hoping he meant in apparel rather than intellect.

# Recovery Run
## Nicky Lopez

As we ran past the gender confused gentleman (confused about my gender, not his, he seems pretty secure in his masculinity) he remarked how fit the pair of us must be. We laughed and made a gag about running towards a giant cake but he was right, we are a fit gang of two. Even on our tiredest days our legs are trained to run for hours along raging coastlines and through neglected estates finding joy and renewal in every step.

The final couple of miles, 'the Tesco Two' as I've christened them were enjoyably tough, a phrase I never thought I would understand. A few hundred metres before we finished we encountered a puddle of Atlantic like proportions flanked with two mud mountains. Seriously, this bastard had a tide and its own economy. It was literally impassible. We eventually picked our way through what felt like a swamp before we rejoined the path and galloped the final few downhill strides with cheery pride. Eleven miles on a school day is serious shit.

Cleo was talking yesterday to me about teaching as a career, she asked me if I was worried that the children wouldn't like me if I had to reprimand them. I told her that my job isn't to be their best mate but to help them to learn and to develop a love of languages that will see them into adulthood. I did however say that reprimanding them for not understanding was useless, the same applies to the running punishers. Shouting at a child for slowing up or stopping during a run is the equivalent of me telling a child off for not being instantly fluent. If they don't know how then the onus is on us as teachers to educate, nurture and encourage.

So for all the wonderful PE teachers out there (of which there are multitudes) I salute you, may you feel a glowing pride in the life enhancing positivity you are gifting our children with. A gift that will stay with them throughout their days and will almost certainly extend their time on this beautiful planet. To the shouters, the barkers and the anoraked hypocrites, you will be sifted out one by one and your damaging and archaic attitudes with you. Enjoy your time on the Devils treadmill.

And finally to the shivery kids struggling to shift their stinging legs through the winter's onslaught, take heart. One day you will run for yourself, just because you can and the same wind that whipped your calves will whisk you along paths paved with joy. No harsh voice will ring in your ears just the sound of your heart thumping full and fast. And on that day, like me, you'll run for your life.

(For the last few years I've run a Reluctant Runners group in school. It's for the kids who for one reason or another don't get on well with sport. Some of them just plain think they're not good enough, some struggle with their weight, some have been bullied, most of them have had negative experiences with sport. Every Friday lunchtime we take to the streets and cover some pretty mean distances for 7-11 year olds. They support each other in the most incredible way with the fastest runners at the back helping and encouraging the slower ones to lead. We run as a team and no man gets left behind. You can't imagine what an achievement this is for them and for their proud parents, most of whom will run with them at a major city event later this year (last year over 50 of them). And what role models they become to the other kids who think they can't do it themselves.

Yesterday this year's new bunch did a mile and a half on their third ever run. This is what inspires me and moves me when I'm finding the going tough).

**Tuesday 26th January 2016**

I looked at my clothes this morning in despair. The week before last I had a major wardrobe cull and what started out as a spring clean became a clothing holocaust. I began by getting rid of things I don't wear followed by things that no longer fit me (I've lost over three stone in the last year so some of my outfits are becoming comically tent like). Bit by bit it descended into anything that I deemed non-essential. After recycling seven bin bags I looked with satisfaction at the tiny folded pile before my eyes, my capsule wardrobe.

And then I shit myself. I had basically thrown all my clothes away. I was left with three work outfits, two pairs of jeans and a couple of vest tops. What the hell had I been thinking? But secretly, shamefully I knew what I had been thinking...I need space to house my unforgivably massive collection of running gear.

I'm not really sure how this has happened to me, running has infiltrated my life in the most insidious of ways and has seeped into every aspect of it. But nowhere more so than my apparel. Ten years ago

# Recovery Run
## Nicky Lopez

I didn't own a pair of trainers, I wore only stiletto heels and I despised sportswear seeing it as the domain of the great unwashed or even worse, the fitness freak. My wardrobe was largely tight fitting, rather glamorous and heavily accessorised. If the occasion involved flat shoes or a fleece you could guarantee I'd find an excuse. Even in school I wore legendarily high heels and a ton of jewellery.

But little by little the silk gave way to Lycra and the slim fitting became compression. The navy and grey turned into the most hideous colour explosions, in the early days the more garish the better. Most significantly the shoes changed. I didn't really notice it until one day last year when I was smart shoe shopping and I found myself compromising by buying some Chelsea boots with a chunky heel. This had become as glamorous as I could be. Last Christmas Day I staggered to the pub (around 250 metres away) in the most beautiful diamanté studded Kurt Geiger heels, shoes that at one time I could have sprinted for a cab in. I haven't worn them since, so scared am I of giving myself sore feet or a sprained ankle that I cannot bring myself to attempt to walk in them again. The sad truth is that running has robbed me of my swag.

And it's not just my wardrobe.

Ten years ago I ate what I liked and didn't think twice. I ate cake, crisps, chocolate and drank like a fish. I couldn't say if my weight fluctuated or not because I was extremely slim. Then I was diagnosed and with chemotherapy came the substantial hit of steroids. Steroids are a bedfellow of chemo designed to help you tolerate the treatment in your system. The major side effect is weight gain, often dramatic. For me it was gradual but substantial and by April last year I had gone from a very slim 8 stone 6 to a relatively chunky 11 stone 7. Running had done nothing to deliver me from lardarsery as I am a serial over compensator.

Now before I go any further I'm completely on board when I hear people talk about not watching the scales, taking body measurements instead etc. and that's cool for those who are looking to change body shape but in April last year after London Marathon I was advised (or rather told) by my doctors to lose weight. It wasn't a body fat thing, it was weight that I had to lose. I had gained it over the years since I had started running. Now I know my treatment and steroids played their part in my three and a bit stone weight gain but you know what? Crisps and cake had a starring role too.

One of the reasons for my weight gain over four years of marathon training was that I was over compensating for my runs. Here's an example, to fuel for a 5 mile run I would have two small slices of malt loaf and would then run, come in and have a smoothie and a pasta meal. Sounds reasonable, right? The malt loaf and smoothie equalled around 450 calories added to around 250 additional calories at dinner time (because I'd earned it for running five miles). The run itself burned just on 500 calories. That meant that if I did that every day and ate totally carefully otherwise I would be eating an additional 200 calories a day.

But I didn't eat totally carefully because I was a runner and I could eat what I liked. It's so easily done, especially when marathon training as you tend to have a high carb meal the night before a long run too. I was put on a low calorie diet which I followed assiduously and I increased my mileage (I ate back 3/4 of the calorie burn from running each day). Over around 6 months I lost nearly 3 stone. I'm not promoting it for everyone but it worked for me.

That said I annoy myself sometimes. I question every bloody thing I eat as to what good it's doing for me. Running started this whole virtuous circle thing and I'm right at the centre of it. That's not to say I don't shovel Burger Kings down my pie hole at a rate of knots and glug vodka in frankly unsafe amounts on occasion but I must admit, those occasions are scarcer these days. Why? Because hangovers ruin runs and filthy food gives me the shits which in turn ruins runs. Not only has running destroyed my wardrobe it has also laid waste to my social life.

And as you might have guessed I'm an interminable running bore. Get me started on the rights or wrongs of a pre run stretch (wrong, just who can be arsed?) or a good discussion about hydration systems and I can go all day. I'm fucking mental at parties, me. So here I am, no clothes save enough spandex to dress a small, very camp, island nation. But here's the thing, I'm a billion times happier than the girl in stilettos from 10 years ago.

**28th September 2015, Happy Birthday Nicky.**

Ten years ago today I was a wild one. I was working as cabin crew and had a four year old daughter. We had a happy but chaotic life in Mallorca. My idea of a good time was getting totally off my face, which I did frequently. I ate crap, drank heavily, smoked heavily and all the rest. I wore activewear to have my nails done (yes I was that girl) and I hadn't owned a pair of trainers since I was at school (and they didn't get much use then.)

This morning I compared photos from then and now. I went for a ten mile birthday run, it's the thing I wanted to do more than anything. And I enjoyed every sweaty, windy goddamn minute of it. The Christmas after the first pic was taken my life changed; I left Mallorca, I stopped flying and began a new career and I started a new life in England. The last ten years have been a mad, scary, roller coaster to say the least but it's been filled with so many blessings. I wish I could tell the wild, long haired girl in the photos from then not to be afraid of the wild bald girl in the photos from now because despite the obvious she is lucky enough to live an extraordinary life filled with incredible people and amazing adventures. And she runs and runs and runs.

**Wednesday 27th January 2016**

Today I was made to feel very guilty about running and not for the first time. There's no doubt that it occupies a lot of my thoughts and that it can be time consuming, I also don't deny that I take a great deal of pleasure in it. The two hours or so that I dedicate to it are selfish, they are all about me. Yes, they add a huge dimension to my relationship with Marc but we'd still be together without it. There's no getting away from it, running is a self-centred, self-obsessed, narcissistic pastime.

And what does that make me? Well according to this person it makes me selfish, uncaring, vain and a bad parent. And I kind of take issue with that. Because I'm a really good parent. Yeah, I may overdo it on the vodka at times and end up having disastrous leapfrog contests at the end of our road at 1am with my mates and our kids. Yes, I don't always get it right with my decisions, most of the time I feel like it's a game of Russian roulette with the stakes being your child's health/happiness/popularity/self-esteem and yes, I'm not always around because for some of the time I'm out running, alone, away.

# Recovery Run
## Nicky Lopez

But ultimately I'm a super mum and no one would argue otherwise and if you asked Cleo who loved her most in the world my name would come up instantly, automatically. We have an unbreakable, untouchable relationship that was forged in the sands of Magaluf where we started out alone. With the addition of Marc we have become a solid tribe, a gang of three. We are Team Dopez and we've come to party.

But there's no denying the guilt I feel about running and I'm not alone. From what I hear other runners feel it too. I hasten to add at this point that it's not gender specific, I know guys who are given as hard a time as women. In fact I've seen marriages dissolve over arguments about running. And it's true, running is an extremely consuming pursuit, much more so than any other interest I've ever followed.

But let's be real, running isn't an interest, it's a lifestyle. In the same way that people turn to religion, meditation, even alcohol, running is far more about adopting a new mindset than it is about putting one foot in front of the other. From the minute we start referring to ourselves as runners we automatically sign ourselves up, we join the club. Of course we may never feel like a fully paid up member but nevertheless we join a tangible team, a living community. It was very much the same for me.

Not long after my first Great North Run I joined their official Facebook page and from that I joined a Facebook group, I'd never been part of one before but I needed to reach out to people who cared about energy gels and gave a shit about compression wear because none of my mates did. And it was there I met a boy, he ran the group I joined and he was annoyingly cocky, which I liked. He was also a Geordie, which I liked. And he was a runner. I didn't realise then the joy, the brilliance and above all the absolute convenience of having a partner who loves the same thing as you do. We instantly understood each other and could speak freely about Imodium, Body Glide and blisters. And joking aside, this shit matters. The fact that we shared such a lot of things that were intrinsic to our lives made us click.

Of course as we progressed we discovered the same inane sense of humour about things that nobody else would understand (eg. Jason D'rulo; an ongoing joke that the singer, Jason Derulo is actually a fat Yorkshire bloke with a penchant for pies) and a mutual vanity despite a deep desire for sleep and junk food. It really was a match made in heaven.

So does that make us both selfish? I guess so. We both prioritise running, it's the thing we most like doing (eating coming an extremely close second). But is that a bad thing? I don't think so. There I've said it. I don't think it's wrong to do something you like, something that brings you joy. So much of our lives are spent in angst and indecision, running is the small part of my day in which I have peace and clarity. I'm not saying that it doesn't hurt at times or frustrate me but for some inexplicable reason it pretty much always leaves me feeling better about myself. And I'm so much better a person when I like myself. Added to that no one can deny the benefits; when I run I feel fit, strong and unstoppable.

Does it make us vain? For sure. It makes me care about what I look like, it makes me want to look toned and awesome. Is that so awful? Not as far as I can see. When I look toned I feel amazing. I'm not talking about body ideals that I can't achieve I'm talking about the best version of me. That's got to be a good thing. And as for being a bad parent? Well we're sufficiently badly behaved that Cleo welcomes a 2 hour break from us a few times a week. And besides, it's often when she's out, in school or asleep.

I asked Cleo one day if she minded me going running and she looked at me incredulously, why would she? She's young and clever enough to remember that doing stuff you like, things that you enjoy are what life is all about. And if it results in Domino's pizza on the sofa at 8pm watching the X factor then so be it, she has parents who are awesome fun and love life. If you want your kids to live a life they love then you need to set the example by living yours the same way. How else are they going to learn?

The person who made me feel bad today sadly was raised thinking that you have to live a life of servitude without any thought to your own well-being. They hold the notion that enjoyment and happiness is a selfish pursuit.

Well I call bullshit.

Life is short.

Hug your kids.

Tell them life is amazing.

# Recovery Run
## Nicky Lopez

Then show them.
Go run.

# 8

# The Cormorant and the Camel Toe

**Friday 29th January 2016**

I swear to God I need to be sectioned. It's ass crackingly cold out there and we've signed ourself up for another 10k next Sunday morning. What the jammy fuck is wrong with us? Firstly as I've stated abundantly I don't even like 10ks and secondly it's in Southport which despite having tremendous charms also has a beach that not only the sea seems to have forgotten but also warmth gives it a fairly wide berth too. It's a flat, sandy plain which stretches out across miles of marshland and the wind roams free as if it were in the Devils playground.

I wouldn't mind but I'm resisting a cold at the moment, I have a faint huskiness of voice that suggests I'm on the verge of developing the mother of all snotters.

Speaking of which I noticed another delightful habit running has gifted me with, namely the apparent nonchalance I have developed about certain bodily functions. I'm not suggesting for a moment that I poo in public and wipe my arse with one of my socks (runners prerogative) or gob on the carpet at will but I did notice the other day in school I performed a shameful and horrifying act. I was doing my usual elaboration of a point (where I become all flailing arms and overly expressive facial movements) when I noticed my nose felt a little runny.

You can see where I'm going with this right? Being used to having thumb looped hands I usually take advantage of the plentitude of fabric and treat it as a makeshift hanky. The only trouble is that this doesn't translate very well in real life. What the children witnessed was a grown woman wiping an enormous slimer straight from nose to the arm of her suit jacket.

The gasps were audible, even the usually rough and tumble, wipe your nose on a wall type boys recoiled a little as they watched their once refined and elegant teacher perform this grossly unattractive not to mention pretty unhygienic degradation. I may as well have puked on the floor and started eating it such was their reaction. I was halfway up my elbow when I noticed what I was doing and had no explanation

86

whatsoever to hand so I came clean. "Sorry guys it's what I do when I'm running" I said as if that was a justifiable reason for this act of depravity. They stared in disgust as I went into a long diatribe about how having a runny nose was dangerous so we always had to wipe it only children have to do it with a tissue and no, we don't need to tell our parents because they already know and we only need to tell them new things and what was that out of the window and look the lesson is finished already! I totally got away with it I reckon.

Anyhow, it's cold, I've got a cold. And we're doing a cold race next week. I'm dreading it. Funnily enough though every time we're out running at the moment and I think I'm finding it tough in the cold I think back to the summer and shudder as I recall the leg destroying, energy sapping heat that I really dread. It reminded me of one run in particular...

Holiday running.

The thought of it sounds amazing. Stretching your legs out for endless miles along golden beaches with nothing to limit you. No time constraints, new horizons. Just you, your music and the open vistas before you.

Only the reality is somewhat more manic and a whole lot less glossy. I know this as I tried it once in Tenerife on a quiet Sunday morning. I did all the right things, I was covered in factor 72,000 from shiny head to nail less toe and I took a bottle of water with me. I'd even got up especially early to avoid the heat of the mid-morning sun. It was a perfect morning, a very light breeze dancing off the palms and the shimmering sea inviting me to gaze upon its beauty as I glided down the promenade. Southern Tenerife is awesome for running owing to a largely pedestrianised stretch linking most of the resorts. Punctuated with small inclines and some challenging but conquerable steps the promenade itself stretches out for miles and runners dot the walkways pretty much at all times.

It was these runners that I had enviously watched on holidays past and wished I had brought my running shoes, this time I was determined to be one of them. So off I went for a modestly paced 5k figuring I'd take it easy, acclimatise and ramp up the distance tomorrow. The hotel we were staying at was conveniently placed at the top of a steep slope, I judged that this would make the first section of my run enjoyably downhill. First major error.

Pavements in Spanish countries are made of rather different material than the gritty, grey concrete we Brits are accustomed to. Canarian pavements are constructed of smooth ridges of almost marble like material and whilst this is probably the more aesthetically pleasing (apologies to any concrete enthusiasts) it also generates considerably less traction hence the first half kilometre of my run saw me sliding at breakneck speeds towards the promenade with a look of absolute terror on my face. I careered towards innocent early birds, out for a peaceful stroll before the throngs of holidaymakers invaded the streets, as if I were wearing a pair of invisible skis. It was as if I had unwittingly taken part in some sort of snowless sled race as I dodged dog walkers and screeched past sun worshippers shrieking and yelping until I eventually reached the horizontal haven of the prom.

Taking a moment to compose myself after my somewhat dramatic entrance onto the Tenerife running scene I turned in the direction of Los Cristianos and started a steady run. After about 29 seconds of running at what I perceived to be around 7 minute miles I decided to drop the pace down a notch, after all I wasn't PB chasing today. I glanced at my Garmin to check my pace and it read 11.29. Some sort of anomaly obviously, my watch is in Tenerife, it's confused and probably needs a little time to settle. I continued on and became aware of someone blowing a hairdryer in my face on full temperature. Where the bollocksing hell was that heat coming from?

I plodded on feeling increasingly lumbersome. The sweat rolled from my head in torrents and into my eyes, as this mingled with the now melting factor 72,000 sun lotion I increasingly wanted to pull them from their sockets. I rubbed at them fiercely and I could feel my mascara smearing across my face. I reached for my water bottle and realised in the hiatus of my opening slalom section I had left my bottle on the prom wall as I steadied myself. My mouth was now claggy and thick and my ability to swallow reduced rapidly leaving my making odd little choking noises every few steps.
This was not going to plan.

The only thing truly keeping me moving (bearing in mind I had covered less than two kilometres) was how friendly and encouraging the locals were. Mustering up as sunny a smile as I could I trotted past cafes and shops waking up lazily in the morning sun, the tenders shouting a whoop, a hello or even reaching out for a high five. I wondered if they were always so friendly but realising that I was the only person, let alone runner, out on the prom that morning I guessed they must have thought me particularly badass with my bald head, in my hot pink vest and matching shorts.

As I approached my halfway point I noticed the prom had been taped off and a crowd of people stood behind. Figuring that some sort of accident had occurred I turned grumpily back the way I came, annoyed that I would have to find a way to add the distance on at the end. My desire for a drink was now becoming urgent, I was no longer sweating and I was looking at the sea with lustful eyes wondering how bad for me it could be to drink. My head was beginning to burn where the sun cream had slid off and my legs were crazily heavy. Suddenly I heard a shot fired and I instinctively ducked.

Looking up after a few seconds I saw nothing, no other person. Was that why the prom area had been taped off? Is that why there was no one else around? Maybe there was a gunman at large. I decided I was in grave danger and my only option was to run. It's amazing what adrenaline can do to a body that you think has done all it can. I began to move my legs forcefully and my feet pounded the hot, smooth pavement. Despite my terror the insane waiters and shopkeepers still cheered and high fived me as I tore past them so I started to shriek warnings at them in garbled Spanish as my head was totally mashed but to frustratingly my cries and desperate hand movements only seemed to encourage their happy waves. I could hear my heart beating in my chest like the roar of thousand feet. I could not only hear it I could feel it, thumping hard like a stampede.
Which was then that I was caught in a stampede.

Out of nowhere a huge mass of people appeared running towards me, this terrified me even further as I knew they too were running for their lives. I ran with every bit of power I had in me, but God I was done in. Along the endless prom the crowd had gained on me and were now metres away, literally breathing down my neck. Many of them started wildly waving and gesticulating towards me and I frantically tried to outrun them. Now stretching my arms and legs at their maximum trajectory I ran with Kenyan like swiftness; agony, effort and fear etched on my face. But it was no good, the hysterical, shouting, pink crowd had consumed me and I was being swept among them.

Did I mention they were all dressed in pink? It was something that struck me as the crowd seemed to slow slightly to my pace allowing me to just take the lead. I also then noticed they were all wearing pink ribbons. And running shoes.

At this point my attention was drawn to the cafes and shops all festooned with pink ribbons tumbling from tables and merrily fluttering along the prom wall.

I was in a race.

I was in a cancer race.

I was leading a cancer race.

For. Fuck's. Sake.

The last kilometre was hallucinatory fun. I grabbed a water bottle and slurped it down while the runners reverentially allowed me to lead. I graciously waved them on past me and they eventually drifted away amidst back slaps and a million high fives. I awkwardly slipped off the side road laughing openly now at the insanity of it all. And then I ran up the skiddy slope like a gladiator running up the travelator grunting and giving a victory roar at the summit.

Then I collapsed into bed for the day and didn't surface till dark. Holiday running.

It's not for everyone.

**Saturday 30th January 2016**

It's been a real sweaty bum flap of a week, it really has. It's been one of those jumbles of days dotted with incidents ranging from ball aches to full on catastrophes and there have been lots of tears. Family life is never easy but when you've got a family as diverse and complicated as ours it's a Basra like minefield. I suggested to Marc this week after another tumult of tears that I thought I was depressed but as the words tumbled out of my mouth across his startled countenance I knew it wasn't true. People who are truly depressed find themselves feeling hopeless for no discernible reason. I don't feel hopeless, I feel stressed. And for lots of very discernible reasons.

# Recovery Run
## Nicky Lopez

I'd decided that I wanted to run tonight. I had comfort eaten all day in work and it had been a long ass day. Cleo was happily ensconced in her phone in the company of my parents and storm Gertrude appeared to have a tolerable window installed at around 7.30 when Marc would be in. It was also Marc's final day in his current job before he begins a whole new role, I knew from today's texts he had feelings of both optimism and sadness. A run would be good for him too. But I knew given my extreme tiredness, the fact that I haven't been feeling tickety boo health wise this week and that I was wired to the point of nuclear meltdown this run wasn't going to be my finest, most majestic hour. I felt I had to do something though and running sometimes feels like the only thing I can still reliably do.

Since finishing my chemotherapy 6 weeks ago I have felt more than a little adrift. One would presume that it would feel like a release and an escape but the reality is quite different. After 6 years of knowing who I was and where I fitted in I now find myself lost and emotionally homeless. Add into the mix a massive falling out with my closest friends, several drastic family arguments and a number of other pretty gargantuan issues and I've started to feel like a stranger in my own life.

My saviours of course are my boy and my girl, as I wandered down to the beach at lunchtime today I breathed thanks to the universe for them. I have shelter in the storm, a place to hide and it's a cavern of raucous laughter and comfortably huge love. It's amazing that no matter how immense your difficulties are if you have at least one person who gets you then you know you're going to get through. And I have two, I'm ridiculously blessed.

So I pulled on my gear. I felt annoyingly uncomfortable. My underwear was bunching, my Garmin couldn't locate, I felt weird and alien. Just as we were ready to leave the house Cleo stopped us to find out how quickly we could clap. She does shit like this and because we're also idiots we are equally enthralled. The three of us stood there in the bedroom frantically clapping as if we had just seen something terribly important and entertaining. Kind of how I imagine Coldplay fans behave at their gigs (I can pretty much guarantee that I shall never know this from my own experience as I would sooner eat my own haemorrhoids). And to be fair it was harder than it seemed. Probably made harder still by my equally clapping bangers which I realised were still hoisted into a push up bra. Thank Christ I noticed.

As soon as I changed into my running bra I felt a little more at peace with the world. As we ran from the front door I felt glad to be out, in spite of dramatic reports of biblical weather it seemed calm and mild. Marc had his head torch on so we made for the canal. He had done his first night run there last week and loved it and having done a recce at the beach today I knew there was a fierce westerly wind blowing. The canal would offer us some respite from any strong gusts.

Running used to be a source of angst to me, a thing to worry about but lately it's felt way more therapeutic and I recognise how healing it can be to my soul in times of stress. The problem is that my body's way of dealing with stress is an entirely less therapeutic and more gastric affair. My worries are realised in my stomach. Now this can be a good thing at times, when I'm stressed I produce wind in immense quantities, I'm pretty sure you could fuel the national grid from a tough week of mine and with often hilarious consequences. Let's be honest, there's nothing quite like a massive, high pitched fart for blowing your own bubble of self-importance. No one can take themselves or their problems seriously when they're trumping like a brass band on helium.

Thing is sometimes it doesn't work like that and it's just sheer pain. Wind can play havoc with your body and if you haven't experienced it then you probably won't believe me but it can hurt like knives. And that's how tonight's run started out. I knew from the outset as my stomach was making the insane noise it does like I'm carrying a bag of water in it, the sloshes and splashes were audible. I have no idea why this happens. I don't drink just before a run, I have taken every proprietary brand of antacid and tried every natural remedy but still it happens. It'll come for a few runs then disappear as randomly. The only common denominator is stress.

The noise soon turned into pain, firstly as a tightness, a gripping feeling around my ribs but the gripping soon becomes painfully long claws grabbing at stomach muscles, kidneys, intestines. The pain twists and changes as it moves upwards causing you to gasp and wince. I guess it's a hangover from six years of a torrent of unforgiving chemicals in my system, something has to give and I think my digestive system has fared badly. But I think my gut is also a sensitive soul and if I worry then it does too.

So how to deal with it? Well sometimes I simply have to stop, grasp my hands into fists under my ribs and push upwards. Occasionally this releases a little wind, enough to get me home. But tonight it began so early on I was in dread, usually it's a halfway point thing but this was in the first mile. I decided to adopt a policy of acceptance and for tonight it largely won out. As the pulses of pain would beat across my torso I reminded myself it was just wind, it wasn't weapons. My body would move it and even if not, it wouldn't kill me, I could do this.

I also focused on what was feeling good, my legs felt strong and I had pulled my Buff from my head to feel the warm breeze. And it was a beautiful night. An indescribably heaven sent night. One that felt like summer despite being in January. Where were the destructive gales, the torrential rain, the devastating storm? In running as in life sometimes we have to look at things with fresh eyes, from a whole new perspective. The whole route transformed for me as if I had never before trodden it. Sometimes we have to step outside of ourselves, away from the familiar and comfortable in order to regain clarity. Marc ran on ahead of me judging when we needed the light which was surprisingly infrequent.

The ambient light from the hidden roads and bridges that overlook the canal created a serene glow across the rippling water. It was a totally different place to run in the night time. Because much of the wildlife was asleep there was little to distract the eye save the play of light on the water. This made us tune in acutely to what we could hear. The lack of rumbling daytime traffic uncovered late night machinery operating in the recycling plants and the distant roar of containers being loaded onto the ships in the docks. It was all deliciously fascinating, like we were intruders in a world the daytime dwellers knew nothing of.

Despite the relatively sedate pace for us I felt like we were racing along. Marc would switch on the lamp at dark or uneven stretches and I had to match his pace to keep sight of the path. This was exactly what I needed. Sometimes I allow myself to drop behind, lost in my own thoughts and pace I happily trundle and I love it. But tonight I had to keep up and the effort it involved given the pain in my ribs started to turn into a steely resolve. Somewhere from deep within my downtrodden spirit was awakening and I was reclaiming where I belonged. And in that moment my heart began to pump with more than blood, my eyes widened and the wind in my face started to slough away my self-doubt.

The pain remained, coming and going in tumultuous waves and dull aches but I began to feel more at ease with it. I guess in we don't always get to be pain free on the run any more than we do in the day to day business of living, we have scars, bruises and memories of hurt. They sit there not as a reminder of our weakness but of our capacity to overcome it. So often we view pain as a lack of strength but after so long of living with it I have discovered that pain can sometimes be a call to arms, a demand to get up and fight.

In life we are faced with so many opportunities for weakness, food, drugs, alcohol. We are accustomed to resisting and this gives us some empowerment but we have few chances to show ourselves how strong we can be. Running presents us with this chance on a run to run basis though, every time we leave the front door we enter into a duel between our heart who believes we can do anything and our mind who wants pie and cider. And pain can teach us. It can knock us down but it also allows us to rise up and conquer. A little hardship can unleash the lion who believed they were the mouse.

I ran through the final miles of the run an entirely different person to the one who began. As we strode from the canal into a wind that nearly took our legs away we realised that we had been in the eye of the storm. Chaos and uncertainty were around us but we had run unafraid into it and found our own kind of peace. My perspectives had altered and I could see with refreshed vision. And I had remembered something - that I can thrive not in spite of difficulties but because of them. My pain does not have to be the rock I perish on but rather the outcrop from which I can leap and find my wings on the way down. And the hurt inside me is not a shout to stop but an order to never stop moving forward. One step at a time. A battle cry from the soul to the sole.

## Sunday 31st January 2016

Ten miles this morning along the canal and as runs go it started out decidedly 'meh'. I guess there's something good to be said about forcing yourself out beyond your comfort zones and pushing on but at the times it just feels like ass. And the funny thing is that ass is largely what I could feel this morning.

Despite having lost a significant amount of weight lately this morning all of my running gear mystically became seven sizes too small for me. I dragged my Skins on as if they belonged to a Barbie doll instead of a full sized woman. Christ knows how but I appeared to have tripled in size overnight and the thong (note: I have more than one of them) that I usually wear with comfort had become a cheese wire determined to slice through my foof like a ripe Edam. In an attempt to right this mediaeval type of torture I spent the first five minutes of my run standing outside my neighbours front window with my hands in my pants. I'm sure it made for an illuminating Sunday morning breakfast conversation piece.

Determining that nothing would solve the predicament I wedged the fabric into a slightly less eye watering position and continued on. It was less than inspiring conditions. Generally I don't mind running in the rain, I've had some awesome runs in tempestuous conditions including one particularly memorable splash fest with Marc in Whitley Bay.

Today's rain was the crap kind though, the sneaky bastard stuff that looks light but gets you soaking wet in seconds. It was like a fine mist of gritty ice blowing in our faces so I pulled my Buff up over my nose to protect myself. I've extolled the virtues of the Buff before, a miraculous tube of material that can be twisted into a myriad of useful devices from a hairband (admittedly slightly useless for me) to a neck scarf or hat. Today I used it under a cap, I like to wear a cap in the rain as it protects from the endless face wiping but it doesn't afford me much coverage behind the ears or the back of the neck when it's cold so that's where the Buff came in. I wore it balaclava like and topped it with a cap. Today it turned me into a badass ninja. Or at least that's how I felt. I realise I don't look exactly like this as recent photos from the Cancer Research Winter Run suggest. I in fact look like a lunatic, albeit a cosy one.

# Recovery Run
## Nicky Lopez

On the whole it was a tough run and we both felt it, sometimes you just can't tune into the rhythm of your own soul and you're hopelessly out of step. We kept on, digging in and keeping steady, for the large part we didn't speak. We silently swapped positions, each leading the other and taking the force of the weather as one flagged a little and needed some respite. Thoughts came and went as my mind wandered to recent events, arguments and worries. My legs were stiff, my stomach ached, and my arms hurt.

As we were approaching mile 5 I saw Boundary Bridge and I felt a little more hopeful as I knew this was our turning point. Then looming above us perched on a light we saw him. Colin the Cormorant. Colin is a bird who has gained some local notoriety by appearing in unlikely places. As we live along a sweeping coastline you would think he would be out there with the gulls and kittiwakes but it seems Colin hasn't yet decided where he belongs. He's been spotted in numerous urban places and I saw him myself last week in the Bootle Strand section of the canal with its slightly dishevelled and litter polluted waters. I love him. He reminds me that we don't always fit in, we don't always belong and that's OK. As long as we find our own stretch of water to love that's all that counts.

My heart lifted when I saw him, proudly staring out way up high, he glanced down momentarily as if he saw something familiar and then it struck me. Colin isn't lost, he isn't searching, he's happy to be wherever his wings take him because like us, he gets to experience life from every side of the water and he gets to see things others of his kind never venture far enough to discover. Colin the Cormorant doesn't sweat the small stuff because he's too busy having an adventure. I'd like to tell you from then on in my legs were lighter and my breathing easier but it would be a lie. But I did hold my head higher and I began to look forwards instead of down, something I haven't been able to do in so very long I've almost forgotten how. And it did make a difference both in my mind and in my body.

The rest of the run was difficult but cathartic, I might not feel strong but that doesn't mean I'm not. I'm happy to be where my feet take me, and they can take me really far. As we ran past the windows of the corner shop Marc stopped briefly to adjust his shoe. I stared proudly at myself, admiring the strength I had built in myself not only physically but also in character. As my eyes dropped they fixed upon the biggest camel toe I have ever had the displeasure of witnessing in my entire life. It was gargantuan, it was akin to a physical parting of the Red Sea. It appeared as though my body was actually separating, the rift that so often causes me trauma in leggings had become a freakish chasm encased in shiny black Lycra. I actually gasped. Then Marc saw it (you couldn't miss it) then we dissolved into creases of laughter.

As I've said before, my life seems to be a series of catastrophes scattered with incidents so ridiculous that there's nothing else to do but raise your hands to the heavens and laugh. My difficulties, no matter how pressing or painful can be assaulted and defeated by the look from a slightly eccentric seabird and the hilarity of a freaky foof. The absolutely nonsensical will always triumph over the seemingly insurmountable.

And no matter what the photos may suggest, I know deep down inside that I'm a cool ass ninja.

And Colin knows it too.

# 9

# You've Got A Friend

**Monday 1st February 2016**

During today's run I was debating with myself whether when you're having a tough one is it better to be running with someone else or alone. I put the question to Marc when we got home (in a very non loaded way-no one likes a psychotically clingy run buddy) and he said the jury was out for him too. Whilst it's awesome having someone to support you, share your woes and motivate you home it's also good to hack through these things in your own time, under your own steam, in your own way.

I know I'm lucky because I get my bread buttered both sides, I get to run alone lost in my own thoughts playing my own preposterous playlist and I also get a super supportive run buddy who knows me inside out. And we both agree that race day is definitely more fun when you've got company.

When I first started out I ran with my work colleague Pauline. A group of us from school had decided to do the Great North Run, they were running to support me and despite not really knowing what to expect (I actually thought it was cross country up till a few weeks before the event) it was exciting. We started off doing the odd run, nothing formal but bit by bit through injury or circumstances everyone had dropped out but Pauline and I. Pauline had admirably kept up some training but reasonably newly diagnosed my treatment was getting to me and my training was sporadic at best. By July I still hadn't done anything constructive and the race was in September. I remember reading the pre run magazine in a state of panic, it advised if you couldn't comfortably run 8 miles by that point then you should seriously consider dropping out. I could barely run three.

I texted Pauline and asked her how she felt about deferring it till next year, she replied saying she felt she would be letting our sponsors down but totally got why I needed to defer, people would understand. The next day I went out and ran four miles, I didn't care how long it took me or if I stopped along the way, I just wanted to see

98

if I could do the distance. Over the next week I dramatically (and foolishly) ramped up the mileage until I felt more confident. Pauline and I began to follow a training programme and took it seriously. I was by far the weaker runner, I stopped a lot and was painfully slow.

Pauline was excitedly enthusiastic and she kept the two of us motivated but I found it incredibly tough. The turning point came for me with the longer runs and I gradually found my feet. On holiday in Dorset I did 8 hard but comfortable miles alone and I began to feel it might just be achievable. We had great fun, we would chat at times and feel pretty invincible afterwards. We obsessed about what the day would be like and spent hours discussing energy gels and correct hydration. We decided to attempt the full distance before the day so that we could go into the race knowing we could do it. At 12 miles it became so tough we were practically running on the spot, I remember clearly telling a flagging Pauline that I could nearly see South Shields (the finish point of the race despite being in Liverpool at the time) and she duly told me to fuck off. A few minutes later I told her my liver had burst although on reflection it may have been a stitch.

The day of the race was incredible, I had never seen so many runners in one place. I still had my hair although it had been cut short in preparation for aggressive treatment so I didn't feel out of place. The race itself was wonderful, our Head Teacher, Michael a former Great North Runner himself rang us at 8 miles to ask if we'd finished yet and we told him where to go. At around 11 miles a roadside supporter offered us biscuits and I laughed as I watched a dry mouthed Pauline politely trying to wolf down a digestive gagging on every mouthful. But the race was joyous, in the final mile a loud Geordie bloke with a booming voice shouted encouragement to us and it carried us tearfully across the line.

We had run a bloody half marathon.

A year later I ran the same race alone, Pauline had the honour of being an Olympic and Paralympic Gamesmaker and couldn't commit to the training. It was a totally different experience, fun but not as much. I had a crashing hangover having had a late night with a crowd of badly behaved runners and one particular Geordie guy I'd met the night before. My motivation wasn't there and despite the incredibly supportive crowd I felt strangely underwhelmed. I was bald by then and my conspicuousness certainly wasn't helping.

Crossing the finish line alone I felt an enormous sense of achievement but as I had no family there to greet me either it was somewhat anticlimactic. Still I had other things to spark my optimism...
I had found a new running buddy but as he lived on one side of the country and I the other our opportunities to train together were limited. Besides, he had been training for Kielder Marathon and was a way better runner.

In the October of that year I did Wirral 10k with Paul, another Running the World member and a fellow Liverpudlian with a number of mutual friends. At the time the 10k was run in conjunction with Liverpool Marathon which Paul was running, it was a lovely event. I had a fab run keeping Paul company for the first hour of his marathon, our pace was comfortable and we chatted along. It was uneventful apart from a stretch towards the end of the race. Every time someone had called our names in support we had high fived each other, as we ran down a busy residential road we knew we were going to get plenty of support.

We weren't wrong, people cheered and said the most wonderful, motivating things. It's no surprise that people are massively supportive when they see a person clearly in the throes of chemo attempting a run and it's been an immense honour to be on the receiving end of that. As we were approaching the end of the road a young lad with his mum shouted my most memorable race cheer yet. He lifted his hand for me to high five it and as I connected with his he roared in the Scousest of accents 'GO ED SLAPHEAD!' I have never seen a mother look so mortified or a youth so quickly admonished in my life. We were destroyed with laughter and as Paul and I parted ways, he to conquer 26.2 miles and me to annihilate a toilet in the local Morrisons (a lethal combination of granola and Berocca so potent I had to text my Dad from the toilet to let him know I was still alive) I was still split sided.

The following April I went on to conquer my own 26.2 with Marc having trained mostly alone. It was the way we had to do things back then. For our second London Marathon in 2014 we tried to do as many of the long training runs as possible but given Marc's mum's poor health it wasn't always possible. It was pretty much out of the question for me to run those sort of distances alone by then so my friend Naomi stepped, or rather cycled, into the breach.

Having been unable to run despite many attempts because of a horse riding injury she offered to accompany me on wheels. Glad of the escort and mindful that her bike had a basket that could carry snacks I happily accepted. The majority of our runs were blissful, I can remember it being a particularly cold but sunny spring and I had newly discovered the bypass and coastal path so we always headed north through the pretty Sefton coastal towns of Hightown, Formby, Freshfield and Ainsdale.

It was a great bonding experience as Naomi rediscovered her love of cycling and I was able to share with her my love of running. It all went well until the 17 miler which nearly ended the both of us. It was a ferociously windy Saturday morning at a time when I was notoriously superstitious and thus inflexible about changing or diverting routes. I also didn't understand how wind works. Now any sane person when faced with the prospect of 60mph winds would avoid an incredibly exposed coast at all costs.
Not I.

My only concession to change was to invert our usual route so we began on the long beach stretch (thinking we could get the hard part out of the way first) and finish coming down the bypass. This was the ultimate in mixing things up as far as I was concerned. Bear in mind at this point I didn't know there was a beautiful, sheltered canal on my doorstep despite having lived there for most of my life. So there we were on a stretch of beach I now avoid at nearly all costs, I should have done that day because I knew from bitter experience the year before what to expect.

But as you know by now, I'm a slow learner. The reason to avoid the beautiful coastal path from Waterloo marina towards Crosby beach in high winds is because the small, rolling dunes that line the narrow pathway are largely unfixed. The soft sands and forcible winds create an extremely beautiful and ever changing environment. The downside of this awesome natural phenomenon is that massive quantities of soft sand are naturally dumped on the path by the winds creating a drastically difficult passage for a runner. Not to mention a cyclist. High winds and shifting sands also make for a very effective however very painful facial as we both learnt that day.

After several miles of carrying the bike through glue like mounds of powder sand we were both in tears of despair. We debated whether we could go any further but we ludicrously decided to continue. It had often been said we shouldn't be allowed out together and this was no exception. We carried on through crosswinds that were nothing short of perilous. At any time we could have left the beach and took a less hazardous, saner route, any other normal person would have. Not us.

We ran and cycled getting blown dementedly from one end of the prom to the next and then onto Hightown. We were so windblown and burnt when we arrived in Formby village we looked nothing short of mad. Like two insane castaways we could barely speak as our sandy faces had been paralysed and we drooled a little as our mouths were so dry. In delirium and pain from the coastal torture we begged the pharmacist in the provincial Boots to give us some painkillers. The poor woman must have been terrified saying she couldn't but a benevolent customer saw our manic desperation and bought us some Co-Codamol. Maybe she had once been in a sandy wind attack, maybe she had trained for a marathon. Whatever it was she recognised our suffering and she remains blessed in my heart to this day.

But it was far from over. I'd say I'd seriously misjudged the wind direction that day but that would suggest I knew the slightest thing about it. As far as I knew, wind blew, end of. And yes, I was an educator of children, take it up with the government next time they cut spending in teacher training. When I reversed the route I presumed that the wind which was blowing into us would blow behind us on the way back. Makes sense right? Well yes unless it was a 60mph crosswind and our route back was parallel to the one we had taken out. But hang on, we wouldn't be going back on the coast this time, being inland would no doubt ensure our shelter and protection?

The A565 aka The Formby Bypass is a godless patch of land that separates Southport from Liverpool. It is a meteorological conundrum in that no matter what season, what time of day or what local weather conditions there is always a substantial gust on that road. That Saturday morning was no exception. As we turned the corner from Formby onto the pathway which borders the dual carriageway our legs and wheels were practically taken from us. The intensity of the gusts was nothing short of terrifying and there were several times I fought to remain standing. Naomi wrestled with her bike heroically to keep it from veering off the path into the fast and steady stream of cars whose passengers eyed us with equal amounts of disbelief and disdain. I mean who the actual fuck goes running and cycling on that road in that weather? Um...we do.

By the time we got into Crosby we were wild with madness, we were like two rabid animals frothing and gurning with stretched faces and wide, blank eyes. The photo we took had to be digitally enhanced dramatically just to make us appear normal but if you look closely you can see it there, a little too much of the whites of the eyes betray a lunacy that lies behind. I'm not sure if Naomi ever cycled after that morning, I know it was the last time she cycled with me. We remained friends but we choose not to speak of the events of that morning again. Some things are just too painful.

These days I run with my fellow idiot and to be fair, he's generally a lot more sensible than I am. He's taught me the benefits of flexibility of thought along with how to read the direction of the wind correctly. He's a superb pathfinder and has mapped out some of the most awesome routes I've ever taken. He is also an expert in planning for weather and I am finally beginning to learn how to avoid the wind or in the very least how to not make it work against me for four and a half hours. And it's true, we make a great team running together. We have developed an instinctive style to our teamwork and most of our communication is non-verbal, apart from the childish toilet humour and occasional grunt.

I know people often say how lucky we are that we both share a passion and whilst we both would never give up the amazingly wonderful experience it is to run alone we both equally appreciate how sharing a run can strengthen and deepen a relationship. That said I often wonder how it looks to passers-by, a couple running together without speaking. I remember thinking about it during the summer when we were coming to the end of a very gorgeous evening run and I had written this later that evening...

**8th August 2015**

One two, one two, one two, one two.

There they go, that couple who run together. I feel sorry for them, they don't speak to each other, they don't even look at each other. They're like strangers, wrapped up in their own thoughts as they run past us. God knows what they're doing it for, they look knackered and they're no youngsters.

One two, one two, one two, one two. I wonder how that poor girl feels running next to him. She's obviously struggling and he's looks intense, almost angry. God I feel sorry for her. And he doesn't seem happy. I suppose this is the only thing they do on a Friday night. Anything to avoid talking to each other. One two, one two, one two, one two. As we run past that couple walking, off out for the night, they stare at us. One two, one two, one two, one two. That's the sound of our feet, hitting the concrete of the promenade of our beach. The beach where we laugh, play, photograph, walk. The beach where we run.

One two, one two, one two, one two. You see that's not silence between us, there are a million words exchanged within that footfall. And though we stare straight ahead I can see inside his mind and he in mine.

I wonder if that couple knows each other's breath so well that they can read it? How the tiniest change in its pattern tells them both exactly what the other needs. Do they know the cadence of each other's step so well that they fall into a natural rhythm together so that the beat of it sounds like their hearts? Are they so wired into each other's bodies that they can detect the slightest turn and automatically follow in line with them?

One two, one two, one two, one two. There's not a word spoken between us but every mile I pass, every hill I climb, every step I can feel him willing me on, roaring encouragement, holding my hand. In the hardest mile home when I know he's working hard I push him on, stretching my legs so he follows, supporting him, and shouting his name in silence.

One two, one two, one two, one two. And so we run, two bodies but one mind. Without a word or a glance to each other we run.

And never are we more in touch, more deeply connected and truly a part of each other.

One two, one two, one two, one two. That's the sound of our souls and we know every step and footprint that carves the pathways to them.

# 10

# Mad Dogs

**Thursday 4th February 2016**

So I have a history of avoiding illness and injury. That's not to say I don't get sick or injured, I mean take a look at me, I'm hardly the picture of health. Despite being reasonably confident that I've beaten cancer (subject to MRI etc.) I have a moderately serious heart condition, am half deaf, half blind and the left hand side of my face twitches uncontrollably. I'm not exactly a model of physical wonder.

What I am adept at though is complete and utter denial of any health condition whatsoever. I swear if my ass fell off tomorrow it would be a month before I'd admit I couldn't poo. And this is particularly prevalent when it comes to running injuries. Historically I put my head down, hope for the best and rely on good luck. Why? Because injury only ever seems to arrive when you're getting somewhere, it's the cruellest irony that when you're at your physical peak you are also at your most vulnerable. And I hate that more than anything because I'm a person who needs to feel like they're winning, not in a competitive 'I'm gonna whoop your ass' kind of way but more of a 'I'm all over this shit' sort of thing. So when it happens to me I tend to play it down or rather, pretend it's not happening.

Last night I'd been writing the section about our second London Marathon (yes, I know it's hard to believe that this piece of literary genius isn't one seamless oeuvre but rather a series of incoherent ramblings sellotaped together but there it is, I'll hand back the Pulitzer) and I was reminiscing about the hip injury I had ignored for several years. Marc came in from work shortly afterwards and suggested a run. The weather was predictably shite but arguably less shite than it had been all day so it seemed prudent to take advantage of a pocket of puke in a river of poo. You can tell already how much I felt like running, yeah?

After the usual 20 minute wardrobe horror I decided I had to wear gloves, it was bloody freezing. I reached up to the designated running accessory shelf (only God can judge my level of anal retention) and there it was, my hip injury, not sitting on the shelf you understand but making itself known across the top of my thigh. I decided that this time the sane thing to do would be to rest it, after all we have a race on Sunday. The sensible thing would be to take some ibuprofen and do some very gentle stretches.

I was still pondering these points as we passed from Crosby into Blundellsands about 3 miles into our run, rain and hail catapulting at our faces leaving icy stings. The weather was annoyingly weird leaving me baking then freezing in relays. As we had left our house and bounded up Brownmoor Lane I was struck dumb with cold, the first silent mile was shivers and resentment but as suddenly as we turned I began to cook and cursed the Gods for telling me to wear a hat and gloves. But the weird thing was I was loving it anyway. I was reminiscing about my first runs when that part seemed like a mountain and I stopped regularly, bending over in puffed exhaustion. Now I could bound up it freely, overtaking other runners and feeling strength in my legs and heart. I had found that sweet spot, that delicious love right at the beginning of the run this time and I was in my groove very early. Yes there was a strong wind and the rain hurt but I felt stronger than anything that could try to deter me. But as I ran along I knew that lurking under that strength there was an old familiarity and as my calf seized tightly my hip began to pull. I did what any responsible runner would do and ignored it completely.

The run itself was pretty nice, we had opted against going to the canal and instead decided to make a route up weaving through the streets of Blundellsands, it's a well-heeled area largely populated by footballers and the elderly so the houses are an eclectic mix of ultra-modern and grandly traditional. It also sits right on Burbo Bank which is our favourite part of the beach and renowned as much for 'Another Place' its 100 Anthony Gormley Iron Men statues as it is for its spectacular sunsets.

Now as you know, I'm not one for making it up as I go along, I like to know where I'm going and how long and far it's going to take me, but I also realise the benefit of a spontaneous route too. An off the cuff run can add an element of fun to a too familiar plod and it can make the miles go much faster. Added to that on a night like last night you can judge the weather as it happens and make decisions as to where will offer the best shelter. Or at least that's the plan. What can happen during these runs is that one runner can have the genius idea of running down the coastal road to catch the tailwind. Actually it did turn out to be a genius idea but for one nightmarish moment before we turned into the road I genuinely believe my head was about to be severed from my neck such was the ferocity of the crosswind. The noise in our ears was thundering as the sound of the gales coupled with the crashing tides made a raucous symphony. But as we turned it was instant, almost eerie silence and the wind was behind us, peacefully gliding us along. And we needed it too, Marc was feeling tired and I was busy trying not to notice how horrifically stiff my hip was.

We ran several loops to cover a ten mile distance which was a tough job not just because of the limited running scope we have when the canal and seafront are off limits. Blundellsands stops abruptly giving way to either the coastal path or miles of fields, neither of which are suited to a dark, gusty night. To the south you can run a mile or so into Waterloo but you really wouldn't want to venture any further than that towards the docks and the city in the dark, to the east are more fields and to the west, the Irish Sea which is damper than you would hope for on a weeknight run. Without the escape routes of the towpath or beach it's a case of zipping up and down local roads to cover the distance. This isn't so bad generally but if you're knackered then it can be demotivating and if your hip hurts then the constant up and down of kerbs and driveways can start to gripe.

Of course none of this was helped by the gooey eye infection I was also ignoring which with the wind and accompanying sand was starting to render me basically blind. My contact lenses had become blurred and I was struggling to make out the pavements along with being randomly slapped in the face by errant branches. As I'm writing this I'm aware it sounds like the world's crappiest run but it really wasn't, I felt pretty good. I just had this foreboding sense of doom that I'd done something stupid to my hip reaching for that bloody shelf and deep down I knew I really shouldn't be on my feet. But ten miles was done on the eve of World Cancer Day, and it felt significant. And now I can't run.

# Recovery Run
## Nicky Lopez

**Friday 5th February 2016**

I'm an idiot.

Right when I'm in the best shape I've ever been in my whole life I decide to screw it up. Ok so it wasn't intentional but leaning for a shelf for fuck's sake? It's such a boring reason that my friends are trying to read some sort of innuendo into it as no one can believe that an injury could be caused by something so utterly banal. What's lingering in my mind is the very real feeling that it would probably have settled by now had I not persisted and run ten miles on it afterwards. Now I have a predicament, my heart and my stomach which ate a ridiculous amount of donut and crispy cake this morning in school say I should get out there tonight and test it out whilst getting shut of some calories.

My head on the other hand is telling me that after a walk at lunchtime I can still feel some stiffness and should therefore rest up. I'm also holding in the back of my mind that we are entered for the Mad Dog 10k on Sunday in Southport. It's a race that I've wanted to do for a couple of years but have always been too far into the throes of marathon training to upset the schedule for a shorter distance. Many runners rate it though in terms of fun, organisation and the all-important goody bag.

A well-stocked goody bag is to me more important than the medal itself. I used to be a real bling girl and wouldn't dream of entering a race without something shiny at the end but after having done countless of the Great Run Series I now own a collection of near identical grey looking medals which along with swag from numerous other races have been consigned to a drawer. I know some people go in for the whole medal display thing but it's never really been my scene, I love looking at photographs from events but the medal itself has lost its attraction for me. The goody bag on the other hand can be a thing of sheer joy…or a collection of the most insane items ever put together in one place. I have seen a lot of things in these little sacks of wonder, the ubiquitous yoghurt coated nut bar, the syrupy sweet energy drink and even a little dried or fresh fruit, all of which are more than welcome as is the little sachet of sweetly scented muscle rub. What is less comprehensible is a bag of basmati rice, some toothpaste, a can of men's deodorant or some teabags, all of which I have found as post-race treats.

The people who put these things together are either slightly imbalanced or having an enormous laugh at runners because I'm telling you now, the last thing I need at the end of a long run is dehydrated food and drink products. For me the perfect goody bag would contain some wet wipes, a drink, some crisps, more crisps, a pie, some vodka and two paracetamol. That's the kind of shit that would have me rebooking a race year after year.

Marc has been reasonably ambivalent about us doing this race, he like me isn't very keen on freezing his bollocks off on an exposed course early on a February Sunday morning. He's assiduously checked the weather reports and remained open minded about our attendance and he's right. I know when I get to Sunday morning I'll curse myself for ever having suggested it. I'll wear three times my usual amount of clothing because I'll be cold and hungover then I'll get all stressed about feeling like I have to run faster than I usually do. On the other hand it could turn out to be the best fun we've ever had.

The race numbers came last week and runners are designated starting zones by dog names, we are Dalmatians. Ok, I probably would have preferred to be a Greyhound or a Rottweiler but at least I'm not a Poodle or a Shih Tzu. From what I've heard, people love this race, rave about it in fact, maybe it'll be the 10k that changes everything for me because as it stands I do bloody hate 10ks. I guess it all pretty much hangs on whether this injury settles and the best possible way for me to make that happen is not to run, whether I like it or not I'm just going to have to suck it up and admit it now, Friday will be a no run day.

**Saturday 6th February 2016**

No run days can be funny old things and sometimes at the end of them you find you've run ten miles down a canal in the dark... Yes, I know what I said about running on an injury but sometimes you have to make a judgement call and rely on a leap of faith. Was there an element of stupidity involved? Well you know this time I don't think there was. OK maybe initially it was a stupid idea, I'd had a long day in work and had taken a walk at lunchtime that confirmed I still had a hip strain. It wasn't pain though, it was just a stiffness, a whisper that things weren't completely right. Am I making a good enough case yet? I'm almost starting to convince myself.

110

# Recovery Run
## Nicky Lopez

Yes, it was stupid and irresponsible and I was playing fast and loose with my legs but I just really felt like running. In my head I had resolved to take it very easy and if it even so much as twitched with pain I would stop and walk home. What I hadn't bargained for was an hour and a half of hair raising scrambling through pitch black tunnels in the driving wind and hammering rain. It was closer to pot holing than running and there were several times I came close to actually shitting myself.

It was reasonably early when we started out and pretty mild. Cleo had gone out to the cinema with some friends so the prospect of a guiltless run was too good to pass up. OK it was a bit drizzly but it felt fine and I immediately felt glad to be out. As we turned toward the towpath we were met with a crack in the face from Mother Nature as the wind tried to blow our asses off along with our caps. Our matching caps. Once again we had unwittingly gone out dressed as the monochrome gimp twins in co ordinating outfits and caps. People must hate us; for the love of fuck, I hate us, smug bastards. But holy shitballs it was blowy, like hilariously windy, I felt bizarrely excited.

I love Friday night, I've always loved it. It has all the promise of an awesome weekend without the slightly depressing whiff of a Sunday to follow. Friday is where the weekend begins in all its full on sparkly sexiness, Saturday is where the weekend rips its tights and gets over emotional and Sunday is the walk of shame home. I've always been a Friday girl and even these days when wild nights have given way to early nights to deal with ass o' clock ice rink duties I still love the atmosphere, it still feels like a low key Christmas Eve. It doesn't seem that long ago since Friday night to me meant a face full of make-up, a skin-tight outfit and a shitload of booze and to be fair it still looks on paper pretty much the same, just with running shoes instead of stilettos.

There's something nice about an early evening weekend weekend run, you catch workers on their way home tired and ready for rest and party people on their way out, girls glittered and hopeful wafting perfume and clean shaven, Lynx smelling blokes strutting purposefully. Everyone seems happier and more smiley, it's a good feeling. For me it's one of my favourite times to run, having put the week and whatever it brought to rest and celebrating in the way I love most. There's no rush, no stress and I smile a lot. I must look mental.

# Recovery Run
## Nicky Lopez

I definitely looked bonkers as night rapidly began to fall. We had left the headlamp at home in a moment of enthusiastic misjudgement and we were drastically regretting it. Four miles in it was raining hard, the path was turning to a river and the bridges that had been illuminated by the reflected glow from the orangey sky had suddenly become sinister caverns with unsteady surfaces. We stumbled and staggered into the five mile turning point until I knew I would have to adapt and survive. My way of dealing with such conditions was frankly ludicrous. Because I couldn't make out the pathways properly I became a little terrified that I was either going to break my foot or fall into the canal, to remedy this I decided the best course of action was to change my gait entirely and adopt a flat footed, clown like running style pushing my legs forward with straight knees and swinging my arms wildly. Marc, usually the sane and reliable one, asked me what the hell I thought I was doing and my answer must have seemed uncharacteristically plausible as he too decided to adopt the same strategy.

So away we went at a fair pace swinging our legs in front of us, leaning our bodies back slightly and dropping our feet like lead weights. Quite what we looked like I cannot imagine as each time our feet connected with the path it would send copious splashes of water flying in all directions drenching us from stupidly matching head to toe. We kept this insane shit up for three miles until I virtually collapsed from exhaustion in a pool of mud. At the Tesco Two I remembered that my hip wasn't hurting, yes it felt a bit tight and my knee and calf were a bit niggly but none of it had got worse.

Turning off the towpath into the country park the path broadens significantly into a wide thoroughfare and its surface appears a bright yellow in the distant street lamps. I think by this time the clown running and the fact that my feet and legs were waterlogged all conspired to disorientate me somewhat. The road seemed to swirl from side to side and I couldn't judge how far the golden Tarmac was from my feet causing me to start staggering and stamping simultaneously. I couldn't have looked madder if I'd drawn a knob on my face and sang 'Come on Eileen' (it happened in a dream once at Christmas and was so realistic I spent a fortnight asking people I'd been out drinking with in the preceding week if it had really happened or not).

As we ran onto the main road I realised how completely manic and wild I looked so righted myself before my watch buzzed and the ten miles was done. We were right outside a Chinese takeaway and the smell of delicious Friday night food filled my every pore. The car lights were dancing in the rain and the streetlights twinkled like an urban glitter ball; standing there soaked with sweat, breathless and glowing I realised that Friday nights now are not so different than they used to be. This is our club, this is how we party, now vodka time.

## Sunday 7th February 2016, Mad Dog 10K, Southport

So we went for it, the Mad Dog 10k, we wanted to see what all the fuss about. It's consistently hailed as one of the top 10k races in the UK and as its pretty much on our doorstep we thought we'd give it a try. When we booked it way back last autumn we accepted that a February race would mean cold weather but we hadn't banked on the multitudinous shitstorms that have graced our shores in the past couple of months.

I swear to God since the Met Office have started naming storms in this country there's been a steady queue of them all lining up to outdo each other. I say we should go back to making the fuckers anonymous again, that way they might piss off and leave us alone or head to Florida to get upgraded with a name and personality. Either way the conditions of late have been a barrel of shite and the prospect of running a 10k on a notoriously exposed coastline wasn't one we were relishing. Besides, I hate 10ks.

So it went like this...

7:45 am (alarm goes off. Ironically my alarm tone is a barking dog. I silence it immediately)

8:00 am  Marc's alarm goes off (futuristic robot ringtone suggesting he may never actually grow up) Marc shits himself as phone was right under his cheek, freaks out for several minutes.

Marc: *whispers* Time to get up

Me: Is it raining?

Marc: (sadly) No

Me: Fuck

The unspoken agreement was that if it didn't rain we would do it. The wind speed was looking catastrophically awful but we could

113

overlook that as long as it didn't rain. So out of bed we staggered, I somehow had bits of crisps stuck to my face and a plate under my nose. Crazy night.

Kitted up in relative record time for us (wardrobe brief was 'bastard cold') we drove off towards Southport, a Victorian seaside resort about 15 miles north of where we live. It was a bright, sunny morning that felt happily mild from the inside of a heated car but as we approached our destination the skies thickened and we stared at the pampas grass on the dunes in terror, it was horizontal. Pulling into the carpark we could see gathering masses of club runners and we suddenly felt out of our depth. In our tiny minds club runners are very different to us, club runners know about fartleks and tempo runs, we only know about tampons and farts. Club runners are serious runners, they run to improve their times, to improve themselves. We run because we really like fatty food and larking around.

I suspect in reality that club runners couldn't give a shit about what we do as it's probably very similar to what they do and I know loads of club runners that are wonderful, well-adjusted people who actively support and encourage other runners in the most fabulous way. But in our heads club runners are the elites, the head boys and girls while we are the plebs, the class clowns. Cleo just misread this over my shoulder as 'class onions' which is a pretty accurate description of us, I'm sure we make a lot of people feel like crying.

So we sat in the car furtively pinning our race numbers on wonkily and cursing the hurricane that was tearing apart the Marine Lake. As we got out of the car we were momentarily encouraged as the actual temperature felt not too bad. Then the wind blew and nearly ripped my nose from my face as it iced it back into paralysis. Deep joy.

Anyone who knows Southport will agree that whilst it's an undeniably lovely place with a delightful beach it's not often that you actually glimpse the ocean itself. In fact it's often so far out that it is no longer visible to the naked eye. Today it was crashing in on foamy white horses. The weather report said 50mph winds, this was going to be nothing short of mental. We staggered over to the buses which would transfer us to the start line and were childishly delighted to find ourselves on the front seat of the top deck. We gooned around like

# Recovery Run
## Nicky Lopez

school kids taking selfies as we trundled past the awesomely named 'Cockle Dicks Lane' and 'Knob Hall Avenue' snorting and guffawing.

The atmosphere on the bus was lovely, everyone was laughing and chattering and it reminded me how friendly and nice runners generally are. We arrived at the local high school where the baggage drop was situated and found ourselves in the midst of a party atmosphere, music was blaring and people were gathered in happy, laughing groups. We both commented how it weirdly smelled like the Great North Run probably due to a mix of wet grass, Ralgex and wee but it felt reassuringly familiar. It was knob shrinkingly cold though and I was dreading parting with my woolly hat and fleece, I even considered leaving them on for one insane second but then I remembered the near heat exhaustion experience that was the CRUK Winter Run and threw them into the rucksack along with my gloves. I did buy a coffee though, a delicious cup of black, hazelnutty warmth that kept us both toasty as we queued for the loos.

Race day portaloos are a hideous rite of passage for runners, the secret being to spend as little time in them as humanly possible without defecating/urinating on oneself which is far more difficult that one might assume. Today I followed my usual routine, one deep inhalation before entering and then do the deed whilst slowly exhaling meaning I don't have to breathe inside. All well and good if you're not wearing slippery gloves or are essentially tied to your own clothes by a series of thumb loops, drawstrings, safety pins, rip cords and staples. It was the smallest portaloo I've ever been in and I felt a wave of claustrophobia as I had to practically tear my clothing off my body to get it to budge whilst gripping my gloves between my knees and hovering precariously over the bowl of steaming wee. I burst out of the terrifying poobox in a state of shock and panic before around 200 bemused runners.

The final call came for the start line and we hurriedly made our way to our pens, we were Dalmations which we realised was the second fastest pen, rather ambitious for us. It was cramped but good natured and predominately populated with worryingly agile looking runners in shorts and vests in contrast to us with mad slogan t shirts and neon tights. We were all told to howl as the starting gun fired which we dutifully and enthusiastically did and off we went.

# Recovery Run
## Nicky Lopez

The pack moved surprisingly slowly at first and we struggled to find space to stretch our legs out. Then we turned left into the strongest and most forceful headwind I have ever run in, along miles of open exposed marshland it was brutal. I am not slightly exaggerating when I say that it was akin to running with a large elastic band around your waist being pulled in the opposite direction, this was resistance training at its toughest. Whether it was because we had grown accustomed to the relentless bastard breeze of the coast or we were just having a good day we both found ourselves running strongly. The wind that used to dishearten and floor me had become a challenge to me and an unbelievably fun one.

I heard a guy say that it was three miles into the wind so I had a time frame and I felt unstoppable. We learnt quickly to tuck in behind the faster pack as much as we could to stay sheltered, yes this meant breathing in a variety of body odours ranging from acceptable to puke inducing but it was worth it to avoid the fist in the face wind that was raging. And rage it did. I could hear runners who looked like they knew their stuff gasping and wheezing, it was insanely tough going. For us, it was nothing short of hilarious and we couldn't stop grinning and giggling. Of course we couldn't speak and I kept making spluttering noises as I tried unsuccessfully to swallow but even that seemed funny.

There were moments of surreal insanity too, the brilliantly organised race featured numerous entertainment points including an incredible drumming band who were being pushed sideways by the wind so kept lurching in different directions. There were also well placed singers belting out adapted classics to motivate the participants, it created an awesome atmosphere of funfair like jollification. One notable singer was the Elvis impersonator along the wildly windblown promenade who inexplicably grabbed a runner and seemed to try to rugby tackle him to the floor. Whether or not this was intentional was unclear but it was hysterically funny to watch if maybe not for the runner himself. Marc was pissed that in the furore Elvis had blanked his high five attempt but I reckon he had a pretty close escape.

All along the route (and afterwards I learnt Marc had too) I had watched two women in front of us. They were charity runners on their maiden 10k (so their vests proclaimed) with awesome paint splashed tights. They had kept a brilliant pace and this really started to piss me off; I began to hate them. How the hell could they be running faster than me? I'd been doing this shit for years. After giving myself every excuse in the book I resolved there and then to own their asses, there was no way they would beat me to the finish line. Clearly Marc felt the same as he had the exact same steely look of hatred in his eyes as I did. I looked at my Garmin and realised we were near the 5k point so we had to turn soon, I started to run harder, determined to get past them and so did Marc.

At that exact point we turned onto what I shall now forever call the roundabout of doom, a small white circular bump in the road that signalled the turn. As we turned sideways to the breeze the crosswind caught our legs so hard that we crashed into each other and lurched crazily towards the kerb, we righted ourselves just in time before we took out legions of insanely scantily clad blokes. One of these blokes followed us onto the return stretch into a ridiculously strong tailwind but where it gave us some assistance and respite it had the opposite effect on him and he genuinely sounded like he was dying. His breathing was so loud and laboured that I turned in fright but he seemed to be relatively healthy, he was moving forward and he wasn't going to bloody well overtake us. He carried on desperately gagging for breath for another two miles before he presumably collapsed and died as it suddenly and thankfully ceased.

In the final mile we were really hammering it at around a 7.20 pace as a bloke in a blue graffiti splashed top sauntered past us like he was off for a Sunday stroll. I eyed the bastard viciously and decided whilst there was no way I could catch him I would not let him out of my sight. I tracked the poor bloke like a hunted animal until I could see the finish line and we powered past it straight into the arms of our mate Lisa from Macmillan (that's not her name by the way, she works for them) who was handing out goody bags.

And awesome goody bags they were too, filled with chocolate and energy drinks and useful stuff (although there was fucking inexplicable dried food again!) and then we got a brilliant technical t shirt that I might actually run in as opposed to use as a tea towel or nightshirt and some socks, and a water bottle, and gender specific deodorant!

It was a brilliantly organised race and fantastic fun, I can totally see why people rate it so much and we'll definitely be back. We bumped into heaps of running mates all with wind-blown smiles and breathless stories and took countless selfies, it was such a happy, friendly morning.

When we got home and consumed twice as many calories as we'd burnt we chatted about how glad we were we'd done it. It was such an enjoyable run and we really did have a brilliant time, we could have so easily have not gone. Marc said his decision was made early this morning, he believes in taking chances (he chose me after all). He thought that given the choice between a routine, mundane Sunday morning in bed (romantic old fool that he is) which would be instantly forgotten or a rock and roll epic in insane weather that we would always remember we should make the smart choice, which is sometimes the mad choice. You only get one life, so always choose the adventure.

In the words of George and Andrew 'Choose Life'. And as with all the adventures we go on together I wouldn't have missed this one for the world.

# 11
# The Start of the Slump

**Monday 8th February 2016**

It's my Mum's birthday today and a day off for me, Cleo is trying to break my heart by filling her suitcase with what can only be breeze blocks judging by its weight. She's off on an incredible trip to the US next week and I must admit I've turned into an over protective annoying Mom who shits herself if her child so much as sniffs. As a result of this she's going away with a sizeable stash of medications and potions, more to ease my mind than to actually treat anything functional (although if she gets gout then she's on top of that shit). I daresay I'm the world's worst role model when it comes to exercising caution with illness or injury, a run I did the day before Christmas Eve was testament to this.

**Wednesday 23rd December 2015**

Ok, I'm going to start with a disclaimer stating that no one should go against medical advice and that mostly your doctor knows best and you should always be sensible etc.
However...

Marc was at work, Cleo was happily ensconced with cool Uncle Lol and my mother was being my mother.
I was crawling the walls at home and I was beginning to wallow in it. I'd had a shed load of injections yesterday so figured they'd have probably had a positive effect on my blood count by now. Added to that I have horrific manflu and I was sofa surfing doing my best Jabba the Hutt impression. I really was beginning to get on my own tits. Besides, how often at this time of year do you get a pleasant, still, sunny afternoon?

So you understand where I was coming from. I was pretty sensible, I dressed warmer than was necessary and took my phone, a million tissues and some money and meds with me in case of emergency. I planned to do maybe 5 miles or 10k but accepted I might need to cut short. I felt a bit dodgy so my pace was all over the place and I knew it. I'd worn a Buff to cover my head but two miles in I wanted to rip it off because I had a temperature. It was kind of a joy to get out though and my nose cleared for the first time in days, I had a lovely tailwind and I began to feel a bit badass.

When I reached mile 4 I converted my Buff to a headband and unzipped my jacket a little, I was going to be fine for another couple of miles. I checked my Garmin and my average pace was 8.10 which was a bit faster than I planned so I decided to drop the pace. I needn't have worried. Turning back to home I ran into a headwind that felt like I had a hand pushing me backwards. Why do I never learn about outgoing tailwinds on beaches? For a mile and a half I fought against it, swearing and sweating in equal measures. My nose turned into the Niagara Falls and my legs became lead. And I was boiling. Alicia Keys was belting out Girl on Fire in my ear, and I sodding well was. I was going nowhere, I looked like I was doing the running man in a wind tunnel.

But then I turned off the beach and my feet found their wings again, I picked up the pace and felt really strong. I had a glorious mile back through the village and felt like a gazelle (although suspect looked a bit more like a gnu). It's amazing how a brief reprieve from the weather can lighten your legs, not even the half mile where I accidentally paused my Garmin (something which would normally send me spiralling into a frenzy of despair) could kill my buzz.

When I finally stopped at 8 miles (8 and a half really but I only believe what the Garmin tells me) I felt happily done in. Ten minutes later and the cold had returned, but it didn't matter.
I'm not sure whether it was the right thing to do but I certainly don't feel any worse for getting out there. Kill or cure? Only time will tell.

**Tuesday 9th February 2016**

I haven't run since Sunday, a combination of drastic weather and being knackered after work has rendered me apathetic. I've been mulling over the weekend's events and I do still feel somewhat victorious, 50.43 was a great time especially in those conditions.

On the way home in the car we had our usual post-race synopsis. This generally goes the same way in that I jabber incessantly about the tiniest minutiae of the event whilst Marc makes random listening noises and eats his body weight in chocolate. Part of our compatibility as a couple I think is rooted in our differences and this is particularly notable in our post-race state. I tend to become very hyper and adrenalin driven (annoying) whilst Marc tends to quieten and feel tired (grumpy). In the same way that we react differently post run we also have very different approaches to race day. It was something we'd talked about earlier that morning prior to the Mad Dog 10k and something I really wanted to work on.

For too long now race day has induced only one reaction in me and that's fear, poop liquidising, gut churning fear. It was only a few weeks back during the Winter Run that Marc had asked me if I was enjoying it as I had zoned out, drifted off and had a look of pain on my face. And he was right to ask because when I look over my race day photos from the last few years, not the posed ones outside landmarks or in beer tents but the candidly hideous ones that official photographers take then charge the kind of money you could buy a small nation with to get them, it isn't a pretty picture and I'm not referring to the foof hoof. On virtually every last one of them I look unwell, upset, destroyed and desperate. I've showed them to lots of people and the general ruling has been that you give it your all on race day so you can't expect to look amazing, these are just pictures of me going for it with everything I've got.

The only problem is, I don't and they're not. That's my shameful truth. On race day, or any other run day for that matter I don't give my best. Why do I hold back? Why don't I run all out? When we were running on Sunday I knew we were making a great pace during the last 5k but there was still more in my legs, but something always holds me back. I watched Marc and I could see him itching as he was in the Winter Run to fire on all cylinders and really tear it down but he couldn't as I was hesitant; fast but not my fastest. And in reality I don't know what my fastest is.

I think much of the reason is tied up with fear of failure. I've spoken before about the feelings of doubt that I get before basically every run I do. I feel that this will be the one that exposes me as a charlatan, the one that proves that all the other runs were luck or weren't real. Sometimes when I'm done I'll check my Garmin several times to confirm that I have got it right, that I did actually do it. These feelings of doubt and anxiety are most prevalent on race day and in some cases have seriously affected what should have been an amazingly enjoyable day. I guess it's obviously a self-confidence thing, rather than a case of 'she believed she could so she did' I'm more 'she thought she had no chance but she did anyway' and like most things I'm sure it's something to do with feelings of inadequacy or failure but ultimately I'm just wired this way.

In the training for Marc's newest position at work he's required to learn how to correctly take a pulse and understand heart rates. He took my heart rate the other day and it was low, around 50 bpm. Now in most cases a low heart rate indicates a high level of fitness, only I don't actually believe that I'm fit. I see people in gyms pumping iron and grunting on spin cycles, friends doing boot camp and millions of burpees and in my mind they're fit. I don't count myself among them though, I tried to do a press up once and it hurt, I tried planking but got bored and burpees are just some form of insane torture. I don't do that stuff so I don't see myself as fit, yes I can run ten miles after work three times a week and a half marathon on a Saturday morning before a day in town but that's not real fitness, that's just running.

Somewhere in my head I'm still the girl from ten years ago who doesn't own a pair of trainers and thinks that she's not cut out for fitness because she won't be able to do it. This self-doubt has crept into my race days and into my head before every run like a new cancer. That's not to say it's terminal though.

One of the things we did chat about in the car on the way home was that Marc said he needed to smile more during his usual training runs. He said on race day he smiled a lot, partly because of the cameras but mostly because of the atmosphere and supporters. He said he needed to transfer this into his training to see if it would improve what had been some tough runs of late. Something occurred to me like a slap in the eye, in all my usual training runs I smile and laugh a lot, even when I'm alone (because I'm a fool). I nod at passers-by and say friendly hellos but even in my solitude I grin a whole lot. I think a great deal when I run and most of it is in gratitude. I focus on how fortunate I am to be running, about how far Marc and I have come, I think about Cleo, about the people I love and I daydream about a happy future.

122

# Recovery Run
## Nicky Lopez

Despite the doubts prior to them training runs are generally a joyful experience and I smile very much.

Conversely on my race day photos I'm not smiling at all. On any of them. Could it be that the mere action of smiling might be the secret to enjoying race day a little more? Well here's the thing. On Sunday as we were on the transfer bus to the start line I decided to chill out and smile, I told Marc this. In my head I had elected a 'fake it till you make it' way of thinking. And it made one hell of a difference.

During the run I made a concerted effort to smile and to tell Marc I was having fun. And the weird thing was that despite it being by far the worst conditions I've ever raced in I ended up having the most brilliant fun and I ran better too. Just simply by pushing my mouth into a smile it had reminded me that I love to run. Now that's only half the story, I still fear failure. I guess I put pressure on myself like everyone does and I worry that I won't be able to deliver. 51.15 seemed really hard at the Winter Run, how was I going to top that? Well I need to start telling myself that I don't have to, no one expects it but me.

On Sunday I think, in fact I know, I could have run sub 50. Would that have made me happy though? Well yes, of course it would, any runner is delighted when they hit a milestone and I'm no different but I don't have to hang my every hope in every race on it. I just need to believe in myself a little more and learn to take chances. So what if I run all out and slow down in the last half mile? I'll know I ran my hardest. Or so what if I larked around with Marc on the John Reid Road, or Tower Bridge and lost a couple of minute? At least we had fun and it was memorable.

Running is a simple pleasure that we can over complicate with our own neurosis and desires. And that's not always a bad thing, for as much as I find myself fearing failure I discover countless victories and I think race day encapsulates that magical dichotomy that running truly is. We hold in our feet our dragons and demons, some of them we trample into the dirt and some of them stay on our soles. But with every run they are ground into a thinner matter, rubbed into a deeper insignificance. And in small degrees the person that we hoped we always could be slowly emerges from the web of doubt that entangled us.

And it all begins with a smile.

## Wednesday 10th February 2016

OK so tonight hurt.

Sometimes no matter what preparation you put in the pieces just don't fit and you end up having one of those runs. Today was a long ass day though; between a job, a business and a busy life I'm stretched in more directions than a very stretchy thing and days like today leave me feeling like I've nothing left in me. I know I also still feel the effects of treatment too, I'm much more tired than I expected to be and it comes at me when it's least convenient. I knew I wanted to run after work tonight so I did all the right things, made sure I ate properly, took it easy on the coffee, planned easy meals and kept well hydrated.

Knowing that I would be feeling tired I stacked as much as I could in my favour. When Marc came in early I was chuffed, this was a good omen, this was set to be a fab run. And if by 'fab run' I meant ten miles of rib stabbing pain in the ass biting cold with hallucinatory sensations then yes, it was fucking awesome.

Literally seconds after we left the house I felt like I had a hedgehog under my ribs, the worst stitch ever. It was like I'd never run before and had tried to leg it for five miles flat out. I tried the mental mantra thing 'it's just a stitch, it'll pass' I told myself. It didn't pass though, it stuck with me throughout the ten miles reminding me that I'm not as badass as I think I am, testing me to see if I really do love running or if I'm just a fair weather friend. It was tough, because of the pain I was constantly altering my breathing so I couldn't get a steady pattern going, I was also struggling to take a full breath. The upshot of this was that I started to feel a bit odd, I began to misjudge the ground beneath my feet which seemed to be moving independent of any control on my behalf and my legs were moving wider and wider apart. I ended up feeling like I was jumping with both feet and legs practically in a split position, I reflected at some length on how fantastic I must look doing my mega squat jumps along the dark canal towpath before it dawned on me I was in fact hallucinating.

I think the combination of pre run meds, tiredness, following Marc's bobbing headlamp and a distinct lack of oxygen all conspired to create the perfect storm and basically sent me loopy. Realising I was essentially on another planet I felt it prudent to stop, this coincided at the exact same time as Marc nearly skidded sideways toward the canal with impressive agility after crashing into the mother of all puddles. We stood breathless and shell shocked, we really needed to get our shit together.

We stayed there for a couple of minutes just breathing and bringing ourselves back down to earth. We set back off under the cloak of a star scattered sky with a little more trepidation in our steps. Marc maintained the lead pulling me along with a steady, supportive silence. I could feel his sympathy for my pain, he'd been there before himself and so I could sense his understanding and yet frustration at not being able to help.

The pain under my ribs remained at a controllable level but by the time I saw the halfway point bridge I was relieved. I stretched, bent over and tried to open my rib cage using a variety of yoga/rave moves but I couldn't seem to get a full breath down. Marc had an idea, he would grasp underneath my ribs and try to force the wind upwards a little. I had tried to do this using my fist but I simply couldn't get leverage. Standing behind me he put his arms round my waist and squeezed tightly, he then leaned forward until I was bent double. Using a rocking motion he gently but firmly attempted to push the trapped wind and hopefully disperse it. We did this for around thirty seconds until it became apparent that we looked to all intents and purposes that we were performing a particularly lewd act in full view and would probably be caught on CCTV and arrested at any time.

Turning for home I started to repeat a mantra in my head 'find joy,' I was hell-bent on taking something good from the run despite the pain in my side and the burn of lactic acid that was building in my calves. I looked at the stars, I breathed what I could of the cold air and gave thanks for my life, the chance to be running ten miles on a Wednesday night in February.

And then I took a deep breath as through the darkness we saw a tall, beautiful heron standing on the edge of the path. As it saw us it launched itself upwards and we watched as it mounted the sky. What struck me most was the difficulty it took to haul itself into the air, it was tangible and it was audible, it was something I'll never forget.

What I had always presumed to be an effortless act I now understand is much more than that, it is something which requires considerable power, force and tenacity. I don't mean to be cheesy and it's not like I have revelations on every run (except about awesome inventions involving magnets, I have loads of those) but I felt like I had seen and learnt something significant. I realised that sometimes to reach the heights you have to push your own limits and physically drag yourself upwards and it's not always as easy as it looks. Once you catch the breeze then you can start to glide but the journey up to it takes hard work and sometimes painful effort.

Coming towards the last mile we were ridiculously tired and I started to do the bizarre wonky leg type run I do when I'm knackered which terrifies fellow pedestrians and pavement cyclists owing to its spontaneous lurches in random directions. We ran with our hearts alone as our legs had long since given up. When my watch finally buzzed at the top of the avenue we both groaned in relief and exhaustion.

Marc said recently that there's no such thing as a bad run, I don't know about that, some of mine have sucked balls in a major way. What I do know is that there's no such thing as a wasted run, there's always a purpose, always a gain. People say that life is tough because you get the test first and the lesson afterwards, I think running can be a lot like that, you only get the wisdom after you've had the experience.

Still, this teacher has taught me more about myself than anything else and as classrooms go it's a pretty good one to be in.
So lace up, every day is a school day.

# 12
# Running with a Cheetah

**Later that evening.**

Not running related but...

When Marc or I see a post in our Facebook group, Running the World, which starts with these words our heart sinks. Nearly two years ago he made me a reluctant admin of the group and now it's my baby as much as it is his.

To be honest I'm more of the Wicked Stepmother, I have far less tolerance than he does but as with any half decent stepmother I try to make sure things are running smoothly and share the load. It's a great group with thousands of members from different nationalities all united in their obsession with the run. Over the years we've met and made lifelong friends with a number of members and Christ, these dudes know how to party.

First things first, you must have gathered by now that this is not an instructional text, this isn't a book about how to run/start running/improve running or any other type of guide. If anything it's more of a series of scrapes, brushes with madness and a whole heap of cautionary tales. In that sense it's far more a book about how not to run, what not to do and what best to avoid doing if you want to get better. I've done all the bloody stupid, idiotic things that you've thought about but were never so foolish enough to actually do and written them down so you don't have to put yourself through them. Think of it more a a compendium of running catastrophes, a diary of disaster that you can refer to on a random basis e.g. If you were thinking of wearing a brand new, untested outfit for a marathon (who the fuck would do something so ludicrous for the love of bollocks?) then you could flick to page 58 and see what the outcome of that insanity would be because as it happens I've done pretty much all the stupid stuff. In many ways I act as a public service, a sort of running superhero only I'm not very good and I do all the shit you shouldn't.

With that in mind I want to remind you of a cardinal rule of running...

## Do not get drunk the night before a big race

It seems obvious enough, alcohol will not only give you a banging head, wobbly tummy and bleary eyes it will also significantly dehydrate you and inhibit absorption of essential nutrients from your diet. Now there is a case for having a relaxing bedtime drink in the evening before, I have enormous trouble sleeping and so on the eve of all three London Marathons I have had a beer before bedtime simply to calm the nerves and so help me to relax. No, what I'm talking about is proper drinking, party drinking, and I don't think any runner who has trained hard for an event would be daft enough to jeopardise the enjoyment of the day for the sake of overdoing it the night before. It actually seems preposterous as I'm typing it out, nobody would be so recklessly halfwitted as to get hammered the night before an event...

It is with genuine shame that I will admit to have being significantly intoxicated the night before at least 7 major half marathons that I have run. It's no coincidence that all of these have been with Marc at whose feet I squarely (perhaps unfairly) lay the blame. I always imagined when I grew up that I would be the type of lady who had decanters and I would share a post work G&T with hubby and perhaps a glass or two of Rioja with dinner. The reality is that we're not that kind of grown up habitual, low level drinkers. We are teenage binge drinkers who consume nothing for weeks, chug everything in the bar over four hours one Friday night then puke on the doorstep into one of my hats whilst trying to get off with a hydrangea. And I haven't turned into a wine drinker (it gives me a crashing headache) like most mature adults of my age. If you asked anyone who knows me what I drink they would be stumped other than knowing it would contain vodka so basically, anything with vodka.

I can remember with nauseating clarity the morning of our first Great North Run together in 2013. Marc had made a breakfast of chorizo style sausage and egg sandwiches and I spent the entire run revisiting that sandwich whilst it relentlessly tried to exit my body via my throat. The night before we had met up with a bunch of friends from Running the World, one quick drink turned into carnage and the next morning saw Marc and I stumbling around in each other's pants, cursing our own stupidity and making foolish breakfast choices.

128

# Recovery Run
## Nicky Lopez

I'd like to say we learned our lesson and saw the error of our ways but we repeated the same mistake the following year on only we upped the ante a little. The Running the World pre Great North Run get together was now an established tradition, meeting up at the Pitcher and Piano on the impressive Newcastle Quayside with an open invitation to all. Being naturally quite socially awkward plebs we had a quick nerve settler, than another. It was at the point when our friend Lee exclaimed 'Let's get pissed!' I realised things had once again gone horribly awry.

Things were equally raucous this year the only difference being we had used the benefit of our experience and arranged the meeting earlier in the day, this would mean everyone home earlier and thus less chance of debauchery right? Wrong. I recall staggering off the Metro in the dark and eating a rather expensive meal in a restaurant I have no recollection of. The thing is as much as we know it's silly and it affects our performance on race day we also like a bit of balance. Whilst neither of us would want to feel so rough it would ruin the experience we also enjoy meeting up with our mates and having a few scoops. We also accept that we're not professional athletes and we're here for a good time not a championship time.

These nights were minor infractions, mere blips on years of responsible running and taking good care of our health. I have to admit that all of these events pale into a collective insignificance when compared to the utter living hell that was the morning of Liverpool Rock and Roll Half Marathon as a result of events precipitated by one Mr Tim Christoni.

We've been lucky enough over the years to meet some truly awesome people and call them friends and we respect each and every one of their sporting achievements individually and without qualification. Many of our friends are super fit, very accomplished sports people and a few of them are what I would term as proper athletes. I'm talking about the kind of guys who take podium places at events and are sponsored by sports brands.
Tim Christoni is one such proper athlete.

An impressive Californian long distance runner, he is preposterously tall and decorated with numerous tattoos that sleeve his arms and adorn his legs. A former US soldier he's a big hit with the ladies; in regular clothing he is a charming, witty guy with a ready smile and a friendly easiness, in running gear he is The Cheetah and his sky high stretch strikes terror into the hearts of lesser mortals. Legendarily photogenic he is as serious about running as he is about partying.

We first got to know Tim when he joined Running the World in 2013 and we instantly became friends. Despite running achievements that most of us could never dream of attaining he became an active and supportive member of the group offering advice and encouraging words with a huge generosity of spirit. With a wicked sense of humour and a colossal heart he's impossible not to like. When he told us he was going to come over to Liverpool for its inaugural Rock and Roll Marathon in May 2014 we were beside ourselves with excitement.

After months of planning we arranged to meet up on the Friday for one or two drinks, allow ourselves some rest on the Saturday whilst Tim caught up with the legions of people wanting to meet and run with him, do the race on Sunday (we would do the half as we are pussies and Tim would do the full as he is basically not human) and then we would party. As it was a bank holiday the next day it was perfect, we had it all covered, we were all over this. There were two important factors we hadn't taken into account: the first is that Marc and I are idiots (no surprises there), the second (and perhaps more surprising) is that Tim is also an idiot and between the three of us how we survived that weekend I shall never know.

It started well, Tim arrived from LA and headed to the hotel mid- afternoon, we had a large vodka and Redbull sent to his room as a jokey welcome drink. We excitedly put on our best gear and made our way to Revolution in Liverpool's Albert Dock where we would meet for an hour or two allowing Tim to then go to bed and for us to take Cleo to ice skating in the morning. We met up around 7pm and after emotional hellos it was as though we'd always been mates. Feeling a bit swaggy we decided to have a cocktail so we ordered some with the most hilarious names, we were delighted to discover it was happy hour so we were given an identical order free. The deliciously sugary drinks went down so well we thought we'd maybe just put one more order in before happy hour ended and then we would all go home. Well, maybe it was safer if we ordered two. This then meant that we had four cocktails each on the table.

# Recovery Run
## Nicky Lopez

Tim, new to Liverpool and not wanting to appear rude placed the same order at the bar meaning that within ten minutes we had 8 rather lethal cocktails each on the now groaning table. Why we didn't leave them alone I cannot explain, what led us to feel we had to actually consume them all still baffles me to this day. What utterly nonplusses me though was what happened when Lisa Wild our good friend and representative for our charity Macmillan Cancer Support arrived.

Seeing us now dramatically worse for wear she realised she would quickly need to play catch up and so placed yet another order. In due time we had another four drinks each in what was now the longest ever recorded happy hour in history.

I am not completely sure what happened after that but if I tell you that to this day it has made me think twice before I accept any alcoholic drink then you might guess the extent of the damage. Based on the photos that we looked over several days later when the trauma had quietened a little we clearly didn't stop there. There were scenes involving jewelled, headressed Mardi Gras dancers, there were photos of me wearing my wig inside out like some bizarre Mohican, there were published videos of us screaming Beatles songs in the most hideously pissed voices, there also appeared to be several major tumbles and a bottle of champagne. I have never seen a group of adults look so overwhelmingly shitfaced in my life, we were quite literally destroyed.

Snippets of the night have returned to me on occasion like flashbacks from a bad acid trip. I recall calling a barman Olaf repeatedly because someone had told me that was his name, I also remember Marc and Tim doing some amazing Latin dancing and my dad appearing somewhere in the early hours of the morning to take us all home like a pack of naughty kids.

The next day was one of the worst of my life. I have suffered greatly at the hands of cancer and chemo but nothing could have prepared me for the way I felt at 8am that morning. Marc and I woke to the alarm fully dressed and sprawled on Cleo's bed. My heart was thumping loudly and I think I could hear Marc crying softly and sorrowfully into his pillow. I tried to lift my head but the pain was so earth shatteringly intense I could do nothing but lay perfectly still. Cleo started stirring and then she must have seen us because she just kept saying 'Oh my God' over and over again. I could see on the floor my inside out wig and a bundle of coats, we both still had our shoes on. I genuinely thought I was seriously ill, I thought something had broken inside. I couldn't see Marc but he sounded shell shocked like he had been involved in some terrible trauma and we both had.

But our parental responsibility kicked in. We had to get Cleo to ice skating she could not be made to suffer for our gross irresponsibility. This was going to involve a car journey and Marc's blood was still running Rum Bongo, I whispered to Cleo to ask Grandad if he could drive but every time I moved my lips the only sound that emerged was 'blurhgydtguj' which is pronounced as it is spelled. Suddenly she fixed me sternly in the eye that was open and said "what the hell is that?" "Issss Marc", I said almost coherently and winced and groaned as I tried to tilt my broken skull towards where she was pointing.

Marc was lying looking alarmingly lifeless with his shirt open and a pirate hat on his head. Cleo stared at us both in a look that was a mix of amusement, disappointment and disgust and said "What the hell happened to you both?"
I can only tell you the same thing we told her.
We'd been Christonied.

The rest of the day was nothing short of brutal. After a silent car journey (my dad said afterwards he thought we might be dead) trying not to throw up we sat in an ice cold skating rink shivering like junkies. Too ill to attempt coffee (I had already disposed of my stomach contents several times that morning without the aid of food or water) we couldn't even look at the ice as there were skaters moving and spinning on it.

I have never felt so absolutely drastic in all my days, my head hurt so badly I actually cried a couple of times that day. I thought it would never stop. Marc looked worse than I have ever seen him and I was scared about him sleeping in case he never awoke. Truth is he had drank so much Redbull he wouldn't sleep for another few days. We got in touch with Tim to discover he had cancelled all his appointments as he had developed a 'sore knee'. Lisa promised us she would never speak to us again. The horror of it all escalated madly when we remembered we had a half marathon the next day. And Tim had a full.

# Recovery Run
## Nicky Lopez

I felt hideous in every possible way as we took to the start line for the first Liverpool Rock and Roll Marathon and Half Marathon. My body ached, my head thumped and I could barely walk let alone run. My stomach had turned to jelly and water and my legs shook. Marc had barely spoken since Friday night such was the state of shock to his system.

## Sunday May 25th 2014, Liverpool Rock and Roll Half Marathon, Liverpool

A bright, warm, sunny morning made the city look particularly gorgeous. Liverpool gets an undeserved bad rap at times because it really is one hell of a city with beautiful, impressive architecture dancing along a vibrant waterfont. I was so glad everywhere looked full of life as I really wanted this race to go well. We had seen so many of these awesome looking Rock and Roll races from our friends in the US, when an English one was announced we were excited and when we found out it would be Liverpool I was jubilant.

My hometown means a great deal to me, a city steeped in history and music it's had its fair share of press coverage over the years. At times it does itself no favours but on the whole it's a brilliant place to live and is full of warm, friendly people. We are also friends with people who work for the UK organisers of the race so we were particularly keen to support it.

The set up was great, a start on the Albert Dock right in one of the busiest parts of town made for a great atmosphere and lots to see, yes it was much earlier than we were used to at just 8am but given the already warm sun we agreed that was a good thing. The half marathon got off to a resounding start with Tim and the other marathoners including another of our super runner friends Caroline Jackson heading off for the full an hour later. It's a great route which took in lots of Liverpool treasures including a run past the Cavern on the Sunday morning sticky Mathew Street and a brief nod to Eleanor Rigby after that the course snakes off towards Chinatown and into Sefton Park the city's largest green space.

The couple of miles to get to the park is admittedly a long drag uphill and there's little to distract from the whopper of an incline that is Parliament Street. It is an utter bastard (although when we ran the race again in 2015 it didn't seem half as bad as I had remembered) but it's reasonably short and after that it's pretty much plain sailing all the way back down to the finish. Along the way we were treated to various bands and entertainers and it really was a new and fun race. The loop down Penny Lane with the eponymous song playing relentlessly throughout was a nice touch and even I felt something of a tourist.

I'd gritted my teeth from the beginning through the vestiges of the hangover from hell but eventually I found my stride, as we were heading towards the promenade I began to feel like we might finally be on the home stretch. But stretch it did. Otterspool prom which was built from the rock pulled out from under the Mersey when the tunnel was drilled is a sweeping rampart that hugs the south of the river into the city, and it goes on and on and on.

We finally reached a mile marker and I was hopefully expecting to see the number 13. When I saw 11 miles in bold letters I dropped the F bomb so loudly you could have heard it in Birkenhead across the river. I was dying and so to be fair seemed to be many of the runners, the long prom and hot sun had sapped us all. It was at this point that Marc got his second (or in fact first) wind and started humming and whistling merrily. If I hadn't have loudly told him to fuck off I swear to God someone would have punched him, I was seconds away from it.

The final mile was an exhilarating rush back towards the Albert Dock by the Echo Arena with a large, cheering crowd and a huge stage set up ready for a free concert arranged by the organisers. It was a brilliant party that seemed to get even better the following year (we also had VIP passes by that time so felt insanely swag) and included a free pint at the end. A fab race which I was proud was held in my home city. If only we hadn't been dying of alcohol poisoning.

Miraculously we made it through the run, I couldn't drink water for fear of rehydrating the alcohol levels and so felt even direr but we managed it in a respectable time. The proposed meet up afterwards went ahead but we were more subdued than usual and headed home around 5pm to die slowly on the sofa. It was around a week before we felt normal again. Tim had a pretty triumphant marathon finishing in some insanely fast time but he too still recoils when anyone mentions the events of that weekend. We're still great friends with he and his new wife Helen and we plan to honeymoon in

# Recovery Run
## Nicky Lopez

Los Angeles. Lisa finished what was her first half marathon and had gone on to complete the Great North Run and the London Marathon. She still hates us.

Lesson to learn. Don't get drunk before a big event. And, if a tall Californian guy with wild eyes and a Boston Marathon tattoo on his leg offers you a cocktail, then run.
Run for your goddamn life.

# 13

# Wind, Turbulence and Altitude Sickness

I've strayed off point again with my non running related post.

Yesterday I made the decision to start growing my hair. It's been stubbornly but patchily coming back for a while but as I may need a small surgery on my brain I've continued to shave it. I didn't want to grow it and have to go through shaving it all off again. I also accept that I have clung to cancer the way one clings to the familiar because it's safe, it's known but I need to let go for my family's sake as much as mine. Cleo and Marc need to look at me and breathe easy, they need the security of normality. And it is time to get back to normal. The thing is though that the return of my hair is a truly terrifying prospect for me as I no longer really know what normal is.

For the last six years I have been predominantly bald and it has very much become my identity, I'm a little afraid of who I'll be when I'm just like everyone else. I suppose in that way it is running related because with the return of my hair I am starting to feel the weight of expectation, after all if she can do this in chemo what can she do when she's well? And the truth is not a lot more.

I have been inordinately lucky, on the whole I tolerated chemotherapy very well indeed and was able to control the majority of the unwanted side effects. Yes there were enormously difficult times but nothing that I felt would defeat me. Was this down to my immense strength of character and indomitable spirit? I doubt it. I imagine it was mainly due to genetic disposition and a sizeable chunk of good fortune. I suspect in good health my athletic performance will be pretty much unchanged, I feel in better shape now at the end of treatment than I ever did in my life so I can't imagine any sudden, life changing improvements.

But in terms of who I am and what I mean to other people, well that is going to change drastically. For six years I've been the girl who runs in chemo; I've been inspirational, strong, tough, unstoppable.

My bald head has represented me more than anything else and in many ways it has defined me. The question is, who am I to be now? As my hair grows I become just like everyone else and with no limitations also comes the burden of no excuses. In a couple of weeks I will for the first time in a long time be just like everyone else. Scary times.

## Thursday 11th February 2016

I just had my ass handed to me on a plate. Comprehensively.

The weather this morning was perfect, windless, sunny and crisp. I had a day off work and there was never going to be any doubt that I was running. I had planned for it, even gone to the anally retentive lengths of laying my gear out with alternatives in case the Met Office were lying to me (again). But in this case the sneaky little buggers had played a blinder and it was spectacularly lovely. In my head I was already athletically leaping over tall buildings and small children in swathes of bright stretchy material covering vast distances. Lately the weather has been such a buttcrack and this first whisper of Spring sounded like a reprieve, time to relax and get in some happy miles. So that was the plan.

A little voice in my head kept telling me to stay in bed today but I ignored it, it was gorgeous outside. What the hell did that little voice know? Quite a lot as it happened.

After a lovely peanut butter, honey toast breakfast I leisurely put on my running gear pondering what route I should take. I strangely really didn't feel like the coastal route, bizarre for me because I'm basically a mermaid (only with less hair and I can't really swim very well) in that I live and breathe the ocean. I was born and raised by it and if I stray too far from it I feel claustrophobic and hemmed in. It's no surprise that I ended up with a boy with an equal amount of salt water in his blood, he feels its call and its pull every bit as strongly as I do.

But today I couldn't hear it, somewhere in my head I couldn't tune my soul into that path. I think I had my heart set on running the eastern route of the canal, the scenic, rural route that glistened in the sunshine like a river of stars. I hadn't run it since November mainly because of the weather, the pathway after the first mile turns to a dirt track for two further miles which in wet conditions becomes a mud bath. At this point the towpath is more stable as it winds directly along the edges of Aintree Racecourse whose wide, flat expanses leave the area extremely exposed to even the slightest of breezes causing it to tunnel into a strong gust. It's basically a run that can only be done in dry, still conditions, pretty much exactly like today was.

I hit my Garmin and strode off excitedly and purposefully and was instantly levelled by a sharp thudding pain under my ribs the same kind as I had felt last night only worse. I could barely catch a breath and I was wincing with pain; I knew it couldn't last though, I would run it off, it would settle. I ran up towards the pylon, my familiar friend of old runs and as I approached I saw a bloody lake spanning the pathway, I shit you not.

This wasn't your average puddle, this was the asskicker of all water features, it was vast. As it reached the perimeter of the pavement it had spilled over onto the field for about five metres in each direction creating a swamp. Seriously there were birds floating on this aquatic bastard. It left me with a quandary; how in the actual crap was I going to cross to reach the towpath? Where was my trusty Geordie pathfinder when I needed him? Seeing as I had left my dinghy and oars at home I cast my eyes down the road to hell, an endless hill stretching off into the distance that connects with the towpath via a preposterously steep slope.

My heart was already sinking but I tried to keep optimistic, it was a perfect day and the canal would be heavenly. But everything hurt, my shoulders, my back, my arms all ached and each step felt disjointed, uncoordinated. At the crossroads leading off to the canal I briefly considered cutting my losses and heading back towards the beach but I had come this far, I might as well go on.

As I reached the towpath I was rewarded with the most beautiful vista. In my absence I had forgotten how utterly resplendent it can be on a sunny day. Every inch of nature seemed to be alive and rejoicing in the cold air and warm light. My heart lifted a little and I pushed on but I was acutely aware that I was indeed already pushing and I had barely covered two miles. The pain would not subside, I just couldn't find a rhythm and I knew there would be more difficult terrain ahead.

# Recovery Run
## Nicky Lopez

Of course I was right, the next mile and a half took me through nothing more than a gully of heavy, deep, sticky mud. It took intense concentration to stay upright as well as keep my bloody shoes attached to my feet, they're super light, knitted and hardly built for that kind of shit. Passing two chemically enhanced gentleman trying to fish with a long twig elaborately decorated with empty hula hoops packets I was momentarily distracted from the pain. They shouted merry greetings in some language not of this planet and I couldn't help chuckle a little, things weren't so bad.

But in fact they were, I was seriously struggling and I had already stopped four times. Looking at my watch I was aware I was running an 8 minute mile, a pace far beyond today's capabilities, I tried to slow myself but I couldn't seem to and my legs moved with rapid erraticism (if that isn't a word then it should be). As each mile passed I debated turning for home but as I would reach the mile point I would feel slightly better and decide to run on only to feel a new wave of despair a minute later.

Finally I reached five miles and I almost tearfully hit my watch for a break. I crouched down to stretch my legs and retrieve my breath, the motorway roared above my head but it was a scene of peaceful beauty down where I was and I gazed at it thankfully. Yes it was incredibly hard going but moments like this make it worthwhile and memorable. After a minute or two I knew I had to get going, one way or another there were five miles left to run and only me to run them.

Five miles, a distance that's normally comfortable, manageable to me had suddenly become gargantuan in proportion and I wasn't sure if I had it in me. I plodded along feeling at times more like I was stumbling than running, intermittently stopping in despair and exasperation with myself. If I could just get to seven miles I would begin to feel like I was getting home, the end would be in sight. 'Hold On' by Drake started playing in my ears and I could feel warm tears run down my cheeks, I missed Marc, he would help me, he would get me home.

Finally I got to seven miles and a turnstile, I leaned over it and breathed for a minute, knowing that I was about to hit the hardest part of the track again. A passing lady walking her dog asked if I was OK and I replied that I was struggling today but I would soon be home. I'm not entirely sure I believed that myself. Over the next two miles I had to use all my energy and concentration to keep from stumbling over and as I eventually reached nine miles I was in trouble. I hurt from the soles of my feet where I could feel every stone and twig to the top of my head which itched and stung from scratching at my new hair growth.

The last mile was probably one of the hardest I've ever done and I will openly say I felt broken in both spirit and body. When my watch finally buzzed I felt huge tears and a sense of defeat. Walking home I began to get my shit together and come back to life, sanity and rational; I had run 10 miles not yet 12 hours previously, it had been a tough week in work and yes, I now have some physical limitations that I still haven't truly faced up to and come to terms with.

Like I said yesterday, no run is wasted and every day is a school day. Today's lessons? Respect the distance, don't always ignore the little voice and above all, never, never, ever give up.

## Sunday February 14th 2016

When I started running six years ago I hated it with a vengeance. I found nothing enjoyable in painful, sweaty, breathless movement. It's fair to say that the only thing that kept me running was a pigheaded attitude and a feeling of total helplessness. Running hurt me but it also brought me a level of self-control that I had been robbed of both physically and emotionally but I wasn't good at it and I certainly had no love for it. Co incidentally I was also single at the time, I'd just come out of a long term relationship that to both parties was self-destructive and ultimately doomed to failure.

In many ways when I first began to run I'd given up on all the things that come with love, things like the soaring heart, the moments of excitement, the anticipation and the feeling of fulfilment. What I didn't realise at the time was that running would bring more love into my life in more ways than I ever thought possible.

Of course there's the obvious, I met Marc through running. Standing bent double at the corner of my avenue feeling broken and defeated, dragging my aching body through six miles in the driving rain training for my first Great North Run, feeling hot, sick and useless during the disastrous, soul destroying four mile runs for my second

# Recovery Run
## Nicky Lopez

Great North all led to my mister, my other half, the Geordie boy. This morning he knew that my confidence had taken a major bashing in my last run so he gently and carefully led me through an absolutely amazing 1.53 half marathon run.

It was a gorgeous, sunny, cold morning so we decided to do ten miles along the beach. As we started out I felt nervous and stressed, my last run had been an unmitigated disaster and I had lost my mojo. Yesterday we had eaten a shitload of Chinese food and lounged about and today I was paying for it, I felt heavy and sluggish like I was hauling myself along and my legs were still stiff from Thursday's calamitous outing. I'd also decided to try out my new running shoes and their pristine stiffness was making me feel like I'd clothed my feet in cardboard.

The worst thing was that I just didn't have any speed, I felt like I was running at the fastest pace I could but I knew I wasn't going anywhere in a hurry. Now and again Marc would pull slightly ahead (conversely I could tell he was on fire today, he was running smoothly and with little effort, totally in the zone) but whereas normally I would stretch my legs and equal him today all I could do is linger behind and wait for him to drop back which he did. At times when he pulled ahead he left a lingering reminder of the colossal heap of crap he too had consumed last night and being downwind was the least attractive place to run.

The best thing I could do was keep my head down and persevere, I could get through this. What I had done right today was take two painkillers beforehand. Six years of treatment and a heart condition have left me with muscle stiffness and soreness and I often neglect to do anything constructive about it. About three miles in I began to feel a little more in my stride, my legs were moving in a more fluid way and my breathing had settled; little by little I was beginning to enjoy the run.

As we passed mile four and were heading toward the halfway point I was feeling more confident so I suggested to Marc we put the extra half mile in to make it 11 miles, he agreed and said it was the best way to put the demons to rest. It's true I think, if you really want to slay the memory of a bad run the best way to do it is to outstrip it. If you can't do it in pace do it in distance. As we ran onto the footpath which borders the firing range I began to find the sweet spot, the happy place where my legs move on their own and my breathing follows.

Marc could definitely sense this and with no hesitation he suggested running on to make it a half. He totally knew what he was doing, he was giving me a route to re-establish my confidence. A half is a sizeable distance and a great way to feel a sense of achievement, I was happy to accept the challenge at that point. I'd justified it in my head by playing a bizarre numbers game which meant I was only really running just over half a mile than I would have (we'd have run to 5.75 for an 11 mile halfway point so it would only be 6.50ish for a 13 miler) and I felt pretty great.

I'd have felt better if Marc hadn't eaten what he had last night but even that foulness couldn't burst my shiny Valentine bubble. What did piss on my chips a bit though as it often does was the behaviour of some cyclists on the route.

Now before I go any further and get hunted down by legions of padded ass pedal pushers I need to make clear that a lot of cyclists I encounter are pleasant, unassuming people who will obey the rules of the road and smile or nod a hello as they pass. There are though as in any collection of humans a number in their ranks who are complete knobheads and we seem to meet most of them on our runs. I can tell from a distance when it's going to happen. An inability to make eye contact along with an unwillingness to divert from the trajectory that they are currently on.

It's at these times I most like to play Twat Chicken. This, one of my most favourite games involves a stiff resolve and a foolish temperament. As the stubborn (some may say ignorant but I wouldn't, obviously) cyclist approaches, the runner (who has previously ascertained that they are occupying the correct side of the path) must wear a look on their face of either complete insanity or a beaming smile, either is effective. The aim of the game then is to engage said cyclist in eye contact and to hold ones ground until a) the cyclist veers or b) the runner is mown down and killed. Now I should mention that in general I have never had a stern enough will to accomplish option b but I have come very close on a number of occasions.

As well as these amusing (I often scream loudly and madly if they get too close) if arse rattlingly annoying jousts I also particularly enjoy it when cyclists travel in groups straddling footpaths like miserable (they rarely smile) chubby butted armies. Today we had an encounter that can only be described as intimate with a ginger bearded misery wheeler as he practically mounted us from behind. I'm not sure he was expecting me to shout 'BELL END!' quite as loudly as I did but given his proximity I felt we were essentially now best friends or lovers anyway.

And while I'm on the subject of bells, why don't these rolling buttmunchers use them? The amount of times I've nearly shit myself because an all but silent vehicle has suddenly appeared less than two inches from my left tit is frankly unacceptable. If you're a cyclist and you suspect you may fall into this category (I would say minority but I'm not entirely convinced) then please, heed my warning before you find yourself one day clotheslined by a butch looking girl in unforgivably bright Lycra. And bloody smile once in a while too, it won't kill you but I may.

As we bounded on we chatted about how we were running faster than I perceived, I still chose not to look at my watch but I knew with his characteristic Geordie understatement we were probably going pretty well. We passed by an elderly lady walking next to her bicycle and she smilingly asked if we'd like to swap, I didn't want to though, I love that my legs can carry me far and freely. I imagine she would have given anything to do what we were doing, to be able to run untethered by pain or limitation.

It reminded me of Marc's mum who had been housebound by her condition, she had often looked at people passing by the window of her house and said she would give anything to just be able to walk to the corner shop. What the hell was I doing whining about lost mojos and bad runs, I have life I have love and I have freedom. I felt ashamed that I had allowed my own defeatism and vanity to obscure the enormity of the gifts I have in my life. I had no right to not acknowledge the joy there is waiting for me in every moment.

By now we had run into territory that we hadn't seen since we were marathon training last year and it was wonderful to see it again. Passing through wheaten fields and over the ambling River Alt the air was full of springtime and the hedgerows were littered with bow headed snowdrops. I began to feel full hearted and glowing.

143

# Recovery Run
## Nicky Lopez

At the halfway point at Formby station we turned and ran back towards home, the sun now on our faces and the wind at our backs. My legs now were stronger, pacier and when I stretched them for speed they responded. We laughed and talked and exchanged cheerful greetings with passing cyclists and Valentine couples out for a walk under the bright blue sky. The hilly footpath felt happily challenging and we pushed strongly both up and downhill until we were quickly back on our own coastal path.

Heading back onto the beach I thanked Marc and I thanked God for this feeling, this unutterable happiness and gratitude for my life and for the love of running with heart beating strongly and filling my lungs with clean, sea air feeling entirely, electrically alive. By now we were fast and strong and we made light work back to the beach. The final mile back home was against the cold wind but it felt like a blast of cool relief from a very warm hearted sun.

We finished particularly strongly feeling like we had miles left in our legs and hearts full of love and hope. We were talking about how lucky we are that we share this passion that our idea of a fun Valentine's Day is to do this.

Although it led me to Marc, running has also led me to love in so many other ways. It has opened my eyes to the beauty of the world and has given me moments of such complete joy as I fell in love with nature and the outdoors. I have experienced total fulfilment and more than that it had allowed me to learn to love myself more, to appreciate the strong, miraculous piece of work that my body is. It's also improved my confidence in myself physically and in terms of self-esteem and belief that I can achieve and succeed.

Running has also softened my heart, it has made me more tolerant, more understanding and more accepting of others. Although it took me a long time to fall in love with running I pretty quickly fell in love with this planet we live on and the people in it, including myself.

So this is what I was thinking about for Valentine's Day, if you can't find someone to love then find something to love instead - a hobby, an interest, a passion. I can't promise you that you'll meet the man or woman of your dreams, if you're lucky like me you might. The thing is though when you open your heart and mind to one thing it's really hard to close it off to everything else. It sets off a chain of happiness and joy seeking and if you can find beauty and joy in as many places as possible then you start seeing it in more and more people too.

And of course when you love something then you tend to start being around people who love that same thing too and a shared interest can ignite hearts in a very special way. It's not just luck that I met Marc, one of the reasons we became involved with each other was this common interest, this mutual madness.

And in turn he taught me how to fall in love with running itself.

I always knew running was good for the heart.

## Wednesday 17th February 2016

We ran last night, it wasn't the greatest run and I don't have a huge deal to share with you about it. We were knackered after getting up at ass o' clock to bundle Cleo off on a transatlantic adventure so we decided that 8 miles was going to be more than enough. Marc wasn't actually going to run but when I told him that I was he changed his mind, not because of any selfless devotion to keeping me company but rather because he he'd look like a little bitch if he didn't. And he's right, if I don't run on a day when he has I feel like I'm failing at life. Such is our relentless idiocy.

So there we were traipsing our weary asses towards the beach in the dark, horrid icy rain blowing in our faces like little wet knives. I'm having hat dilemmas right now and I was torn tonight between hat and cap, I favour a cap in the rain but my head was cold. I second guess a lot of things at the moment, apparently it's to be expected.

Yes my hair is growing back but six years and a lot of stress has taken away my deep, dark brown and silver plated it which highlights the extra years that are sitting at the corner of my eyes. It's fair to say that externally the glowy faced, bright eyed girl has been sacrificed and an older, war wounded woman has occupied her space. Internally give or take a few battle scars the girl lives on. My digestive system has taken the knock too as I've mentioned before and I seem to suffer from crippling stitches and wind pains with reasonable frequency.

The thing is I'm adjusting to a new normal, learning how to live with the new, old body I've found myself in and it'll take a while to find my feet if you'll excuse the pun. And I do struggle to find my feet literally at the moment, one of the side effects of my very long term chemo has been peripheral neuropathy, a condition which also affects diabetics. It causes a feeling of numbness in the extremities which means that I need to constantly check my feet for signs of cuts, blisters etc. as I can't always feel them. I'd ask Marc or Cleo to check but they both have a pathological fear of feet which involves expressions of disgust and repulsion when I attempt to wave my run ravaged trotters in their faces.

I'm finding increasingly when I run that I have no feeling in my feet for a good portion of the time and it's madly disconcerting, causing me to change my gait at times and affecting my rhythm. Plus it's just weird, it feels weird, it's like running on blocks of wood. That was one of my bothers last night along with a lump of pain under my ribs and the general shitty weather.

We were running pretty quickly and I was wondering how long I could keep the pace, I still haven't got my head around speed training but I may try a little in the summer or far more likely, I may not be arsed to. I tried a few different breathing patterns to see if it would help which if nothing else served to distract me. I found that the deep breath in alleviated it a little so I tried doing this then releasing my breath in short sharp spurts with pauses in between. This not only sounded bonkers but it also made me a bit dizzy which coupled with my clown feet made me start running pretty strangely.

I then decided to adopt a similar technique to one I'd used when I was in labour with Cleo. I was in a pretty bad way having somewhat optimistically opted for a natural birth (seeing as at the time I would cry if I broke a nail) and Entinox just wasn't cutting it. Speaking of cutting it at one point a poor unsuspecting student doctor was pushed through the door to deal with me and I asked, nay begged him to cut me open and remove the child. He explained something about I was too late for an epidural and therefore he couldn't do that, I told him I didn't care and to cut me open anyway and I wouldn't tell anyone. I'm not sure how I expected him to conceal this surgical nightmare but like I say, pain was not my strong suit.

So next a midwife came in, not one of the lovely, sweet, holistic type of practitioners that you get these days, no this woman was the type who would slap the baby's arse then tell you to get back down the mines. Anyway she told me the best way to deal with the pain was to make some noise, as much as I liked, nothing good would come of holding it in. So I did; I roared, screeched and mooed like a cow. I made noises that I didn't know a human being could make. Deep, primal roars and squealing grunts, the other patients must have been fucking terrified. I did however cope and out popped the CleoBeast, all nine pounds eight ounces of her, the same kid who had just texted me the most mind-blowing pic from the top of the Empire State Building.

So I thought it might work with the wind pains while I was running, obviously not on the same scale. As the pain rose to a less than acceptable level I would let out a sigh or a quiet groan to try to release a little of the tension in my torso. I guess I must do this quite often anyway as Marc didn't even flinch let alone mention it. I do know from running without my music on when I'm with Marc that I do tend to make noises that sound a little bit like I might actually be dying so I reckon the extra effort with my grunts and moans didn't faze him at all.

It did help me a bit though, it must have as the final few miles whilst still tough were nothing like as hard as the first. I guess the mere vocal acknowledgement that I was finding it hard going gave me a bit of relief and comfort and thus the impetus to carry on.

Whilst I was running I was thinking about the multitude of online articles I'd read about how to cope with tough runs and the one phrase that repeatedly came up was 'embrace the suck'. It's not something we do naturally, we live in a society where everything is improved, facilitated, user friendly. What do we do when the run we're in starts to malfunction and for want of a better phrase, goes tits up? Well the idea is that we carry on regardless, embrace the suck and keep moving forwards.

I imagine at this point you may think I'm a hypocrite, here I am evangelising about the importance of enjoying the run and being kind to yourself whilst I'm also advocating the idea of toughing it out, hanging in there, embracing the suck. Well I kind of think that the two aren't mutually exclusive, I think it's perfectly possible to treat yourself nicely and also to push on, in fact I think it's one of the most valuable runs you can have.

Because the truth is that some of your runs are going to be like last night and if my gut feeling is anything to go by I think I've got a lot of tough runs ahead of me. The only possible way I'm going to get through them without destroying my confidence or my love of running is to embrace the suck, to remind myself of how strong I am for continuing and of how much I am growing both as a runner and as a person by strengthening my resolve, building my resilience, honing my badassery.

When we did Birmingham Half Marathon in October it turned into a very tough run and despite me getting a PB I seem to have whitewashed it a little from my memory. I think I was on such a high from my last Great North Run in September (which I'm getting to tell you about) it was going to be impossible to live up to. Mad really as in hindsight I learnt such a lot from the day but it was a new run for us and Marc had begun the weekend with the cold from hell…

## 18th October 2015, Great Birmingham Run Half Marathon

So, a very emotional day today and I learnt so, so much. Firstly, I need to do more hill training. I obsessed about that hill, studied it and let it get inside my head and what gets inside my head inevitably makes its way down to feet. I have a history of self-doubt when it comes to running and in the past I've let races get the better of me as soon as the going gets tough. So secondly, I need to work on my mental game. In the first mile I lost track of Marc and started to panic, my common sense flew out the window and I was ready to quit until he found me.

Up to mile ten was great and I had bags of confidence, I was running fast and strong and had a ton in the tank. At mile 11 I had a blip and I momentarily lost the plot, with the run, with Marc, with myself. I need to keep things in perspective, it's a bloody run not my final judgement day. Thirdly, my peripheral vision is shit. At mile 11 I ran straight into an official holding out water at the water station, the bottle hit me straight in the face, not only did it hurt like hell but I was also embarrassed and shocked. I think I had some sort of panic attack, I started crying, I couldn't breathe and was shaking.

Fourth, I need to chill the hell out, it's just a bloody run. The fifth thing I learnt was that runners are wonderful people. The amount of support, love and concern I was shown at that point by total strangers was moving beyond words. I can't thank them by name but I will never forget that. Penultimately, I learnt that I'm a really good

148

runner and I'm turning into a smart one too. I have strong, fast legs that work even when I'm not feeling great. I know my shortcomings and I accept them but I've got real strength. I finished another sub two half marathon, this time in 01:56. And I love running, it makes me happy.

Finally, not so much a lesson learnt as reaffirmed. I am so lucky to be blessed with Marc, he is the greatest running buddy and partner and not only would I never want to run a race without him, I simply couldn't. He has the most immense strength of character and humility along with a bravery that constantly challenges me to be braver, stronger, better.

So I'm trying not to fear the sucky runs from now on because out of them can come the most incredible achievements. Maybe instead of hating our demons we should do something different and see if they behave differently when we try a little tenderness, give ourselves kudos for the story so far. It's just possible that the power is in our own minds as much as it is in our legs, or feet or stomachs to turn a bad run good. And if all else fails, embrace the suck.

# 14

# The Geordie and the Gym

**Thursday 18th February 2016**

A run can mean all sorts of things, it can be a celebration, a commiseration, a mood booster or a stress reliever. That's the wonderful thing about running, it can be whatever you want it to be on any given day. In many ways it's like a high class hooker only without the risk of infection, the price tag (although my running wardrobe would suggest otherwise) or any moral issues. Tonight's run was all about confidence, it had been a tough day for Marc so I wasn't sure if he'd want to pound it out on the streets alone or have some company.

He opted for the company option and I was glad, so often when I've had a shit day I've appreciated the sound of his footsteps next to mine even if we haven't exchanged a single word, sometimes a silent presence is enough. So out we went towards the Leeds Liverpool canal into the stingingly cold night. There was no chance of talking as the shock of icy air took our words away until we were deafened by nothing more than the sound of our own breath.

I'm not sure or not whether I like listening to myself breathe, I still haven't made up my mind. Sometimes I hate it, I become overly aware of what should be automatic and natural and from that second it becomes stilted and out of time. Other times I love it, the strong, steady beat playing in my head and reminding me how absolutely and essentially alive I am at that moment. I guess it's tied up with how I'm feeling, what sort of run I'm having. Tonight I was in between, not sure whether to trust what felt comfortable or fear what felt like effort.

It was colder than we had accounted for and as we swung onto the canal I knew we had got there pretty quickly and my legs were a little stiff from sitting in one position at my bench all day. When I'm not attempting to enlighten children with the joys of conjugating irregular verbs I have my own business making jewellery, much of it for sporty types and runners.

It began as a half-baked idea borne from a gift I had bought Marc, a stamped metal keyring with some nice wording on it. I knew runners would love stuff like that but it was impossible to get hold of. After failing to encourage an existing businesses to do it I decided to look into the possibility of doing it myself. Long story short after a very steep learning curve and a huge amount of independent learning I now have a happily small but successful business called Run Bling which I love.

Returning to the original point, I had pretty stiff legs after a busy day so I was feeling the pace. The thing is though I wanted the run to be all about Marc, I wanted him to lead and I would be there to nurture, support and encourage him. What I hadn't accounted for was quite how nippy the little bastard can be. As we darted onto the canal he switched his headlamp on to illuminate the pathway and then started to disappear into the pitch dark distance. I stretched out my legs and pushed down on my feet to gain ground but each time I did he seemed to find an altogether different level of speed. I started sprinting hard and breathing heavily to keep him in sight but he was away like a Geordie Usain Bolt only shorter and with a lamp on his cap.

I could hear panicked sounds escaping from my mouth betraying me as the wuss I really am, approaching the second mile I wailed "Marc, I can't keep up with you!" He was sorrowfully apologetic, he was feeling stressed and his legs were taking over, it was then I knew what I had to do. Waving him on ahead of me I knew it was right to let him run on, set him free, stretch his legs and spend all of the pent up frustrations of the day on the towpath. I knew it would be best if I held back, had my own run within tonight's capabilities and we would meet at the end knowing we had both achieved in our own ways, he with speed and strength and I with...um...

And that's when I started to put my foot down, because this run wasn't about what I could do but it sure as hell wasn't going to be about what I couldn't do. For ten hard, sweaty, intense miles we pushed on faster and faster until I felt like my legs were spending more time in the air than they were on the floor. As the miles whizzed past I wondered just how long I could keep this up, doubt crept into my ear and whispered that I was going too hard, too fast.

At the halfway point we stopped momentarily where I had a hallucination that I could see satellites moving all over the skies. It was in reality an optical illusion caused by the quickly moving clouds but for one brief moment I was fearful something extra-terrestrial was about to happen to us. I really shouldn't tell people what's in my head until I've ascertained it's real or sane. With a demonic 'HOWAY!' from Marc we resumed our hellish pace hurtling under bridges and past the unsuspecting heron who leapt to the sky with her powerful grace.

At times it was very tough, I ran mile to mile keeping an eye on the ever diminishing pace and with each mile I could feel him coming back to life, confidence growing and spirit strengthening. And for what it was worth mine was too because I felt so grateful to be strong enough to keep up with him, to be able to let him rip it up and have the strength to stay by his side because I knew in a heartbeat he would drop the pace and sacrifice this boost to make it easier for me.

But tonight I wasn't going to let that happen, as we reached the final three miles my hip began to feel tired and I started to doubt whether I could maintain the now sub 8 minute pace for another 5k so I began running mile by mile and breathing strong and hard. My legs didn't let me down and at every turn they responded with power and speed pushing me beyond my comfort zone into relatively unknown territory.

This is what it feels like to let go, to run hard and to keep running hard. I kind of liked it and the voice of doubt that had been raging in my ears was quieter now. As we turned from the canal onto the broad pathway my legs found a new strength and I stretched them to match Marc's pace. For his part he was on fire, there was actual steam coming from him yet he appeared to be making very little effort, whatever was going on inside him had put strings of pure steel into his legs and his heart. We finished the ten miles in 1.22 which is damn good going by our standards.

As we wandered back to the avenue we talked about the phrase 'go hard or go home'. It's one that's never sat well with me, I'm more of a 'do what feels right at the time' kind of girl. When I asked Marc what he thought he said his phrase would be 'Go hard or just do whatever' and I love that. He didn't go out tonight to break any records, to settle any scores, he just went out and ran as well as he felt he could. And I could see in his eyes that something had changed, something had galvanised deep down inside him.

# Recovery Run
## Nicky Lopez

About an hour later while he was studying and I was wrestling an avocado in the kitchen he sent me this quote in a text, 'Being defeated is temporary. Giving up is what makes it permanent. Never give up, stay dedicated.' It's hard not to love the boy.

## Sunday 21st February 2016

I like my comfort zone, in fact I love my comfort zone and it's the area I most inhabit when I'm running. My comfort zone generally lies somewhere between the 8.50-9 minute mile, it's the place where I can find my groove and go into cruise mode. I say generally because as with all things in running my comfort zone changes, sometimes with frustrating inexplicability; what felt smooth and easy on one run can be my top level of effort on another. In fact it can often change several times within the same run, the goalposts constantly moving sometimes closer, sometimes beyond my grasp.

I see a lot of quotes and hear people talking about how growth only happens outside the comfort zone, I'm not so sure about that. My steady improvement over the last year has had far more to do with consistency than challenge, rather than pushing myself harder I just did more. I think for a person like me that kind of strategy works well, I've never been good at gritting my teeth through great discomfort, I do it but it's always with a certain uneasiness as to how much benefit that actually is.

Of course as a runner you have to learn resilience but I think there's a gaping chasm between challenging yourself to do a little more or hang on a little longer and pushing yourself through barriers of physical or mental distress. And I think that's the whole comfort zone thing, yes it's great to leave it once in a while and test your limits but don't go so far from it that you can't get back there if you need to in a hurry. And it definitely is a journey. Taking ourselves beyond what feels safe and familiar can be scary stuff, for me definitely.

My runs are pretty much always well within my ability level on roads and routes that I know and whilst the outcomes can vary it's often pretty predictable. Having never gone for it in an all-out run I have no true idea of what PBs I'm capable of or where my limits are. That's why runs like Thursday night are so important as they put me through my paces without leaving me feeling exposed or doomed to failure.

Of course the journey beyond your comfort zone should be a short one where you always keep your point of origin within reach, moving too far from what your body is comfortable with is reckless and invariably leads to injury. But there's beauty to be found in that little extra stretch and it leads you to destination of self-discovery and renewed enthusiasm.

A run beyond your comfort zone whether it be in distance, pace or terrain can bring a whole new dimension to your running and can lift you from a funk if you've become bogged down in routine or monotony. As with any journey you have to plan in advance, a longer run will need more in fuel and hydration, a faster run may need you to attend to any existing injuries and new terrain needs attention to correct clothing and shoes.

But there's something truly awesome in getting out there and shaking it up a little. Thursday night for me left me feeling exhilarated and certainly pretty damn smug like I had pulled something new and special out of an old bag of tricks. And no, I did not just refer to myself as an old bag.

The only downside is that a walk on the wild side can involve risk and where risk is involved a sacrifice may be necessary. Anything that pushes you beyond your comfort zone can potentially lead to problems and you have to not only try to counteract that as much as you can but ultimately you have to accept it. If you run harder, faster, higher or further than your muscles are used to then there is a significantly higher chance of injury. Yes take every precaution available and listen to your body but in the end the possibility still exists.

For me my fast run on Thursday finally brought to a head the injury I've been avoiding for so many months and as much as it frustrates me I know it's probably a good thing. In the final mile the pain that had begun in my calf last year and travelled through to my knee a couple of months ago culminated in one sharp and searing jolt through the back of my leg making it hard to bear weight.

So here I am, grounded for a week, compressed and depressed. The thing is that this was a ticking time bomb and would have eventually happened regardless of a fast ten miles. Running involves injury, the trick is handling recovery. And this is the most important part of the journey away from the comfort zone, when something goes wrong knowing when and how to find your way back to it without losing your spirit in the process.

I'd better start walking.

## Monday 22nd February 2016

I am shit at gyms.

One of the issues I have with injury is that much as I'd happily sit on my arse eating Frazzles and pawing SunPat straight from the jar into my trap I have developed runner's guilt. I daresay my catholic upbringing had already conditioned me to feeling bad about pretty much everything I've done since 1983 so it shouldn't really surprise me that I now feel a creeping sense of shame when I don't run.

As with most things running related it's basically irrational and inexplicable, there is no good reason why I should feel bad about resting, taking a break and recovering...but I do. In all other aspects of our lives Marc is supportive, caring, loving and generally wonderful but in this one aspect alone he is a complete and utter twat. When I'm on my third Reese's Peanut Butter Cup he will give me exaggerated looks of disgust, if I cry off a run for any reason other than a severed limb he will say something like 'it's OK, I'm sure no one will judge you' or something equally knobby which means I have to drag my sloth like arse through the door.

To be fair to him it's this no nonsense attitude towards my apathetic moods that helped me through some of my most gruelling treatments. Where other people would readily accept my bullshit excuses for not getting out of bed he would push me on. That's not to say he is harsh or unsympathetic, he's held my hand and stroked my head through days I didn't think I'd see the close of but he also knew when I was using cancer as an inadequate reason for not actively continuing to live. He simply refused to allow me to stop being alive. Sadly he applies the same ass kicking attitude to gym days and it makes me want to kill the little shit sometimes.

It's not as if we don't have fun at the gym, we do, but that in itself is a problem because it raises a very important question. Why are people in gyms so fucking serious? Most runners I know are pretty dedicated to the cause, they train long and hard through all weathers and struggle through injury and fatigue to improve and succeed. But they usually know how to have a good time too and certainly at races and meetings they are on the whole a friendly, fun loving bunch. Whilst very committed to their sport even the most serious runners I know also know how to party and even at high level events have got time for shits and giggles.

In the gym though it's a different matter altogether, all I see are stern faces often contorted in pain accompanied with grunts and in some cases pissy tantrums with the equipment. Maybe because gym work is such an introspective activity it can stop people being aware of those around them but in our gym people rarely smile or make eye contact. And I suppose that really works for a lot of people, in our busy lives we can become flooded with company as in today's customer oriented environment many of our jobs involve more and more contact with the public.

The attraction of shutting off from the chaotic world and plugging into your own thoughts and movement is often what draws people to exercise and certainly as a runner it's one of the things I enjoy most. Working with kids is a great honour and I mean that sincerely, kids are rarely complicated or bitter and they take you as you are with an implicit trust that you're going to help them navigate through the unpredictable ocean that is life. But they're noisy little beggars and teaching a subject that has to be constantly spoken makes for a cracking headache at the end of a long day. Sometimes a long, silent run on the beach can do more for me than three glasses of Grigio and a chick flick ever could to de stress.

I totally get how people would go to the gym after a long day at work to zone out and work up a sweat, what I don't get is the intense seriousness of it all. Our gym is a lovely gym, it's terrifyingly expensive and much like childbirth in that I blocked out the pain of joining so instantly I have never revisited my bank statement to see what my monthly fee actually is (just to clarify I have actually tended to my child in a moderately more responsible manner than to my bank balance). I suspect if I were to find out it would be very difficult to justify so I prefer to live in poverty stricken denial.

# Recovery Run
## Nicky Lopez

On the subject of denial we also joined Cleo to the gym at the same time, In my head I had visions of weekend family exercise sessions followed by skinny lattes in the cafe (I don't even drink milk) and matching active wear (now that shit we've got down to a turn). Our weekend reality is bollock o' clock ice skating shovelling down bacon and egg butties followed by traipsing around town whispering 'for fuck's sake' every time I see a price tag. We also hot foot it to Newcastle and binge eat fish and chips (Harbour View Seaton Sluice-best chippy in the known universe) and breakfast on hot macaroons (Tynemouth Market-to die for) with a half marathon thrown into either for a good measure. Cleo has little interest in the gym save for the possibility of even more clothing to own.

But nonetheless it is a great gym, one of those airy, open plan type setups with family areas, women's only gym, (don't men like to exercise with their own gender group too?) studios and a mega swimming pool equipped with a huge bubble contraption area. I genuinely would spend more time there if it wasn't for the fact that
a) I'd always rather be running and
b) I can't gym.

I was on the Stair Master torture machine last week busy watching my heart rate increase to dangerous levels trying to detach my toe from the step before I got horrifically mowed down or sucked under whilst rapidly and painfully giving up the will to live. Directly across from me in the opposite studio was a spin class, it was one of the most exhausting and terrifying experiences I have ever witnessed and that was just watching it. The participants in this cycling class from hell seemed to be high on some sort of illicit and incredibly potent amphetamine, or maybe I was, either way the pedals on the stationary bikes were turning 8 times faster than their traditional, freewheeling counterparts and what's more they were maintaining this phenomenal speedy cycling seemingly without pause or variation.

As the bloke at the front with the headset shouted at the manic pedallers the music thumped. At one point they all stood up from their seats, still cycling like the clappers, while gobby headset bloke insulted them a bit more and then had another drink and a stroll. As my tethered foot became dangerously chewed up in the Stair Master so my fascination with the screaming session of torture in the facing studio grew. Every now and again the admittedly packed class would alight from their steeds and perform a series of burpees, squats and on the spot sprints while gobshite in a muscle vest snarled in their faces then disappeared out of sight, presumably to eat a pie or a baby or something.

The thing is that the people in the class looked absolutely traumatised, they spilled out half an hour later in a state of shock clutching various limbs like they'd been involved in a car accident. Now I know some people, loads of people, adore spin class and I can absolutely understand how highly charged, intense exercise can be massively thrilling but these guys just looked distraught, like something bad had just happened to them and it's that I don't get.

Let's be honest, I'd be a hypocrite to evangelise about something as basically bonkers as running and then disrespect another person's choice of exercise, as far as I'm concerned if you're out there moving you're doing something awesome. I'm just putting it out there that a lot of people in gyms look in pain, stress and a bit grumpy. And what the fuck is with throwing the weights down on the floor and shouting at them after you've lifted them?

I think much of the problem is me though, I have a natural propensity for messing around a bit. Just to clarify I'm not a twat, I don't describe myself as 'zany' or 'wacky' and I don't go in for disrupting or disturbing people trying to go about their business without bother or hindrance. I do like a chat though, a smile and the occasional lark and in our gym that's banned. I discovered this on my first day there when whilst waiting for Marc to finish his abs set I busted a reasonably flamboyant move to a song that was playing. Tumbleweed...

Marc stared at me in horror as if I'd just smeared poo across my face and started yodelling. I swear to God the entire floor of the gym stopped dead, I believe the motorway traffic outside ground to a halt and someone, somewhere arranged to have me sectioned. Marc whispered quietly but firmly 'please stop' with a look in his eyes that was so full of torturous pleading I desisted immediately. Apparently you're not allowed to dance in a gym unless you're specifically instructed to do so. The same thing applies to singing, chatting, smiling at strangers or commenting on their active wear and this is all totally alien to me.

As a runner I've always hugely enjoyed the social aspect as much as I've valued the solitude so I'm completely at odds with the notion of entering a total me shaped bubble for my time there. At first I shamefully thought it might be a guy thing but I tried a little chattery in the ladies gym and found the same there, no one was rude they were just so highly focused on what they were doing that they couldn't actually see me, dispelling the inordinately vain notion I had that everyone in the gym would stare at me. The truth is no one intentionally stares at anyone as they're all so concentrated on what they're doing, if they do look it's on a completely subconscious level and you can bet that rather than judging your form they're actually thinking about cake.

In fact interaction in general is a rare thing in our gym, either that or I have disgraceful body odour, it's totally possible. But despite not being able to gym properly I do sort of enjoy it and it's definitely a saviour when you're injured. When I first heard about cross training I dismissed it as something only proper runners do as well as fartleks and cross country (although to be honest that shit still baffles me) but in tiny increments I have opened my eyes to the possibility of doing complementary exercise. And it's definitely highlighted some growth areas; I have the weakest arms imaginable, they're like threads of cotton with the tensile strength of candy floss. I also lack core strength and this often came up on long, marathon training runs where my midriff had ached like a bitch the day after.

In truth I don't get there often, time is a luxury item in my life and it's in constant short supply, if I do have time for anything solely for me then it's running, any other space occupies a very narrow margin indeed. But every week or two when my shit looks like it may possibly be somewhere approaching together then I hitch a ride with the mister and make it to the gym. And what's the first thing I do when I get there? I hit the treadmill, the fast moving instrument of certain death from either catastrophic fall injuries, drowning in sweat or just consumptive boredom. I bloody hate the treadmill, I wobble, stumble, can't look up and feel like I'm running seven times faster than on a road. But as soon as I enter the gym and I get that noob panic I retreat to where I feel safe, to what I know I can do, and I run.

It's a primal thing I guess, revert to what you know best but after around a minute and a half of semi controlled falling at speed I get cheesed off because ultimately treadmills are shit. The thing is, as an action in isolation running is a boring ass activity, despite my poetic ravings on the subject if you put me on a treadmill in a silent room these days, blindfolded me and didn't turn the air-con on I suspect I'd last less than a mile because the actual motion of running is repetitive, limited and pretty tiring.

What makes running such a joy to me is a complicated thing but I'm pretty certain it has far less to do with the physical motion and far more to do with the environmental and emotional aspects. I'm lucky in that I live in a place where I can access safe, attractive running routes with relative ease but I've discovered even the most seemingly dull surroundings look entirely different when you throw a bit of fresh air and pace into them. Yes the action of running offers a rhythmic kind of therapy but I think this is improved dramatically with changing scenery and a connection to the natural world regardless of how rural or industrial your route is.

Of course there is the whole aspect of challenging yourself but if that's what you're into I'm telling you now there are a cornucopia of ways of achieving that a billion times more fun than dying of boredom in a pool of your own sweat on a treadmill.

There are however exceptions where the treadmill is a beacon of light, a lifesaver and your greatest friend. I have a number of running pals who live in rural areas that whilst breathtakingly beautiful in the sunlit days of summer become harshly inaccessible, pitch black and therefore downright dangerous in winter months. And sure, winter can be another great reason to hit the tready, whilst some runners love nothing more than freezing their split shorted asses off in hammering rain and thick blizzards, icy roads and dangerous gales can make the treadmill the safest option.

And most importantly I know many runners, particularly those just starting out, who lack confidence on the streets for fear of judgement or worse. It's defeatingly sad that people who are bravely trying to improve their fitness and health could face the possibility of being publicly jeered or mocked but some people poke fun at what they don't understand. And some people are just wankers. For people who either fear or who have experienced this kind of shit (which is thankfully becoming less common as far as I can tell) the treadmill is the perfect way not only to run uninhibited and unhindered by knobheads but also to build a decent level of running fitness and confidence to get out there on the open roads. And this ties back into the whole reason I jump on them first at the gym, it lifts my confidence and makes me feel less of a noob.

And there are parts of going to the gym I do like, in fact pretty much all of the exercise we do there is enjoyable in a gruesomely painful way. It's a totally different physical experience from running and I enjoy the variety. I like to do 10 minutes each on the cardio stuff like the rowing fish game, Satan's staircase and the upright non twirly wheel bike (apologies if my language is overly technical, as you can see I'm a pro) but I do not use the cross trainer.

The reason I do not use the cross trainer is that it openly exposes the fact that I have no co-ordination whatsoever. One of the reasons I have never learnt to drive is my inability to synchronise arm and leg movements simultaneously without accident or injury and the cross trainer relies heavily upon this seemingly elementary skill. The first time I tried a cross trainer was in my friend's house several years ago and I was actually rather good at it, I quickly developed a smooth, fluid style and found it enjoyably challenging. This positive experience must have stayed, deep rooted in my psyche as when I joined the gym I was itching to hop onto it and show off my natural prowess.

At first things seemed alright, it was slightly less co-ordinated in style but I assumed that it was down to a difference between models of machine and I would adjust momentarily. As my speed increased things started to deteriorate rapidly, my feet kept sliding on the insanely long foot beds (whose foot is actually that big for Christ's sake?) and so I started doing bizarre little jumps to get back into the right position, the problem with that was in order to jump I needed a bit of leverage so I was pulling on both handlebars at the same time to raise myself up. This caused both of my legs to randomly shoot in front of me at the same time as if I was on some sort of swing. I started to panics so I tried to get some rhythm back by moving my feet faster but I had forgotten that the pedals and handlebars were connected and as I pushed on one the other would react with opposite force. This sent my confused body into a mad frenzy giving me the appearance of a cartoon character that had slipped on ice.

I maintained this ridiculous motion for another minute or two before my foot slipped completely and I went crashing off the whole machine sideways and landing heavily on my arse. I was baffled as to why I had fallen so dramatically from my initial cross training throne but then I recalled that my maiden outing had involved several bottles of wine and a couple of shots. Perhaps that's where I had gone wrong. Either way, I think the streets are a safer option.

# 15
# Adapt and Survive

**Thursday 25th February 2016**

It's a week since the back of my leg exploded because Marc tried to break the land speed record along the Bootle stretch of the Leeds Liverpool Canal. It's been a bloody tough week in countless ways including two separate car recoveries (one involving an inexplicable diversion to Gretna Green) and my dad temporarily being a missing person. Cleo came home from America exhausted and sick and I've had a letter for an operation I don't want to have. Oh and my eyelashes have fallen out again which is pissing me off no end as I have about three spiky hairs left on each. Quite why I keep putting mascara on them I have no idea but it's making me look a little bit mad.

Added to this the Brits were on last night and Coldplay won best group which just about finished me off (Chris Martin, in the unlikely event you ever read this please know I'm sure you're a lovely person, it's not you, it's me). So the best cure would have been to run only I couldn't because I have an injury. To be honest when we were in Newcastle at the weekend we were glad we couldn't, the weather was pretty horrid with a strong, cold wind that would have made it perfectly horrible. We also ate to the point of embarrassment which would have rendered us incapable of walking let alone running.

But since we've been home I've been itching to get out, especially seeing as the weather has taken a slight turn for the better (by which I mean as far as I know there isn't a severe weather warning in place) but for once in my life I've practised a little good sense and given myself a week of rest. I've done some walking which I always enjoy, I'm lucky enough to work pretty much right on the beach so my lunchtimes are spent in happy solitude save some seagulls and the occasional dog walker, breathing in the ocean air and letting it refresh my mind.

Marc and I have been walking in the evenings too (he's taken a brief and uncharacteristic break from running and the gym while he devotes his evenings to study for his skills tests) and it's been a relief to at least be moving. One night we ended up in the local park playing on the outdoor gym. I love the whole notion of outdoor gyms and I applaud whomever pioneered the initiative, they give people experience of and access to basic gym equipment which is both useful and awesome fun. My heart sings when I see people using them from kids to the elderly.

After a brief but hilarious workout in the dark we moved onto the main park and played around like toddlers on the slide, see-saw and swings. I'd forgotten how much fun the park is, how great it is to run and jump and skip and sing for no other reason than the enjoyment of it. Something mysterious happens to you as an adult, fun turns into exercise and exercise turns into work. It's like we can no longer do things unless they have a definite purpose, a fixed outcome and at the same time as this happens in our minds our bodies change too, jumping off stuff becomes dangerous, skipping becomes stupid and swings start to make us queasy. It was a wakeup call to my soul to stop with the glorification of busy and start doing stuff just for the hell of it.
So today I ran.

I was hoping that after a week of rest I would feel massively refreshed and with boundless energy and for the first mile it definitely felt that way. I'd put on my sure fire, no nonsense running shoes and headed for the beach, there would be no pissing about with boggy tow-paths today. I was so glad to be running again, I felt a sense of relief and release as my legs moved steadily, smoothly and without pain but as I hit the two mile point I had to admit to myself I felt a little tired

I'd overlooked the fact that taking a week off running isn't the same as taking a week off from life. For once in my annoyingly rigidly ordered psyche I hadn't set a distance, I would see how it felt as I went along adjusting my effort and pace where needed. Marc has taught me a whole lot about running according to effort and it's one of the most useful things I've learnt. The idea is that you run according to how it feels, how much effort you're putting in and maintaining a steady rate of effort despite the terrain (this is a simplistic way of explaining it but hey, I'm a simpleton.) For example slowing down when you tackle a hill so that your rate of effort stays the same as when you were on the flat.

It's this kind of technique that's really improved my running as instead of setting pace for myself (which I tend to obsess about) I set myself a level of effort. It's valuable because your perception of effort can change drastically from run to run and this can be demotivating if you only rely on pace, sometimes an 8.30 mile is a breeze, other times it's an agony. It's a chance to cover up the Garmin and use it only as a distance marker, feeling the reassuring buzz on my wrist as each mile passes (a bizarre comfort as I pretty much know how far I've ran at any point on my route through over familiarity!)

Generally I try to run at moderate effort which I translate as steady but slightly challenging, other times (although not often I admit) I opt to run at a hard effort level meaning that my run is around the top of my tolerance range. Today's run was to be easy, very comfortable and with minimum effort. As I felt myself speeding up I would deliberately slow down to keep it as relaxed as possible and for the large part I managed that. There were some other difficulties though...

As it felt rather chilly I had 'double buffed' for the occasion, one on my head and one on my neck. I say Buff but one of them was not an official product rather a replica produced by a low cost high street retailer and called, somewhat disturbingly, a 'boy's chute'.

By mile 3 I was pouring with sweat and considering stripping down on the coastal path in fact the only thing that stopped me was the insane number of thumb loops that were tethering me. I couldn't wait to reach the half way point. The only problem was that the halfway point is a military firing range, one that today sounded particularly active so perhaps not the most appropriate place to strip down to my arsehole.

But something had to give and so the boy's chute became the sacrificial lamb of the run. I tore it from my neck and stuffed it into a bush with some insane notion that I would return to reclaim it on another run (I won't because I will never be arsed to). After a brief and ludicrous conversation with Cleo about sausages and sanitary towels I made for home. Within ten seconds I'd stopped again, the chute disposal had obviously effected a catastrophic imbalance in the earphone wire equilibrium which was now whacking me rhythmically in the face. I shoved it up my other Buff and carried on.

Approximately three seconds later the new phone armband I'd been testing started slipping down to my elbow, curse my skinny arms, this is God's way of punishing me for not spending enough time in the gym (he totally cares about shit like that, he's a crossfit fanboy). I carried on with the most effeminate running gait imaginable for another mile clutching the strap at my elbow and holding my hand out in a teapot pose swearing repeatedly until I reached the Plinth of Awesome. I dragged the armband from my arm pulling the earphones from my head. My language was hideous, I strapped it as tightly as I could and angrily marched on my way. About five minutes later it felt like a tourniquet or like that puffy sleeve that goes on your arm when you're getting your blood pressure done and the doctor starts pumping it and you're thinking that it's going to actually burst your veins. I de-strapped and readjusted but by that point my key and a twenty pound note were making their way off the edge of the path towards a ten foot drop to the beach. I rugby tackled them both and stuffed them along with my earphones into my head Buff using the type of profanity I reserve only for cyclists and Coldplay (sorry Chris).

Finally I discovered some modicum of comfort and struck out for the last couple of miles, my spirits settled and I found my stride. As I ran along the prom the resting seagulls took flight and soared alongside me making me laugh out loud. The air was bitingly cold now and the right side of my face was frozen solid into a bizarre snarl making me look like a spandex clad Billy Idol to the bemused ramblers out for their afternoon gathering. I tried desperately to smile but the non-frozen side of my mouth just hung open in contrast to the contorted right side and was drooling heavily giving me the expression of a slobbery chopped boxer dog.

In the end I held my arm to my mouth to disguise my terrifying deformity and stem the flood of gob that was streaming behind me. Turning towards home for the final mile I started to feel triumphantly tired with a mild but manageable ache in the right calf.

It was a test drive, a stretch of the legs and I was relieved to feel nothing like the pain I had encountered last week.

It's still there though, tweaking at my leg to alert me to its existence, it won't be ignored this time. A good run though in a surprisingly fast time despite the whole effort versus pace quandary. And amidst all the lunacy I had a new and joyfully novel experience, the feeling of wet hair at the nape of my neck.

**Saturday 27th February 2016**

So I quit my job.

After 11 years in the same, small school with people who have stopped feeling like colleagues and become more like family, with children I adore and walls that have felt like home for so long. Why?

Because sometimes families don't work, they fall apart and they can't be put back together and happy homes become broken ones and when that happens sometimes a person has to leave the children they love in the hands of someone else. Sometimes the only thing a person can do to save themselves is to run.

This morning we woke to blazing sunshine as if God had woken up and smiled right at us, the light spilled in through the curtained window calling us to come outside. But I didn't really want to go, yesterday was a tough and traumatic day by even my standards and I felt nothing short of bereft, the last thing I wanted to do was go outside. Over the past few years life has been so unsettlingly chaotic that I've clung onto what little stability remained with clawing fingernails; letting go of a cornerstone of security has left me feeling exposed, unnerved and afraid.

But as I've also learnt life is a series of kaleidoscopic changes and with each turn there are equal portions of beauty and chaos, the only thing a person can do is to appreciate the loveliness and trust the disorder will settle into something wonderful. Stepping outside today would involve the risk of bumping into people I hoped to avoid for maybe the next twenty years or so, it would also might mean being near school which could stir up all sorts of emotions.

Running was not high on my agenda today, hiding was top of my to do list and I had planned a full weekend of it but the sunlight and promise of crisp, cool air pulled at my sleeve and tempted me outside into the scary, uncomfortable world. Marc had already made the decision before I crawled from under the duvet, it seemed futile to protest and besides I was too exhausted to put up a fight. I ate my favourite breakfast amidst deep sighs of resignation, I had no desire to put makeup on but I found myself on autopilot circling my red, lashless eyes and pinking my cheeks. I stared at my lined, weary face in the mirror and my steel grey hair with the startling white flash above my right temple. When had I become so very old? I gazed at myself for a while and as I did I felt a slight shift in mood, I can't explain why as it was so subtle but I looked deeper into my eyes and I softened a little towards myself.

As I stared I wondered if we really do look that different with make-up on or if we just become more accustomed and less critical of our faces over the time it takes to apply. Yes I look much older but I'd been through a long war that was still forcing me into battles despite what I'd thought was a resounding victory.

As I got dressed I began to feel like I was putting on armour, I looked at myself in my black compression gear and my figure was lithe, athletic and toned. If nothing else I had the appearance of a fighter. With that in mind I tore a t shirt from an envelope I had intended to return and pulled it over my head, dressed unusually for me all in black I looked tougher, somehow more resilient.

We ran our own familiar route towards the beach, Marc hadn't run for ten days because of work commitments so he was moving with speed and enthusiasm. For my part I was neither here nor there, the legs were moving, the lungs were filling and I felt no discomfort; for today that was enough. At the point on the road where we traditionally separate, Marc stayed by my side, symbolically supporting me and I breathed a quiet thank you.

Heading onto the coastal path we checked our pace and at 8.15 we slowed it a little knowing how tired we both were after yesterday's upheaval, it was a gloriously bright morning with a steady yet icy breeze which I was glad of. As we approached the four mile point my legs were looser but I was feeling fatigued, I stared at the bracelets on my wrists I had worn to motivate myself and tried to commit their words into my stormy heart.

We didn't say much but I could hear Marc's steady breathing at my side and it comforted me, I began to feel brighter as if the sun had found its way in through some small gap in my locked up spirit. As we reached the halfway point we stopped momentarily and laughed as we saw the 'boy's chute' I had stowed in a bush on Thursday, I vowed next time if it was still there I would collect it.

Before turning for home I glimpsed again at the words on my bracelets, 'life is too short to wait' and 'the best is yet to come', I had to believe that they were both true. I looked at Marc and remembered that so much of the goodness in my life had been the result of great change. At the Plinth of Awesome, Marc's phone rang and he stopped to take a call about a car we had looked at following our current car's demise last week, as he talked I sat a moment and stared at the sun pouring a glittery trail along the swelling water and I felt a little joy creeping in.

We took some photos and goofed about, it's a relatively deserted spot so we can usually behave like idiots to our hearts content but today it felt like we had gate crashed some sort of bizarre get together. Firstly as we were taking a selfie with the sheer, craggy drop behind us a woman appeared out of nowhere and photobombed us. I would swear to God she had scrambled up the rocks behind but she was dressed in completely inappropriate clothing.

Following this another two people on bicycles appeared and stood insanely close to us despite there being vast expanses of unoccupied land around us. The gentleman offered to take a photo for us and we reluctantly agreed. I say reluctantly as both being enthusiasts, Marc and I are notoriously anal when it comes to photography, we trust no one but ourselves to take pictures of us. This selfie hostility doesn't just extend to strangers, close friends and family but also to each other, I trust him to take a decent picture of me no more than he would trust me to take one of him. The result is that we basically set our own shots up and grudgingly ask the other to press the shutter.

So when this kind sir offered his services we were less than excited, what didn't help was that this bloke was tall and I don't mean lofty I mean inordinately, uncommonly, freakishly tall; he was some sort of medical phenomenon. As he soared over us we smiled graciously like two Oompa Loompas, I have never felt so minuscule and at five foot eight I'm hardly a shortarse. We cheerfully accepted the phone back and oohed appropriately about how excellent the photo was. As they rode off into the distance we were creased with laughter as we viewed the snap of a wide sea vista with two little heads popping up at the bottom of the frame, so gargantuan was he that he had missed our bodies completely.

As Marc set the camera to take a shot two springer spaniels appeared from nowhere and jumped all over him, I do believe the words 'fuck this shit' were uttered as he stuffed his phone away and then shouted his customary 'HOWAY!' to mark our final stretch.

# Recovery Run
## Nicky Lopez

Running onto the prom towards home we crossed the pathway I walk every working lunchtime to reach the beach, I had expected to feel a flood of emotion but instead I felt a surge of relief and a tingle of excitement about what the future held for us.

The prom was busy with walkers and cyclists all profiting from the brisk, golden morning and we weaved purposefully but politely between them dropping to single file to allow plenty of room for our fellow pedestrians. At the final turn of the prom we saw two younger runners, a couple, ahead of us.

It's always a bit awkward to overtake but judging their pace we knew it had to be done. As we approached them they started to speed up and the bloke began taking running jumps up and down the prom wall like...well like a complete twat. The mature way to deal with knobs like this is to let them showboat, allow them to be tossers and ignore them. As we're utter children we decided to overtake them. By the sound of the grunts behind us they were not happy, the thing is though that based on their clothing and appearance they a) were twenty years younger than us and b) hadn't already run 8 miles. They were not going to make it easy for us.

We held them off valiantly until around five metres from our final turn off the beach, a moment I will always regret and Marc may never forgive me for. I was just too tired today and I was so bored of knobbery. Besides, they clearly were inexperienced as they carried onto the path that turns into the dunes of hell, the swathing drifts of soft sand that would consume their legs, dash their faces and blind their eyes on this blowy day. Good luck to the little fuckers.

Into the final mile my legs began to ache and I turned my mind to just keeping on going, I told myself that I was strong and that I had this. I repeated the words that were on my t shirt over and over in my mind and I believed them, yes it hurt but I am strong enough to deal with hurt. I was right this morning, I'm not the girl I used to be. That girl would have stopped, taken the easy route and given in.

The woman I am now with her wrinkles and silver hair endures and conquers, she has become a warrior and a badass one at that. Above all though I reminded myself that no matter how hard things get I no longer do them alone, at my shoulder is a man who doesn't just pull me along precarious paths and push me up the steepest of hills he also guides me onto kinder roads and smoother surfaces. He knows that while he can't always do the tough stuff for me he will always do it with me, at my side breathing strong and steady and when I stumble he's swift to catch me and carry me home.

Runs that I think are insignificant often surprise me on reflection as they're frequently the ones I learn the most from. Today was no exception in that I remembered how important it is to mile by mile reassess how you're feeling and adjust accordingly; over ten miles a lot can change and accepting that is as important as reacting to it. Change is difficult for me at times but running has taught me to adapt and survive and it's a skill I must now apply to my life. Much like running, life is a constant pursuit of whatever horizons I choose to run towards, all of it at my own pace and in my own way with the greatest of travelling companions.

And when the road gets bumpy or the hills high I need to recite the words on my t shirt and believe in them like I did today, like I have done for 6 years.

'Don't Stop, Don't Yield'.

# 16
# Missing In Action

**Friday 11th March 2016**

When you love running, when you've really fallen in love with the dull ache in your legs and the feeling of a lungful of deep, cool air it's hard to imagine ever not wanting to run. But in the same way that your love didn't make an announcement of its presence it doesn't always fanfare its departure either. For the past week or so I have lost the will to run, I have dreaded it, avoided it, made excuses and given myself reasons not to go. With each bedtime I have vowed to take advantage of the cool, spring sunshine the following morning yet as the day breaks I have found myself so desperately unwilling to lace up.

And the worst thing is that there's no apparent reason; physically I feel OK, a bit tired but in truth I've been a bit tired pretty much every day since I was twelve. I can't blame the weather which is my trusty usual suspect when I'm run dodging and in terms of time I suddenly find myself with a lot more of it on my hands. In saying all this I can counter every point I've just made with a 'however'.

Physically I'm not on great form, without anything specific I just feel off. The weather has picked up, it's no longer monsoon season in Liverpool but nonetheless it remains bap shudderingly chilly and I groan at the prospect of feeling shivery and uncomfortable. And as for my new found employment freedom I have put a possibly undue amount of pressure on myself to work even harder with my business. I guess it's the old Catholic guilt thing again (funny it never bothers me when I don't go to church or binge eat during Lent) and I feel the need to overcompensate by working three times as hard. Whatever it is or it isn't my head tells me to run but my heart has absconded.

My doctor says I am stressed and I wonder what came first, the lack of desire to run followed by a feeling of stress of is being stressed out making me not want to run. Yesterday in hospital I popped my head into the Macmillan advisor, she's a lovely lady who I often chat to and I really was just intending to say hi. What I ended up doing was standing there blurting out things I didn't know I even felt. While I was

172

meaning to briefly pass the time of day I could suddenly hear myself saying how I was struggling to adjust to life after cancer and finding life in general somewhat difficult.

It's a very tough thing to explain as I'm in danger of sounding ungrateful for the gift of my own life and believe me, I'm poignantly aware of how precious and fragile a gift it is. Today Dawn, an old school friend and sister of our dear pal Tony is back in chemo with secondary breast cancer. It's hard not to get the feeling that it's everywhere. The thing is that if you've had cancer you tend to come into contact with lots of people who have too and collectively we have a shocking mortality rate.

I've always been reasonably philosophical about cancer; it's an illness, a mutation, natural selection if you like and I didn't take it personally. Even when it seemed unshakable from my bones I didn't give it a personality in the way some people like to as I didn't feel that connected to it. I was sick, the same way loads of people get sick, I wasn't being picked on or singled out and I don't remember thinking why me, it was more a case of why not me? I think (and I'm aware I'm veering off point here but stick with me, I'll get back eventually) one of the most pivotal moments in my illness was in the first half hour after the Great North Run.

I sparked up a fag almost instantly after finishing, I still somewhat insanely hadn't considered quitting at that point and I wandered across Gypsies Green, a vast field exposed to the North Sea coast which serves as the finishing area of the race in South Shields. It's notable to most runners as the place where a phone signal on any network does not exist and also home to the infamous beer tent, it's also where the charity village resides. As I looked down on the hundred or so tents, each dedicated to a different condition or illness a terrible thought crept in - you can't cure them all. Looking at myself against the thousands of people who all had their own journeys with disease and mortality I began to feel pretty insignificant. It also struck me that if we did find cures for all of these conditions we'd have one hell of a population problem.

I guess it was at that point I developed a more pragmatic, less personal attitude to cancer and it stuck with me. It was also shortly after that I began to run for Macmillan. Now I must say I totally back anyone who supports research and cure hunting, absolutely I do but I'm also aware that we all have to go of something, sometime and in the meantime I wanted to do something practical to help people to cope with living with cancer.

Macmillan were all about that. Finding ways to help people with the day to day issues that arise when you have a serious illness is a passion of mine and I have dedicated my running to further that cause. Like I say, I'm also a great supporter of research particularly given the benefit I've had from it over the last six years but my heart lies in trying to ease the burden of cancer in practical ways such as financial and emotional support, therapeutic care along with advice and the general feeling that you're not drifting out to a stormy sea untethered and alone because that's often how it feels. I keep dodging the topic though, the nagging voice in my head that keeps telling me that I don't really want to run and it's scaring me if I'm honest.

Today I pushed myself out again, this time alone. The morning was too beautiful to ignore and if ever I was to fall in love again then today was the day to do it. I've been reading a lot about finding a new normal and one of the strategies is disassociating with things from the past for example perfume, music etc. With that in mind I used different deodorant, made a new playlist and wore my new ultra-boosts, anything to shake the feeling of apathetic gloom. The first two miles my legs felt tired and sluggish but there was no way of stopping the kaleidoscopically beautiful morning from creeping into my heart and waking it up a little.

In slow but glorious stages I began to find my feet and with it my joy. At the 5 mile turning point I was blisteringly hot and heavy with sweat but glowing and smiling, as I turned into the cool headwind it felt like grace seeping all over me and I felt tears gather in the corners of my eyes. Running along the beach I genuinely felt connected to God, the universe, whatever name you care to call it and I gave thanks. The sunlight on the sea was incandescent and the air was cold and smooth. In the last mile as my legs ached I pushed harder and as my watched buzzed at ten miles I had done enough. I felt like I had come home emotionally as well as physically.

When you exercise, your muscles suffer thousands of microscopic tears that given rest and recovery go on to rebuild stronger and more flexible than they were before. I think life is much the same, as we go through hardship we tear apart only to repair with more strength, more resilience. What didn't kill me will surely make me stronger.

Speaking of honesty I've got to tell you that it's now 22nd March, Cleo's 15th birthday has come and gone along with the accompanying pizza/Nandos fests and a trip to Newcastle. The truth is that I was afraid to write because I was afraid of what I was going to find myself saying. In the same way that I stood in Sharon's office that day unwittingly blurting out how I felt about recovery I was terrified of what would spew onto the page if I resumed writing. I think my biggest fear was that following the statement that I didn't really want to run would come the life altering, mind blowing word 'anymore'. The finality of that small word with its immense implications was more than my fragile mind could handle.

So I stopped typing, stopped thinking and tried my hand at surviving. What I didn't stop doing though was running. Before that run I had already done several others, I just didn't know what to say about them as I no longer knew how to express how I was feeling.

Having a little time out has given me space to think about what I learnt, if anything, from those few runs and as usual it's been so much more than I realised at the time. So here for your reading pleasure (and just to confuse you a little!) is what I shall henceforth refer to as 'funk week'. Not because of the amazing dance shapes I cut over those seven days (although I fancy there were many) but because of the overwhelming sense of slump I felt during that period which is still faintly echoing through my legs and heart even now.

## Saturday 5th March, Sefton Park, Liverpool

For so long now I've wanted to run through Sefton Park, it's one of my favourite places in the world. North Liverpool where we live has many great attractions, it's close to the countryside and of course it has an incredible, sweeping coastline with the most unbelievable of sunsets.

What it doesn't have though are the vast, open parks that the south of Liverpool boasts and Sefton Park is the most famous of all. Hugging the outskirts of the city centre on the edge of infamous Toxteth (which in many parts is rather more attractive than the derelict ghettos of yesteryear) it is a grand and imposing piece of land flanked with opulent gates and tree lined avenues. The park sprawls into the more wellheeled area of Mossley Hill and on towards Aigburth. As well as a variety of unusual statues and a distinctive and rather beautiful glass palm house, one of the most appealing features of the park is the lakes and streams that wind through it. Cleo was spending the day in the city centre with friends and we were struggling to find a space to fit a run in as it was a gorgeous, sunny day.

In all honesty I was neither here nor there about running but I found myself suggesting we throw our kit on and go for a run while we were out. I figured if I had to run I may as well make it worthwhile and besides, it would probably be quite a short one. Marc concurred and so we bundled Cleo into the car after she had undergone several thousand changes of clothes, makeup and hairstyle and headed off for town.

As we approached the city I realised I had already made a fashion boob, as Cleo was meeting her friends at Central Station which was essentially inaccessible to parking I would have to walk with her across town. She looked at me in horror as she took in the neon orange and bright purple ensemble I had so carefully put together. My t shirt rather wittily read 'You might want to take notes', what it should have said was 'I have forgotten how to dress like a normal person'. With a pained expression on her face we raced across the streets faster than I have ever seen her move before although to be fair she never once mentioned the outfit or hinted at any embarrassment, I was just Mum and this is what Mum looks like. Mum is a clueless dick with no fashion sense.

Leaving her to have a thankfully fun day I made my way back to Marc in the car feeling hugely self-conscious and strangely exposed. It's funny how I had become so out of place in an environment I was once so completely at home in. Mental note: I need to buy some normal clothes that normal people wear for when I'm required to do normal person duties. The struggle is real.

After Marc had lost his way to our usual spot (4 years and he still can't navigate Sefton Park, it's like the Bermuda Triangle to him) we eventually parked up opposite a pretty hotel which stood on a long road bordering the large boating lake. I felt my usual pre run nervousness bubble in my stomach and rest in my windpipe. It had an air of race day about it, possibly due to the fact that most major Liverpool running races have a Sefton Park section as it's so close to the city.

We headed off past the obelisk and downwards into the expanse of green. The grass was littered with crocuses, their purple and white heads reaching upwards and their orange tongues drinking in the cold sunshine. It was Saturday afternoon and every pathway was populated with children on tricycles or scooters, bandaged in scarves and woolly hats with red cheeks and white breath. It was difficult not to feel happy, there seemed so much of it about. We kept the pace low and explored avenues and glens winding up and down.

We giggled as we clumsily slid across stepping stones and we stopped frequently, sometimes to watch a rainbow in the glistening spray of a fountain or marvel at a trio of wild parakeets noisily gossiping in the trees above us, sometimes it was just to breathe and be grateful. In between stops the miles slipped by and before long we were at 9 miles so we decided to make it 10.

The last mile weighed on our legs and we fell more silent than we had been but it was an appreciative quietness too, yes we were tired but it had been a holiday of a run, a happy break. No great change ever happens entirely overnight, it is these small steps that we take in the hope that collectively they will amount to a larger leap, we just have to keep the faith.

## Sunday 6th March 2016 Mother's Day

I don't usually run two days in a row, as of late my runs are longer so I try to leave a 24 recovery gap in between. That said I don't usually get woken with a delicious cooked breakfast barm from my favourite sandwich shop along with a bunch of sweet smelling flowers and a box of fudge-the Geordie did good.

As the three of us sprawled on the bed munching happily the sun streaked in through the curtains. Cleo looked as if she was ready to drop off again so it seemed a great opportunity to enjoy the morning. We headed off towards the beach but as we did we noticed a cold, strong headwind had picked up. It's not like us to be all spontaneous and flexible but we're also wimps so it seemed the most sensible option to turn and head for the shelter of the canal. As we passed our avenue again I noted that the full circle we had come was exactly a mile, I felt oddly satisfied at knowing this nugget of wisdom whilst simultaneously realising I had turned into a complete nerd.

When we reached the canal the sky had dulled a little and I was aware my spirits had too, it was phenomenally cold. I had worn a base layer with a t shirt over and whilst it looked pretty it was going to be woefully inadequate for the temperature. We picked up the pace a little to try to warm up but the pair of us were fatigued from the previous day and my legs flailed a little making my feet unsteady on the gravelly path.

It was good to be out though, we swapped leads at times but mostly ran together. I was aware that since losing his Mum, Marc finds Mother's Day understandably difficult and so a run would do us both good. Colin the Cormorant swooped by with his huge span of feathered power and we watched him soar into the distance before us. It was far from easy and at times the atmosphere was eerily solemn, our breathing was heavier than usual and the miles were not ticking along with their usual brevity.

There were moments of beauty as always, we passed families of ducks and geese, the mothers swimming proudly with their tiny fledglings in their own celebration of the day. As we passed Bootle Strand I realised we would need to adjust our usual turning point to allow for the extra mile we had already covered. Now as you're reading this I know you'll be thinking how easy that calculation is, they've run an extra mile so they need to knock off half a mile either way to accommodate it, simple huh?

Well not so much. It would seem that not only does running in the cold relieve me of the ability to speak like a sober person it also renders me utterly stupid. Honestly I've tested this theory out on a number of different people with exactly the same results, try to remember song lyrics, do simple maths problems or talk with any degree of articulacy after 5 miles of running in the cold and you're essentially screwed. I'm sure, in fact I know, that there is a simple biological reason why this happens but when it does it's the weirdest thing. It took us nearly half an hour of complicated equations along with numerous discussions and arguments to work out where we needed to turn. In saying that we had no problem remembering the

Yoda song we had been singing that morning which was now playing on loop in my head, intellect is a strangely selective thing.

Turning for home the cold hit us full on and for the first time in ages my arms actually stung with the icy air, it did serve to quicken us a little but by mile 7 I was really feeling it, we both were. Colin the Cormorant sailed by once again and in my weird little head it lifted me. I felt like he had been with us all the way, watching us from above and was now leading us home.

We pushed on and in the tough, final mile the sun cracked through the clouds and burst across the sky turning the fields golden. Ten hard miles but still they were done and we stumbled home with an aching sense of relief.

Later as we three sat together feasting on roast dinner and coffee and cheesecake I looked around and felt a sense of calm contentment. I looked at Cleo and remembered how grateful I am to be a Mother and I hope she sees me as one she can be proud of, not because of things I do but because of what I am. I find that often in life as in running the joy is not to be found in the grand gesture but in the small detail; a swooping bird, a sunny sky, a box of fudge, a slice of cake. It's these tiny moments that become the lasting memories and the big issues become less overwhelming, more insignificant.
Here's to the small stuff.

## Wednesday 9th March 2016

When Marc came home tonight and said he was going to run my spirits sank a little. Well actually they hit the floor. Whatever had gotten into me I just couldn't summon up any enthusiasm to run at all, in fact it was the last thing I wanted to do. What I really wanted to do was lie in bed and do nothing at all.

There is a bigger picture that I haven't really told you about too. Earlier this week I wasn't feeling great, I put it down to running a lot over the weekend but inside I knew that wasn't really the problem. What was the problem was my heart was beating unusually slowly and my doctor couldn't work out why. It's not a mega serious thing but I knew it would entail a change or tweak in medication and historically that usually leaves me feeling dank and lousy. I'd been to the hospital that morning and had a decent chat with my doctor, he'd said I was ok to run as long as I felt good and took reasonable precautions. I was kind of disappointed.

In my heart I'd hoped that he would say I couldn't run, that there was a reason why I felt so apathetic and unwilling to get out there and more than anything that there was something he could do to make it stop. But I've discovered over the years that things don't work like that, there are rarely definitive answers with sure fire remedies or instant cures. Instead there are educated guesses, generalised treatments and ongoing adjustments. My only course of action was to keep going because the notion of not running anymore seemed so wrong.

So I went with as much enthusiasm as I could find which was arguably negligible but still vaguely impressed with myself for my commitment to what was rapidly feeling like a lost cause.

The watery winter sun had melted to dark in the frankly ridiculous amount of time it took us to decide what to wear, I confess most of the dithering about with my outfit was based on what would match best. I've mentioned it before, when all other things are going to shit if I can pull out of the bag a well co-ordinated running outfit I really feel like I'm winning at life.

Our options for running in the dark are pretty limited when Marc isn't wearing the head torch and sometimes he really can't be arsed with the faff of it which I totally get. Our usual course of action is to head towards the beach and then do loops and circuits of the long roads that lead from it. I used to hate the idea of this kind of running, it seemed aimless and boring (I'm a sucker for a straight route) but I've learnt to love weaving through undiscovered avenues with grand houses and previously unnoticed parks.

Running like this has not only added a whole new scope for distance for me but also taught me so much more about the area I live in and given me a greater appreciation of it. If like me you're used to running a regular route then I strongly recommend mixing it up now and again by darting down a road you've never ran before or even just the opposite side of the road. I guarantee you'll start seeing the place you live in a whole new light and it's an awesome way to add a little extra onto your run without really feeling it. It's particularly awesome at Christmas when houses become ultra-twinkly and brilliantly distracting.

# Recovery Run
## Nicky Lopez

Leaving the house we realised how bloody cold it really was so bolted back inside for reinforcements in the way of gilets and hats, this involved my changing my tights for the fourth time that evening and I was even beginning to piss myself off by now. Back on the road again I was finding it tough going, the first mile had felt breakneck but when I glanced at my watch it was much closer to the slower end of my usual pace.

I found myself in slight struggle mode where I seem to be attacking the run instead of relaxing and enjoying it. As we turned onto the main road that leads to the beach I glanced upwards, the sky was the most brilliant, deep turquoise brushed here and there with a sweep of purple cloud and studded with the first stars of dusk. It was so vivid that I was compelled to keep looking skywards and I reminded myself that even in my most ambivalent moments this is why I run, this is why it's always worth it.

We ran down towards the beach but we knew with the rapidly darkening skies it would be impossible to take the coastal path as it has no lighting at all for a mile and a half and is the night time dwelling place of the lesser spotted no lighted cycling twat. We lingered for a moment staring out to the cobalt sea watching a liner glide past silently and then headed back up to the residential streets with their grand houses and high fences.

It was one of those runs where you just seem to plug away at it, our legs were tired and our breathing not comfortable enough to allow any coherent conversation. We communicated in sighs, points and the occasional grunt, each knowing that the other was too tired to respond in any other way.
Then Marc fell.

In my head it was in slow motion but the funny and rather shameful detail I recall most is that before helping him I stopped my Garmin. What is it with us that we have become so innately conditioned to technology that we respond to it as automatically and natural as breathing? I found it pretty unsettling that my foremost instinct was not to immediately stoop to the floor to check if my partner was harmed but to hit the button on my watch to preserve my pace. The only comfort I can glean from this shameful reaction is that I know that Marc would do exactly the same thing. He is as monstrously lacking in humanity as I appear to be. This somehow makes me feel better.

In all seriousness though it was a shocking thing to witness and my heart was thumping in my chest. Marc picked himself up and rubbed his hands together before checking himself over, he told me he had fallen the previous night too at exactly the same point in the run in exactly the same way. He was tired, not concentrating and literally forgot to pick his feet up high enough from the uneven pavement. I felt shaken, really upset, he was absolutely unhurt but it had touched a nerve with me as falling during a run is a huge fear of mine. The problem is that I've never actually done it so I feel a terrible sense of the inevitable, sooner or later it's going to happen. It's like Russian roulette only without the guns and in active wear.

The rest of the run was tough and in the final mile my legs hurt and my brain was screaming at me to stop. It hadn't been a bad run, it had just been a run.

One of the best things about reflecting on a run afterwards is that it gives you opportunity to think about what you can take from it. For me I had the azure sky and the relief that Marc had escaped unscathed, and I had put another run I didn't want to do away. I did not let the voice in my head talk me into submission.

And that for today is enough.

**Tuesday 15th March 2016**

Another solo ten miles today in an attempt to regain a little confidence. On the whole it was a pretty good run but holy mansacks the weather is difficult to judge at the moment. I went from practically licking the pavement in an attempt to stave off heat exhaustion to shivering my baps off in the cold wind. And with unpredictable weather comes the first world nightmare of choosing what to wear.

This has recently become compounded as nature has turned my usually silky smooth scalp into an Axminster carpet which has raised my temperature several degrees. Damn you wonder drugs and your life saving, hair growing properties.

I took the usual coastal path today to take advantage of a nice crosswind and I was surprised how tired my legs were at 3 miles. At first I considered stopping for a break (I have two words for people who think real runners don't stop mid run) but I was a bit pushed for time so took the pace down a little and decided to hold on until halfway. After a minor duel with a driver who was apparently amused at me running twice around a roundabout to make up distance I gratefully stopped and tore the goddamn Buff off I'd been wearing as a headband. I was boiling. I wiped my ever drippy tap of a nose with the Buff/snot rag then pulled out my phone for a selfie to send to Marc.

God's teeth I looked abysmal! Now I know I'm no spring chicken but I looked like one of those 'after' photos on warnings about the effects of crack cocaine, I'd aged significantly in approximately 42 minutes. Scaring myself to death I opted to not send it to Marc for fear of him never returning home and so I headed back toward the beach.

The wind which was now in my face offered blessed relief from the warm day but I was knackered and I started mentally creating milestones to reach for in order to get home. As I hit the prom the tide was in and the path was strewn with walkers all smiling and strolling along with drinks, burgers and ice creams. Bastards.

I pushed on into the final mile, my legs were shredded and chest heavy but I felt somehow triumphant, another run done, another battle won. I think at the moment my runs are as much about slaying the demons in my mind as much as the ones on the road but that's OK. With every step I take my heart and spirit grow a little in stature and at every ten mile buzz of my Garmin another ghost is defeated.

Neither running or life are always an easy thing but they are always a wonderful thing and as long as you approach them with a song in your heart, a little determination and a good dollop of nonsense you'll be sure to enjoy the journey no matter how adverse your conditions.

# 17

# Awakenings

**Thursday 17th March 2016**

I saw a thing on Pinterest recently (I'm so rawk and roll) that said 'you will never always be motivated, you have to learn to be disciplined' and it pretty much sums up my runs of late. It's hard to explain, whilst I always love my runs for the whole getting outside amongst nature and shit I have also felt a bit numb about them recently too.

It's not a physical thing, everything feels fine; but fine is about as much as I can muster up in enthusiasm. Sure I've had my own stuff to deal with lately and I think that's part, if not most, of the problem. Whilst running is awesome therapy there's also a lot to be said for just letting it go and running away from it all...literally.

Tonight I wanted to catch the sunset so when Marc came home from work we headed out pretty much straight away. It was butt shudderingly cold, much colder than we'd bargained for but as we neared the beach we could see that the sky had turned to gold and it seemed to lighten our feet. My breathing felt a little sticky, I think I'm getting Cleo's mega cold, and both of our noses were so drippy it was like a snot rocket competition but it was a glorious night.

As we turned into the coastal path it was ridiculously cold, I mean nonsensically freezing and my right thumb immediately lost all feeling poking upwards like I was having the most awesome run ever. The sunset was everything it promised to be throwing a rich, scarlet curtain across the sky draping the sea in shimmering tassels of gold. We stopped briefly while Marc took a photo and I whispered aloud the words on my bracelet 'make this moment count', I must have looked bloody mental. After another snot rocket contest we ran on chatting at times, shooting the breeze and whinging about the cold.

As we passed a well to do looking couple walking their well to do looking dogs the inexplicably orange coloured man said "come on guys, you're supposed to be out of breath!" I let out an involuntary and utterly bananas sounding laugh somewhere between hysteria and evil genius. It struck me though as we were on our way back that we weren't breathing heavily in fact we were pretty much silent. For a brief moment I entertained the thought that maybe I don't try hard enough, maybe I should push myself more but then I dismissed it because the truth is, I've had enough of pushing and hurting and testing my limits.

On our way home we talked about it and I decided that I think I need a really slow run, a totally relaxing, sedate, leisurely trundle. I've been pushing myself onwards for so long I've forgotten how to relax, how to let go.

The last few miles were challenging but I felt strong and comfortable. It had been a good run, a fun run, a worthwhile way to spend an hour and a half. It always is. No matter how ambivalent I feel about getting out there once I do I come alive, my soul wakes up and my spirit feels unencumbered. I'm looking forward now to my experiment, my slow, steady, plod. I'm thinking it'll involve photos, maybe an ice cream, a little walking. Who cares? All I know is that I'm looking forward to it, and that sounds like victory to me.

## Sunday 20th March 2016, Newcastle

This morning I didn't fancy getting out of bed, I knew I had to run but I was bloody cozy and besides, who cares if I run today or not? Marc casually reminded me that it was not only the first day of Spring (after me moaning relentlessly about winter) and the sun was pouring through the windows but also it was international happiness day (or some other nonsensical crap). No pressure then eh?

He was right about the sunshine though, the world had woken up in full bloom, everything was sparkly fresh and new as if nature had scrubbed everything clean overnight. My stomach was making alarming noises so I eschewed my usual peanut buttery breakfast for a slightly less claggy and slightly more random ginger macaroon along with a large side order of Gaviscon. If I'm ever to be arrested by Vice police they'll undoubtedly find on me some fairly weapon grade painkillers along with more packets of tissues than any human would ever need and every antacid and indigestion cure known to man. My mother calls me the walking apothecary.

We headed off to St Mary's Lighthouse in Whitley Bay, the starting point of my most favourite running route ever. The sky had clouded over but rather than dull the vista it gave an air of wild drama to the magnificent coastline. For the first few miles my legs felt heavy, my knee hurt a bit, I had a twinge in my side and about eleven thousand other niggles that all started whispering my name at the same time.

It's remarkable how much of a hypochondriac running has turned me into, I have become ultra-aware of even the tiniest ache from my little toenail to my eyebrows (yes, even they hurt on runs sometimes too). I spent the first half hour diagnosing myself with conditions that ranged from scurvy, typhoid and septicaemia to dropsy, gangrene and fin rot. Is turns out I was just being a little bitch because by the time I had got halfway I started to feel OK. I even felt OK when Marc suggested tagging an extra half mile on to take us to an 11 mile distance. What caused my OK to be tested was when Marc led us towards what he referred to as a 'slight incline' at the end of the Fish Quay near to the ferry port.

Now if I may refer you back to the other times when Marc has taken me on 'undulating' routes that involve 'inclines' and I can tell you without hesitation or doubt that he is a barefaced, pathological liar. Borough Road unfolds itself from what I presume to be the highest known point in the solar system and tumbles down at a near vertical gradient to the banks of the River Tyne. Any hill that you can't see the top of from the bottom is in my opinion not to be attempted without the help of a motorised vehicle, in fact as I stood at the bottom staring towards the summit I watched a bus hauling itself up it, the driver red faced with fear and oxygen withdrawal. Marc just stood there grinning mentioning words like 'adventure, epic and hilarious' and of course, he knows I'm a fool.

Within about ten metres of the start of my ascent my legs began to stiffen and my assbaps shudder in the most horrifying manner, I was leaning forwards in an attempt to propel myself with a little more power until I was practically bent double. In the opposite direction a cyclist tore past, face frozen with fear, careering downwards towards a bloody and certain death and still we moved higher. By the halfway point I was running on tiptoes, wheezing and folded at the waist like an arthritic Darth Vader. As we finally reached the summit, shrouded in clouds and delirious from altitude sickness I turned to Marc expecting high fives, cheers, maybe even tears of pride. I was not expecting him to say "whoops, no point going this way, we'll miss the good hill by the waterfront" and then disappear back downwards towards the icy depths of the North Sea. Its times like these I could willingly hang the little Geordie bastard. I had no choice, it was either run through the streets of North Shields or plummet to doom; I chose the safest, easiest option and headed away from the terrors of North Shields back down the hill of death.

From there on in everything seemed a little more intense and so a lot more exciting, the lack of oxygen had gone to our heads. We made light work of the next mile before we began the climb back into Tynemouth. Marc in his infinite wisdom had decided that short and steep trumped long and steady so we found ourselves once again pained and dizzy heaving ourselves up a sheer slope until we reached the welcome view of Tynemouth Priory.

The rest of the journey back was nothing short of incredible, the tide had come in and was crashing with gusto against the outcrops of rock that are sprinkled along this part of the coast. If you ever want to feel truly connected to the universe I'd advise you to run next to a wild coast on a spring day, it was one of the most exhilarating experiences of my life. We raced along smiling broadly, our lips crisp with salt and raw with the whip of the wind, not taking our eyes from the silver sea. About a mile from our finish point we ran down onto the sands and then along the tide's edge as it chased our feet and made our faces wet with spray. It had been an epic run, a grand adventure and a moment to remember.

Sometimes we spend so long focusing on the minutiae of own being that we forget to look at what's happening on the outside of it. The wonderful thing about running is that it flings us headfirst (often literally) into the face of nature and forces us to turn out eyes outwards back towards the world; its only when we do that can we truly find our place within it.

## Tuesday 22nd March 2016

When I left the house last night I wasn't expecting much of my run. It was late, well after 7 and it had been a very busy day which had left my legs feeling stiff, aching and not in the least bit inclined to start pegging it around the mean streets of Blundellsands. I had however eaten a gross of peanut butter and a particularly filthy Chelsea bun and so there really was no choice, I had my raw sex appeal to preserve. Besides, Marc was already out running and so I felt the weight of expectation (my own I should add, no one else would give a jiggery shit if I ran or not) on my knotty shoulders.

My Garmin ominously took nigh on a lifetime to connect as I stood angrily pacing around in the cold night air glaring at it. Marc came striding down the street, steam coming off him in such quantities I expected him to toot like a train. I felt a sudden pang that I wished he was coming with me, my confidence has been off lately and it had been a long time since I'd had a run on my own this late. But I knew I had to go so I waved goodbye and set off into the dark alone.

As I couldn't take either the coastal path or canal towpath alone at night my only option was to zig zag through the streets and along The Serpentine, the road that rises above the shore and overlooks the beach. The first mile taking me through houses and driveways saw me grappling with the arm pocket in which I was carrying my phone, in my haste to leave the house after the tardy Garmin incident I had grabbed Marc's armband instead of my own. Given that he is considerably more dedicated to the gym than I am the difference in our biceps measurement is similar to that between a tree trunk and a McDonald's fry, this girl does not lift and it shows. The loose armband kept annoyingly sliding down to the point where I considered turning back to change it, after a few minutes it rested near the crease of my elbow and I decided I would fool myself it was tolerable.

Then something happened...Suddenly without reason or warning my lungs opened, my legs loosened and my spirit soared. I was less than a mile into my run and I felt like I had been catapulted into pure, sweet happiness, the air felt heavenly cool, my clothes loose and comfortable and my feet light and powerful. I simply cannot define it, it was the closest I can describe to a religious experience but I felt unutterably happy and my body felt like a symphony, every limb working smoothly together moving me forward with joy and positivity.

Now I'm an untrusting bugger, I told myself it was because I'd got my outfit spot on, it was because my new earphones were great, it was because my legs had been stiff, any second now the slump will surface and I'll be plodding again. My watch buzzed one mile and I

188

resolved not to look at it, I didn't want to know my pace, I wanted to treasure the feeling for what it was because I had a sneaking suspicion it was going to be an awesome run. And it was.

As I ran along The Serpentine the sky was awe inspiringly clear and the whole city glittered before me next to the thick, black darkness of the Welsh hills. I felt drenched in fresh air and I felt clean and free. It was the run I've been needing for so long, ten glorious dark, cool miles of deep, clean breaths.

Not one incline did I notice, all I felt was the coolness of my wet hair on the back of my neck along with fast and steady footfall and every song seemed to reach into my soul and mean something. I sang aloud and in that moment I remembered I hadn't sang aloud during a run for a long time, I hadn't laughed out loud on my own for a long time, I hadn't stretched my legs, kicked my feet and let my soul free for a very long time.

My body and soul had thrown me a lifeline, a way back from the abyss that had been choking me and I was ready to grab it. In every sense possible it was a recovery run; a recovery from the tough, routine miles that I had been dutifully putting in, a recovery from the shackles of stress and fear that have dominated so much lately, a recovery from the aftermath of all that has happened. It was a phenomenal relief, every muscle in my body felt some sort of release, everything relaxed and I began to breathe easier, more easily than I can remember in recent times. I can only liken it to finally turning and walking away from the devastating wreckage of a car crash you were in and had been stuck fast and staring at ever since. It was closure and an opening all at the same time.

I didn't stop once, I felt the most overwhelming sense of freedom and when I finally stopped at ten miles I was laughing and I hadn't even realised. Sometimes it just happens that way. I thanked God, the Universe, Nature and life itself for bringing me back to life because that's exactly how it felt. I don't think until that moment I had realised how lost I'd become.

I spoke recently about how I was trying to be disciplined as I wasn't feeling motivated and I can tell you that for me, it worked. Plodding on in the face of apathy and dereliction of spirit can seem like the most soul destroying pursuit but it's quite the opposite. I believe in those hard, empty steps I ran through the last month I was building a ladder and climbing it. But remember that climbing involves great effort and determination. The reward is that at some point you will rise, because once you fully commit to the ascent, the only way is up. Stay patient and trust your journey.

**Wednesday 23rd March 2016**
This morning was mostly spent with a doctor's finger up my bum, there really isn't much I can add to that.

# 18
# Endurance

**Thursday 24th March 2016**

After the bum finger incident I found myself unwell, I mean really unwell. I'm sorry to be the bearer of TMI but imagine if you will what six years of almost constant chemical trots can do to a butthole and you'll have some sort of idea the problems I'm currently facing. Suffice to say it's a war zone down there and the things I'm having to do to try to resolve it are less than fun (unless you're into anal torture in which case it's right up your alley so to speak).

As I've mentioned before when I get stressed I get wind; not farty, hilarious, fun wind but big painful pockets of the stuff that hurt like punches to your ribs and back. This week it's been awful and on Wednesday evening I spent pretty much the whole night bent double and crying. It was the first time since chemo I felt despairingly unwell and it was hardly my finest hour. Thursday I resolved would be better, Marc was working late and we had planned a twilight drive to Newcastle as it was Easter this weekend and he had both bank holidays off as he was training.

I busied myself throughout the day trying to ignore the muscle clenching discomfort in my torso, I ate little and packed bags. I was still on an immense high from my wonder run and so grateful of it I was prepared to take the hit of not having run for the following days. We drove down that evening happy and peaceful, making plans for the weekend despite my having an ominous feeling I wouldn't be able to run. I guess it seems stupid that I would be upset about it but I love the place so much it hurts me when I can't run in it.

Both Liverpool and Newcastle feel like home to me and I'm deeply connected to them. The land and sea of both coasts seem to call to me more than any other places on the planet, it's hard to explain but it feels almost primal. I suppose running has become my way of honouring and celebrating the places I love, it's an expression of how tremendously important they are to me. When I run I feel completely in touch with and a part of my surroundings and it can be something genuinely emotional so to not be able to run when I'm there leaves me feeling like someone shat on my birthday cake.

The other looming issue is that to all intents and purposes it looks like we have finally sold the house, Marc's childhood home, his most recent home and our Geordie bolthole. Selling up has come with mixed feelings. Because Cleo was at school in Liverpool and my job was there it was natural that after Marc's mum died he would make his life with us however since I no longer have a job and school life is difficult for Cleo the parameters have changed. A move across to the east coast was not only possible but preferable. This coincided exactly with Marc landing his dream job in Liverpool, a job that currently doesn't exist in the North East. Lady Luck is one hell of a broad but her timing sucks.

So the prospect of cutting our immediate ties with Newcastle is a very scary and also sad one, the three of us adore the place and long to spend our lives there but for the next few years at least, it can't be so. As a result of this we like to spend as much time there as we can, eking out what we can while we can. And we like to run there whenever we can so feeling unwell for what could possibly be our last extended weekend there was potentially the downer of the century.

Waking up on Good Friday I knew that today was not a running day, my stomach muscles were cramped stiff and the toilet beckoned repeatedly. It was a perfect, gloriously sunny day, the weather reports predicting an otherwise washout of an Easter weekend and I was angry inside with myself. The only thing I could think of was to switch Saturday's plans to today so at least we could enjoy the sun.

We ended up having a brilliant day with an amazingly memorable lunch overlooking St Edwards Bay followed by a fun walk along Tynemouth Longsands and cake on the beach as we watched surfers coasting in the fading Spring sun. The evening was spent munching snacks and watching trashy TV whilst just enjoying each other's company, it really had been a Good Friday.

## Saturday 26th March 2016, Newcastle

Sometimes when difficult things have happened to me, often if I'm honest, I laugh them off. I'm not good at the whole facing up to things routine and so my default mode is goon, if you can't beat it then at least

# Recovery Run
## Nicky Lopez

you can make a joke about it. And in general it's served me very well, cancer is a crushingly devastating disease and humour is one of the few ways of levelling it, diminishing it to a manageable size.

But sometimes I can't joke no matter how hard I try. You'd have thought the whole finger in bum incident would be a mine of tasteless guffaws and howlers for someone like me but it has made made me feel horrifically vulnerable, exposed and wanting in confidence.

I was well on my way to curling up into a ball like I had done a couple of years ago when for about six weeks before Christmas following an operation I hid from the world in general, unable to face anybody or anything that didn't exist within my own home. It took months for me to normalise and regain confidence and I was damned if I was going back into that safe, comfortable but ultimately unhealthy place without a fight. So I knew it was important to try to get out for a run even if it was only a small one, just to tell myself that things were going back to normal on my own insistence.

It was an overcast but mild morning so we knew it would be safe to head to St Mary's Lighthouse for our favourite route. That's what I needed, a gentle, ambling pace along a picturesque coastline to renew my confidence and bring peace to my troubles. What I didn't need was a force seven gale blowing directly at me from the outset. It was so strong that it was laughable and laugh was all we could do as we battered our heads against the full strength of Mother Nature, inching along the weather beaten coast. Down to the Port of Tyne we ran, and such was the gale we didn't linger to take our usual photos. My butt hurt, I had a dull ache in my glutes and a sharp pain in my lower back so I told Marc I needed to take it slowly and steadily.

A kind and gentle man in any circumstances his compassion towards me that day was beyond words. Without saying too much knowing I was still acutely embarrassed about what had happened he shepherded me for the rest of the run in the most inexplicably tangible way and I felt completely safe. On my instigation we ran up the hill to the Priory on the way back, it's an ascent I can never fully complete running due the steepness but today with slow determination we did it and I felt a sense of overwhelming pride.

# Recovery Run
## Nicky Lopez

We stood at the top of the hill overlooking the mouth of the majestic Tyne and let the powerful gusts hit us as it took us back downhill and along the beautiful coast road past Longsands and Cullercoats. As we approached Whitley Bay there were two girls in front of us and although I don't particularly like overtaking other runners (unless they're twats in which case, game on) we knew we would have to as their pace was significantly slower than ours.

As we ran past and said a cheery 'Hallo!' we saw a look of pure, venomous spite on their faces that was all too familiar; these bitches wanted our asses. We ran on but we could feel them quickening, their breathing and footfall gaining on us, getting ever closer. Eventually the four of us were flat out sprinting along the road, them trying desperately to catch us and us frantically hoping to stop them gaining. Pedestrians and dog walkers leapt out of the way as we all hurtled down the pavements with increasing velocity, mothers grabbed their terrified children, dog walkers scooped up their pets and mobility scooters went careering into the main road to avoid a head on collision with this pack of psychotic running hooligans. Eventually Marc shouted 'Fuck this Shit!' veered right and I followed, a blur of hi viz orange and ponytail swept past us as we turned onto the prom and bent double trying to stop our lungs from bursting.

When we recovered a little we wandered onto what looked like an old, disused platform and decided to take a quick selfie with the wild North Sea as a backdrop. True to form in the middle of all abandonment a bloke appeared out of nowhere with a dog. The dog, Fred, was the most precocious canine and decided that he too would be a part of our tableau posing cheekily with his toy. In the end his owner took a pic of the three of us together while we marvelled about how utterly bizarre our world is.

Heading up onto the road and down into Whitley Bay we spied them, the orange bitches. Presumably equally destroyed from the breakneck shenanigans that had taken place they were sitting on the wall sucking down water and adjusting their stupid ponytails. They hadn't seen us. Swooping out of nowhere we soared past shrieking 'Hallo again!' and kicked for home, they turned to run but they had nothing left and we pulled away from them and sped off into the distance. No one in hi viz fucks with us.

Running along the sea wall as close to the ocean we could get we let the air fill our lungs and the beautiful, fresh, salty smell brought us back to life. The vista was nothing short of magnificent and it demanded to be looked at making us raise our heads for the whole of the final mile.

Marc held onto me for a good while as we finished and I didn't speak, I just felt safe and home and it was all I needed. When we got back to the car we larked around in the spring sun taking pics across the car park which was festooned with daffodils, my back still felt painful and as I put my hand to it I realised why. Marc's car key had worked its way horizontally in my pocket and was wedged into the lowest disc of my spine. So much for post examination trauma, turns out I'm suffering from terminal idiocy. It was funny though and when we laughed I didn't feel the heaviness in heart or spirit that I had when I first came out.

This was a world I wanted to be in, be a part of. And on a day like today who wouldn't be? Sometimes even the most horrible experiences can be turned around by a word, a smile or gesture and even though the world may not understand what's happened to you it's enough to know that someone in it wants to make you feel better. If in doubt, try a little tenderness.

**Thursday 31st March 2016**

When Marc texted me this afternoon I had already decided I wanted to run, the sky was all sunbeams and wispy clouds and begging to be seen from a beach. I think he was kind of hankering for the gym, he's a lot more committed to it than I am and as much as I try to appreciate the benefit of cross training the truth is I'd pretty much always rather run.

I should also be honest here and admit that I had taken delivery that same day of some new running tights and a t shirt. They weren't just any tights either, these tights were miracle tights (and I'm not being hyperbolic, that's their actual name.) These suckers promised to lift my droopy ass (not that I have a droopy ass you understand), tone my thighs and elongate my legs. I made my mind up that if the tights made good on these promises I'd be eating a shitload more Pringles from now on. So I texted Marc back with the one request I knew he would never refuse 'Come run with me'.

As sunny as the day was I'd made something of an error of judgement as it was ball numbingly cold, the two of us launching out in short sleeves had realised pretty sharpish that profanity was going to make up the majority of the first 5k. In a last minute moment of bonkersness I'd suggested we try the Go Pro, a swaggy, sports camera that I'd bought for Marc for Christmas to film our runs. We're both pathetically vain and arsey about photography in general and it's the one area of our relationship where we are fiercely, often violently competitive. I have known Marc to physically launch himself at me to deter me from getting a good shot and likewise I've rugby tackled him on beaches for the chance to fuck up his frame. But in fairness we do take a nice snap so it seemed like a brilliant choice compared to my previously somewhat patchy success in gifting, I have slightly avant garde ideas in terms of presents and they can often be total fucking monumental episodes of idiocy.

I won't drag you through the scrapbook of shite that is my bestowal history except to say that I once bought Marc two jars of his least favourite peanut butter for Valentine's Day making the Go Pro look like a sodding Ferrari by comparison. I'd even remembered to buy him the accessory kit with its accompanying bells and whistles hence finding myself sporting a slightly bulky chest strap which resembled some sort of S&M underwear article (so I hear).

When I mentioned to Cleo I was dabbling in fetish gear and jumped in front of her clad in turquoise Lycra and black webbing she gave me a weary look and sighed as if her world had gone slightly but terribly wrong. As we ran through the door and past our neighbour he enquired how far we were going 'Just a quick ten miles!' I trilled like the self-satisfied, odious little twat I am. I got my comeuppance. About 200 metres later when my miracle tights had become miracle leg warmers and were flapping around my ankles leaving my droopy ass exposed to the elements and the general public. Grabbing them up to my nipples and waddling for dear life we made it back to the house where they remain to this day flung unceremoniously in the corner (I honestly will tidy up one day).

New, safer leg wear on we headed out for the second time screeching swear words at the increasingly icy air. It was gorgeous though, the late evening light was golden and flooded the beach with gilded beams. Marc was finding it tough, his breathing wasn't right and his legs felt heavy. I don't think the stiff chill was helping any either.

The beauty of having the Go Pro with us though was that it forced us to keep stopping whether it was to take in the full scope of the shoreline or just to catch a different angle or perspective and in doing so it made us acutely aware of our environment and of how incredibly beautiful it looked. We couldn't have chosen a better night to try it. I was aware that it was bouncing around a bit, I'm not the flattest of girls in the chest area so there was a fair bit of turbulence.

On our return leg we ran off the coastal path briefly through the dunes, it was the first time I'd ever done it and it felt exciting, exhilarating and new. The sun was by now setting and I wanted to catch every second of it on film which involved me running sideways, backwards and spinning around in an attempt to get awesome, arty camera angles. I have no idea why but every time we stopped to take in a view I felt the need to put my hands on my hips and thrust my pelvis forwards as if the Go Pro was in some way being guided by my vagina as opposed to my hooters.

We decided to run down onto the beach, the tide had gone out and the sand was comfortably firm, it would look incredible on film. Marc by now was shattered and feeling every step of the last two miles so we paused for a minute to regroup. As we did a parascender appeared from across the shore and dipped low into the horizon creating the most spectacular silhouette. Naturally I stood, hips splayed whilst fanny cam recorded it all.

We dragged ourselves through the last mile, I'd forgotten to restart my Garmin (which inevitably turns me into a tantrum throwing child) and the Go Pro ran out of power about the same time as we did. Finally with cracked lungs we stopped running at ten miles and stumbled home in an exhausted stupor. It had been hard and testing but the sheer beauty of the evening had been enough reward. Besides, we had some amazing footage. And amazing it was.

The Go Pro lens is awesome at capturing the view in a broad scope and the sunset and light looked breathtaking, it's just a shame that it was only visible for around 20 seconds. The rest of the footage (and Christ knows there was a lot as we'd filmed in real time not time lapse) was essentially of my arms and fists accompanied by a soundtrack of heavy breathing, wheezing, farting and an awful lot of bad language. If I hadn't known better I'd have sworn I was being pursued by zombies such was my breathlessness and frantic fist pumping, it was like the Blair Witch Project for joggers, only longer and more hilarious.

Martin Scorsese, you can sleep easy tonight.

### Sunday 3rd April 2016

Sun's out, buns out.

It was flipping boiling today so I decided it was time to crack open the shorts drawer and unleash my assbaps on the poor, unsuspecting residents of North Liverpool. After a minor mishap with some fake tan leaving my ethnicity in question I donned the summer gear and headed through the door feeling positive and looking forward to a fab run.

We headed for the sheltered prettiness of the eastern, more rural route of the canal, it had been November since we had run it together and several months since I'd had the run that nearly ended me there. It's a beautiful stretch taking us past Aintree Racecourse and past jolly canal boats and open fields. It was warm, very warm indeed and within seconds the Buff around my neck (what the fuck? Who wears a scarf on a hot day when they're running?) was transferred to my hand.

We had sketchily planned to do a half marathon so we kept the pace nice and comfortable and at five miles I felt pretty damn awesome. Yeah I needed a wee but it wasn't bothering me too much. Just before six miles we had an idea, we'd go a bit further today, whipped up by everyone else's impending marathon fever it seemed like the most awesome idea. We keep saying we should go longer than 13 more regularly and today was the perfect opportunity, the weather was sublime, a bit breezy but nothing to stress about. So yeah, after all it was only really an extra mile each way, it was a brilliant plan. Until at 7 and a half miles I began to feel thirsty, really bloody thirsty. Then I remembered I'd only had 4 hours sleep because we'd picked my folks up from Manchester Airport early this morning. And then I remembered I'd only eaten half a sausage roll. And drank a small cup of black coffee. And my painkillers had worn off. And I really needed a God damn wee.

# Recovery Run
## Nicky Lopez

At the turning point I tried to put my fears to the back of my mind, I stretched out my calf really well to deal with the injury that must not be spoken about because I am pretending it isn't real and I told myself that it would all be OK. I even had a wee, shamefully shaking the lettuce because I refused to convert my Buff to toilet paper. Without divulging too much information I should have realised then that the tiny, burning dribble suggested I was already dehydrated but then I'm good at ignoring stuff like that.

We ran on but at nine miles I wanted to stop, I wanted to tell Marc my spirit had gone, that fifteen miles suddenly seemed like a very long way indeed. I didn't have to though, he knew. With incredible kindness he hugged me and gave me a ton of options which ranged from a walk break through to a taxi, I went for the plod on and stop when I needed to option. I stood for a while and reminded myself it was only six miles that I regularly run half marathons without a drink, that I was letting my head take over the run and I should just give it back to my legs.

We carried on for a while but my mouth was cotton wool and I had stopped sweating, this was not a good sign. I had become fixated on a bottle of Oasis, full sugar, with ice. It was all I could think of. Marc remembered that nearby the racecourse there was a pub, we should go there for water.

The next half mile to the pub was determined and uncomfortable but we got there. I'm not sure if you can imagine what a Liverpool pub is like on a warm Sunday afternoon in a relatively working class area but let's just say when a butch looking scarlet faced lass with her bum hanging out of her shorts staggers in covered in sweat, panting and begging for water, eyebrows are a little raised by some folk. I don't think I've ever felt quite as conscious of my own idiocy in all my life. The fact that Marc had bright blue compression shorts and a t shirt emblazoned with 'Shut Up And Run' did little to help.

But Oh. My. God. That water, it was so good I practically inhaled it. We legged it out of there and I felt confident I could handle the final five miles now. But I was wrong, it was too late. As we hit twelve miles I was done in, we were running into a strong headwind and my legs were burning with pain and I was thirsty again. Marc was endlessly reassuring and supportive but the next two miles were nothing short of a series of agonising stop starts.

The thing is I didn't beat myself up about it like I used to, I think I'm finally learning that sometimes you have a crappy run. Today I knew the reasons why and I accepted it. But I also accepted that continually stopping wasn't making my legs hurt less but it was making it so much harder and longer to get home. I was resolved, no more stopping.

The final mile was intense, I was much slower but so much more determined than I have been in a long time. Marc repeatedly said how proud he was of me (although if I was him I'd have wanted to repeatedly punch me in the face by this point) and I kept whispering thank you because his gentleness, understanding and care had brought me this far. I sectioned the last mile into milestones then minutes, to be truthful I felt proud of myself, the old me would have quit at ten miles.

As the Garmin finally buzzed at 15 miles I couldn't speak, we held hands and walked silently and slowly for a good few minutes. It had been oh so tough but I was strangely glad.

It's easy to get careless, to fall into a pattern and never divert from what feels safe and comfortable and there's nothing necessarily wrong with that, safe is good, comfortable is lovely. But every now and again it's well worth having your back against the wall and being in a position where you have to tough it out and deal with it, today was that day for me. Lessons learned:

1. Preparation is everything, when it comes to hydration you simply cannot wing it.
2. Always carry a tissue, grass has zero absorbency.
3. When it comes down to it, you can do it, you will get through it and you have got this.
4. Full sugar Oasis is like God in a glass
5. I have one hell of a running buddy.
6. She who endures, conquers.

**Tuesday 5th April 2016**
After Sunday's tough 15 miler I approached tonight's run with a sack load of trepidation. It was only till I said to myself 'stop being daft, it's

not silly mileage, just a nice steady ten' that I realised just how very far I've come.

Heading out into the breezy early evening we decided to take the western, urban route of the canal to take advantage of the late sunshine. At first the legs felt heavy and we were both very warm but as we settled in we started looking upwards and noticing all the incredible signs that nature had woken up and was ready to get its bloom on.

Before long we were gossiping happily, larking about and having a generally lovely time. Colin the Cormorant made an unexpected and spectacular appearance and we stopped to wave him as he vaulted the clouds above us. At the halfway point I needed to stretch the injury that I'm ignoring (sshhhh) and then we turned and ran towards home while the sky was illuminated with prisms of colour from the setting sun. We picked up the pace and it felt right, comfortable, and easier somehow despite our tired legs. The air cooled and the wind picked up but so had our spirits by then, we dialled it down in the last mile as we were tiring and we trundled happily home.

What struck me most about tonight was how different in attitude and approach I had been from Sunday, I'd had it at seven miles with nothing left in the tank, tonight although I was tired I was positive and confident that I could easily make it home. Maybe it was the security of knowing it was a shorter distance or maybe the fact that I'd eaten and drank more sensibly but either way my head was in a whole better place and I was grateful.

So much of what we don't do in our lives is because of what we tell ourselves; we're not strong enough, pretty enough, rich enough, slim enough or clever enough. It's the same in our runs, how much more enjoyable it is when we believe we can, when we trust in ourselves and defy the limitations that so often only exist in our minds. 'Whether you think you can or you think you can't, you're right.' Henry Ford

**Saturday 9th April 2016**

Due to a blessed scheduling error today was the first Saturday in like, ever that we haven't had to be up at a time that most people would consider the middle of the night to go sit in a skating rink and pretend to be good parents. We had the world at our feet and the duvet over our heads, nothing was going to interfere with this unprecedented Saturday slobfest.

Except maybe the fact that we both woke at 7am like hyperactive three year olds unable to sleep. Sod's law. So what do you do when you've got an unexpected free Saturday morning? Do you chill in bed with breakfast and trashy TV or lounge around downstairs still in PJs? Maybe you take a leisurely stroll around the park. What you don't do, what no sane human beings do is decide to run a half marathon. Normal, well balanced individuals simply do not do this shit and Christ knows how but I've begun to view this behaviour as acceptable. Why?

Well firstly because I'm a fucking idiot but more importantly because running is a very real obsession. When I say obsession I don't mean a half assed hobby that you pick and choose to do when it suits, it's something that infiltrates and insidiously takes over your entire life. It's a whole assed pursuit.

We had intended to run along the canal today to shoot down the terrors of last weekend's 15 miles but as the canal runs adjacent to Aintree Racecourse and today is Grand National day the towpath was closed. The weather was still, cold and sunny so we headed towards the beach pulling our long sleeves over our hands to muster up a little warmth. We decided to be strict about our pace today and keep it as comfortable as possible, I wanted to concentrate on my foot strike correcting the heel strike that my new Ultra Boosts have induced.

The first couple of miles were essentially a nasal tsunami, both of us streaming, sniffing and swabbing at our drippy hooters. I have tweeted Mo Farah about this problem to ask his advice, Marc seems to think this is a world away from sanity but I'm of a mind that if anyone knows, Mo knows. That said he hasn't replied, I'm guessing that it's to do with having a busy home life and the demands of training. I can relate. If however I discover by way of non-stalker means that he has simply ignored my message then he needs to watch out the next time I high five him at a race he starts
#snotsleeve #justsayin

Anyway at the beginning of mile 3 Marc said his legs felt heavy. He's had an intense week full of tests and exams which I'm super proud to say he passed but the studying and stress have caused some sleepless nights and now he's mega tired. We walked a little, the sun was strong on our backs and we both felt uncomfortably warm but we cracked on to the seafront and hopefully some cooling air. That didn't happen and so at mile four where the coastal path winds away from the beach momentarily into the dunes we decided to ditch our base layers and stash them for our return.

You know how I've mentioned that even in the most secluded and isolated of places we end up being surrounded by people? Today was no exception, apart from the fact that Marc was barechested and I had my top pulled up over my head exposing a very pink bra. He was hauling me around by the arms of my unfeasibly tight compression top which had been anchored to my wrist by my Garmin. This was all done to an audience of about 17 cyclists, a team of ramblers and several gobsmacked courting couples.

But when we finally did get them off it was pure bliss, I felt about a stone lighter as the breeze rippled through my t shirt and Marc developed a familiar spring in his step. It was amazing the difference it made, we felt refreshed and reinvigorated and with it came a happy positivity. We ran onto the footpath which runs adjacent to an MoD firing range and breathed in its straggly beauty, my calf had tightened but I knew it would be ok till halfway and besides the sky was so majestically beautiful all I wanted to look upwards and try to commit it to my memory forever.

Past smiling amblers with their flappy tongued dogs and young boys whooshing up and down the undulating footpath on their bikes we ran and chatted and let the sun reach inside and light us up. At our halfway point I stretched my leg thoroughly, both my calf and hip were had whispered an ache most of the way but it was gaining volume and needed my attention so I contorted myself into a series of yoga poses while Marc the twat took unflattering photos of my arse.

The way back was awesome, the trains were full of Grand National punters and we waved furiously at them like two utter dickheads but we were free and happy and slightly delirious with dehydration. As we clamoured back up to the coastal path the skies ahead told a very different story, dark and tempestuous, we had to get a move on. We ran down onto the prom and noticed a slight difficulty, the tide was in and crashing over the pathway. We debated running up onto the road, away from the raging, bubbling sea and then remembered that life is short.

So we got soaked.

Passers-by on the road above us laughed and pointed as we ran laughing hysterically though showers of salty foam, it was one of the most fun and life affirming things I've ever experienced during a run, yeah we were wet and cold but we were glowing-red faced, breathless with exhilaration and our faces ached with smiling. Like I say, this is no normal pastime.

The final mile I began to feel fatigue creeping in so I followed the advice of an article I'd read recently which suggested when you're tired to try running faster. We pushed a little harder, pumped our arms a little faster and without warning the Garmin buzzed at 13.1 miles.

Running is a daft activity, it's moving your legs to take yourself somewhere only to run back home again, it doesn't make any sense. I was thinking today how no matter what distance you run, the miles you should be most proud of are your first and last, the first because you made it out of the door, away from your comfort zone and the last because you made it home, you endured and you conquered. The thing that makes it all worthwhile is what you learn between those proud first and last miles; some new wisdom, some gained experience, a painful lesson, some wonderful memory.

Today's learning outcome: Take chances, have fun, be happy.

# 19
# We Can Do Hard Things

## Wednesday 20th April 2016

Today's run was a mixed bag to say the least, I've had manflu this past week but was feeling moderately less mucous ridden today so decided to venture out. I also couldn't resist the amazing weather and the chance to finally wear a vest so off I went towards the beach.

Within about half a mile I was berating myself for wearing long tights (fake tan to facilitate the wearing of shorts is a pain in the arse and no matter how much I run outside my leg colour never diverts from that of a particularly anaemic goth) and my mouth felt ominously dry. It was gorgeous though and I sadistically enjoyed the feeling of practically melting in my shoes. As I turned towards the shore I was hit by a stern but nonetheless welcome breeze just as I'd alarmingly realised I felt completely knackered already.

My legs quadrupled in weight as I approached the coastal path and I started to make that noise that only runners make, the one that sounds like you may actually be in the throes of your dying breaths. I'd also begun to emit quiet but terrifying groans of desperate hopelessness. My manflu had reappeared with gusto; in a gruesome attempt to stem the nasal tide I blew a snot rocket but what ejected from my face was fluorescent green ectoplasm which in turn caused me to start retching and dry heaving. What a classy broad I am.

It was then that S Club 7 (I was despising the jolly bastards by this point) were silenced by the ringing of my phone. It was Cleo's school and they never call me (I used to work there so they know my all-encompassing evasion of phone calls - if you need me, text me). I panicked as I desperately tried to communicate with the caller via means of telepathy whilst I wrestled with the one of 79,000 audio outlet choices iPhone was presenting me with. In the midst of my snotty panic I finally heard Cleo say 'Mum don't kill me but...I broke my phone'.

Now normally I would have killed her and violently, probably several times and then revived her so I could kill her again. She has dropped that bloody thing so frequently and from such heights that she now breaks the damage to me in terms of the distance it has travelled from hand to concrete; I've been to the Genius Bar so many times that Apple and I are on first name terms, I'm going on the Christmas staff night out with them.

But today I was so glad to stop, so overwhelmingly overjoyed to take a break I just didn't give a shit and so I soothed and comforted her to the point she became almost suspicious of me. After she rang off, baffled by my Zen like acceptance of imminent bankruptcy I sat in the sun and just breathed for a while. And when I began running again things didn't seem so bad, the breeze blew in my favour and it all seemed more manageable, I was on the verge of enjoying myself

Heading home and back onto the beach I deemed it wise to grab a drink, I was extremely thirsty and running into the sun with nearly three miles to go wasn't going to improve the situation. I ran to the ice cream van and slurred in my run drunk vernacular to the man that I'd like something wet for a pound. I've since discovered that in other parts of the country asking for this will get you something altogether different and possibly less welcome after a long run. He looked at me with a mix of terror and disdain and handed me a lukewarm blackcurrant Fruit Shoot. It was by far the best thing I've ever tasted in fact I don't know why pubs don't serve that shit, they'd be constantly sold out. They do? Then I'm going to start ordering them, only with vodka.

Set for the last leg I ran onto the promenade and made for home, I was tired but the wind felt so wonderful against the heat it was hard not to enjoy it and the beach looked magical amidst a veil of sparkles. In the distance I watched a girl on the sand doing some fartlek or interval training, running short, fast bursts. As impressive as it looked it seemed like way too much hard work for a day like today.

I turned off the beach and headed up towards the railway hill, a small, tough climb giving way to the generous reward of a fast, steep downhill sprint. Sometimes I relish it at the end of a run and I power up it then swoop down on the other side letting my legs stretch as far as they can until I really do believe if only for a moment that I am a 'proper' runner. Other times it is Kilimanjaro, a looming, gargantuan ascent that tears my legs and lung apart.

# Recovery Run
## Nicky Lopez

When I first ran it with Marc he laughed about it saying it was nothing but a slight bump compared to the mythical North Eastern mountain ranges he scaled in his everyday runs but now even he approaches it with trepidation at times. I think if you run any route often enough there will be parts of it that you come to loathe and to fear if it's a tough day, Mount Crosby (self-titled) is my Everest. Today I was OK with it, I just pumped my arms, pushed my head down a little and powered to the fence at the top that signalled the summit. And then the wheels fell off.

Instantaneously I lost every bit of power in not just my legs but my arms, neck, head, my entire body. I can only liken it to a battery running flat in that there was no recovery from it, no strategy I could adopt. I'd hit the wall. The last three quarters of a mile were a gritty mental and physical battle, every inch of my body and mind were screaming, begging me to stop. My legs moved so slowly it felt like they were sticking to the pavement, my arms so weighty I could barely swing them. My breathing became deep and painful and I was getting nowhere, I felt like crying.

Finally, finally, finally I stopped at ten miles dead and crumbled onto the pavement where I sat dazed for an indeterminate amount of time. When I did eventually get up to walk the last few hundred metres home it was by way of a slow, dazed stumble. Ten miles done and an important lesson: by the time you feel really thirsty it's too late and you're in trouble.

Also, phones should be made of rubber.

The toughness of that run stayed with me and it reminded me of all that I'd been through. My thoughts went back to last year and of the two events that had been the most significant in bringing me to where I am today...

## One Year Ago... 25th April 2015, Facebook

## WE CAN DO HARD THINGS

It's a poster that I saw during the worst of my treatment and it rang true, especially for us.

Because despite everything that life has thrown at us we are still here, still standing, still smiling. We didn't break, we didn't give up. Because we want to pay tribute to you, every one of you who has supported us, sponsored us, loved us, sent us messages, waved at us on a run and carried us through the hard times. Our friends, loved ones, those we have lost. And Cleo. This one is for you. Because we believe that the human spirit is stronger than anything that can happen to it. Macmillan always believed in us, supported us, said we could do it and did everything they could to help us make it happen. Rob Bason, Lisa Wild (and Sue Blunt) and all at Macmillan, this one is for you.

A lot has happened, there has been pain, loss, sadness and grief. There's also been friendship, laughter, hope and an engagement ring. This run isn't about pace or time or competition to us. This is a victory lap for us, all of you and for Macmillan. Because of us, because of all of you and because of Macmillan, together we have proven... We can do hard things.

**26th April 2015, London Marathon, Blackheath.**

The day itself started in the cold and rain on Blackheath, Marc and I huddled together under a disposable raincoat like two vagrants. It was the first time we'd experienced anything other than blazing sunshine at London and we were taken unawares.

In the preceding months my chemo had been intense and along with it my intake of steroids which had meant that I had gained significant weight so my typically skimpy hot pants had been replaced by more substantial capri pants to tether my hair raisingly large thighs. And my word I was glad of it that morning as my legs stung with the sharp, cold drizzle. I'd also opted to wear a cap for the start of the race, I was feeling unusually self-conscious and I guess it was a form of disguise, a way to blend in.

We sat wrapped up in plastic like two fake tanned turkeys and shivered wishing we'd brought enough money for a coffee. Trying to distract ourselves from our imminent deaths from pneumonia we chatted about the previous night's events. We had arrived in London early and with Cleo who usually joins us after the race with my Mum. This year as a treat we'd booked into the super swanky Park Plaza Westminster Bridge for the two nights so that Cleo could chill out in bed whilst we were running but we also wanted her to get a sense of the event and feel a part of it so we had made plans upon our arrival in

# Recovery Run
## Nicky Lopez

London to go to the Macmillan Pasta Party. We had been the year before without her and knew it would be something she'd enjoy.

One of the most wonderful things about running for a charity is the feeling of being part of a very real team and we wanted Cleo to know that she was just as much a part of that as we were. It was a brilliant evening hosted by Rob, the Challenge Events Coordinator who has over the years become our friend and also featured some words from a couple of their celebrity runners, the actress Helen George and the Olympic athlete Iwan Thomas.

Now I've always admired Iwan; despite me having a less than glittering athletics career myself I was an avid armchair supporter and Iwan was one of the runners I'd always followed so I was keen to have a pic taken with him. After his talk a group of people formed around him for an informal meet and greet. Seeing this as my opportunity I edged towards the huddle and waited my turn.

As I approached Iwan with Marc at my side (Cleo was cringing at the table whilst shoving pasta down like she was the one running the marathon) I prepared myself for what I would say (must not fall over, must not swear, must not be overly tactile as can frighten people). It was at the exact moment we came face to face with Iwan that Kevin, a wonderful bloke from Running the World leapt from the line and shouted our names so loudly the room came to an almost standstill. Iwan looked on in baffled amazement as Kevin and his lovely wife placed a camera in his athletic hands and asked would he mind taking a photo of us. I was genuinely unsure whether to die from embarrassment, laugh hysterically or apologise to the world class athlete now standing taking a photo of two socially awkward idiots, I attempted to explain what was going on to Mr Thomas but he remained understandably nonplussed however gracious and we slunk away until we returned to our table and pissed ourselves laughing.

Since that time our paths have crossed a few different celebrities, the gorgeous Sarah Millican a great Macmillan supporter whom I'd met when I was fundraising at one of her shows not only remembered us on the day of the marathon and tweeted good luck but also sponsored us very generously. Both Liz Yelling and Nell McAndrew tweeted some wonderful words of support and congratulations after the Great North Run. In a time where people in the public eye can be vast canyons of shallow crap it's hugely encouraging to know how caring and generous of spirit some famous folk can be.

That said, none of their warm heartedness had any effect on the level of discomfort we were experiencing on the soggy hell that was Blackheath that morning. The cold (either that or my advancing years) had also brought on the irrepressible urge to wee which presented a variety of horrific toilet options.

The portaloo queues were immense; endless snaking lines of white, quivering legs taped, bandaged and strapped in such varieties the area resembled some sort of post-apocalyptic field hospital. It was to be my first and to date, my last experience of female urinals. The term itself conjures up mental images that challenge and confuse me still but at the time I had no idea what terrors awaited me. Picture a row of bright pink arses greeting you whilst their owners try to grapple with cardboard boats desperately trying to direct their wee downwards, this was what I was I was confronted with as I entered. True to form rather than remain respectfully and maturely tight lipped and discreet I burst out laughing. I quickly mastered the delightfully and aptly named P-Mate and found the experience rather novel, no wonder blokes go to the loo so much! Still hysterical after using it I then found myself having to rather explicitly show a French lady how to use one. When I emerged from the urinals shrieking and babbling Bonne Chance wishes to my new best friend Marc threw his hands up and said 'I don't even wanna know how that works'.

With not more than a few minutes to spare we scuttled to the start line which felt weirdly unfamiliar to the usual Greenwich. It's not funny how the tiniest change of routine can unsettle me but I felt elated when we saw the smiling face of our friend Mark Ward, a long standing Running the World member and gloriously amiable Londoner. He was desperately searching for his wife so we chatted briefly before the group shuffled together and we heard the roars that herald the start of the race.

Here we go again.

The run itself began strong and well. We were running comfortably faster than I had expected, largely driven on by an incredible crowd, music blaring from the roof of every pub we passed.

It was still pretty parky so I'd kept my hoody and cap on knowing I could easily discard it when I thawed out a little. A guy dressed as Spider-Man was running at pretty much the same pace as us but around three steps ahead which was a fabulous incentive but also a complete pisser when it comes to much needed crowd support; that and the fact that on the rare occasion someone did call my name out they inexplicably decided I was called Vicky despite having my name emblazoned in giant letters across my t shirt.

Eventually we ditched the glory guzzling web slinger and started to find our groove, the weather levelled and I threw my cap and hoody to the roadside. We were laughing and chatting with other runners and really getting into the whole celebration of the day, we had decided to take selfies at any iconic points along the way, it wasn't about getting a good time but about making memories.

At Cutty Sark where the crowds are thick and deafening we stopped briefly and the emotion began to sink in, the magnitude of our whole journey started to really hit home. I began to focus on what had happened over the past five years and how I'd got to where I was and I started to feel that maybe, finally we had turned a corner. I looked unrecognisable to the girl I once was but my life had changed for the good in so many ways and here next to me was this Everest of a man, smiling and proud.

On towards Tower Bridge and the support was unfathomably massive, the noise was just thunderous and tears hammered down my cheeks, we stopped for another photo and ran towards the gates. I'd forgotten the bloody hill it took to get up to it though and my legs started to feel the whisperings of fatigue, thank God the breeze was behind us and lifted us towards the roaring crowd. Bit by bit tiredness was creeping in but still we were buzzing with positivity.

Coming off Tower Bridge we had the Tower of London to our left and an unbelievably huge sea of spectators and supporters before us screaming our names. In the midst of the ocean of faces we caught up with our lovely mates Amanda and Rob, another Running the World love story (and no, we're not starting a running dating agency, not ever). Seeing people you know at such a huge event like London is both amazingly gratifying and utterly surreal, the familiarity is simultaneously welcome and strangely alien.

We continued on feeling rejuvenated by our friends but as the miles went on my hands began to feel odd. I couldn't bend them into the loose fist I normally adopt whilst running and something just didn't feel right. I started to get the feeling that as well as having massive, lumbering, purple thighs (the resulting photos from the day have borne this out to be true) I had also developed huge comedy fat hands like the kind you see at football matches and on TV shows. Rather than the graceful gazelle I had hoped I would be when I began my running journey all those years ago it appeared that I had morphed into a mega fisted Michelin Woman striking fear into the hearts of race spectators everywhere.

By mile sixteen my fingers were freakishly puffy and freezing cold and I started to feel not just fatigued but completely shattered. Marc was both supportive and concerned, he was struggling with a really sore foot himself, marathons definitely take their toll. We decided to stop for a short while to catch our breath and think straight about what best to do. After a drink and a talk we decided to run to the next St John's Ambulance stop and ask their advice. Still the crowds roared, it's amazing how even when you think you can't be surprised by it any more you still are. You're moved beyond measure by the kindness of strangers, the look when you meet their eyes, the belief and the pride they have in you.

St John's Ambulance confirmed pretty much what we knew, chemo and dehydration are not the best combination. I'd suffered badly with the effects of chemo in the last couple of days leading up to Sunday and it had played on our minds how I'd cope. I'd been consuming electrolyte sachets and Imodium by the truckload to keep it under control. The simple advice they gave was keep hydrated and finish safely. That was good enough for us.

On we went, buoyed up by the masses of running friends we met along the way, the cheers of support, the laughs between each other. The surreal futuristic cityscape of Canary Wharf and the Isle of Dogs at around mile 15-20 was electric and I felt more alive than I had ever been. We were so elated to be lucky enough to be here, to be breathing and running. I felt so proud of what Marc and I had achieved and so aware of what it had taken us to get there.

But God, I was tired.

At one point out of nowhere a reporter started calling to us and asked us for a quick interview. I cannot remember the exact wording of the exchange but I can tell you the pair of us were literally shouting utter bollocks into the journalists face. Don't ever let anyone tell you that running sharpens the brain, it turns you into an incoherent dickhead. Suffice to say (although sadly as it would have been hilarious) it was never aired on television.

By the time we met our lovely mate Nici at mile 20 I was destroyed. Nici is a no nonsense, highly experienced trail runner who regularly marshals at London Marathon; true to her style she gave me an arse kicking and a hug. We stopped a short while to call Cleo who was, as always, hilariously nonchalant and reassure my mum that I was OK.

Then we knew what we had to do.

We struggled along and eventually caught up with our dear friends The Bennetts around mile 22, Steph was beaming and shouting proudly while her lovely dad Tony quietly hugged us. I was in floods of tears by this point, it was emotion though, not sadness. Our epic journey was coming to an end and I began to feel the first pangs of the grief that massive change in your life can bring. Through to the 'Tunnel of Yes' which this year was clean, knob free and the thumping music and motivational placards were welcome inspiration.

Finally out onto the Embankment we realised that a walk run was the most efficient way for us to finish in one piece. I was deathly tired and not prepared to start beating myself up. And we breathed it all in. We waved, took selfies, thanked people, smiled and ate jelly babies. I nearly had a pint before Marc justifiably told me I was being insane. As we ran past Big Ben and the Houses of Parliament onto Birdcage Walk I tired again and began to walk but the noise from the crowd was intense and people were actually screaming our names, telling us they loved us and were proud of us.

It was the most overwhelming feeling of support and encouragement I have ever known outside of my own loved ones and I was broken with tears then rebuilt with a desire to respond, so we began to run again albeit slowly and painfully. Marc took my hand and raised it in the air, the crowd just erupted and I was filled with the most insane pride and emotion. I had a lump in my throat the size of Mars and my eyes were blinded with tears. Onwards to Buckingham Palace and another emotional hug from Amanda and Rob where I may well have smothered a bystander with my bosom. We shall never know, but if she went, she went with a smile.

Then the final selfie outside Buckingham Palace, a huge group of spectators roaring 'SELFIE!' with the Queens abode as a backdrop. I like to think she was having a poo at the time and popped her head out of the window to see what the fuss was.

The last few yards and we grasped hands, held them them high and ran over the line. We were done. We had drawn a final, full hearted line under London Marathon.

It was painful, epic, desperate, joyful, emotional, hilarious and agonising and if you asked us to do it again on Sunday I'd tell you to go fuck yourself...then lace up my shoes.

## Sunday 13th September 2015, Great North Run Half Marathon, Newcastle, Facebook

On Sunday 13th September 2015 I completed my fifth Great North Run, it was a run that changed my life and not just because I met Bob from Emmerdale.

I completed the Great North Run in 01:59:03. Any race, particularly a half marathon is an achievement but a sub 2 hour half marathon is a particular milestone amongst runners. For me it was a rite of passage I've waited a long time for. I ran a half marathon in a really good time. Not in spite of cancer or chemo, not in spite of a heart condition, not defined by anything other than myself. It wasn't an easy course, the weather conditions were far from perfect. Without qualification or caveat I ran a really good run.

You can't imagine what this means to me. For the first time I am not defined by cancer, I'm running on my own terms and earning my stripes.

That's not to say I did it alone, far from it, I have the most incredible running coach. We spoke little throughout the run but we communicated constantly. He let me run slightly ahead and ran like an angel on my shoulder throughout. He knew without my saying what I hoped for and how I was feeling at every mile. At mile 10 when I had run for too long without drinking he knew it wasn't weakness but good sense to walk a little. He knew just before mile 11 that an ice lolly was going to save me and cool me down enough to finish the race. At mile 12 he told me what we needed to do to get the sub 2 and with 600 metres to go when my face was on fire and my legs burning he took my hand and said 'let's bring this bitch home'. We crossed the line hand in hand at exactly the same time, because we are a team and everything that led us to that finish line was a joint effort. He believed I could. So I did.

I cried a lot that day. I cried for all the shit I've been through in the last six years and for what it's taken from me. I cried for what it has done to Marc, to Cleo, my friends and family. I cried for Caroline, I had felt her with me all day but I'm still bitterly angry about her death. I was so proud that the run we had dedicated to her was the best of my life. I cried like it was a birth and it was, a rebirth for me.

There were so many people who said hi, hugged us, supported us and cheered us on. I'm so sorry that I didn't stop and thank them at the time, my heart was on fire as well as my feet and my scalp. I pray they know they made a huge difference and lifted us up so very much.

Fall down seven times, stand up eight.

Despite having completed other races in faster times since that day nothing can ever compare to it. It was the race where I started, the race that kept me believing in myself, the race where I fell apart, the race where I fell in love. A sub 2 had been my secret hope, harboured silently for so long I stopped believing I could do it. On that day I stopped with the self-admonishment and I allowed myself to shine. I finally accepted myself as a runner, not just a chancer with a fighting spirit and a shiny scalp.

# 20

# In Running We Trust

**Back to today...**
**Friday 22nd April 2016**

As I knew Marc had a day off I had planned one myself today too, my fingers were raw from hammering metal and to be honest if I'd hammered the phrase 'London Marathon 2016' one more time that day I'd have been tempted to hammer it onto someone's face, I needed a break from work, I needed a break from the marathon mania that I wasn't really a part of.

It was a beautiful day, full sunshine and virtually no breeze which was begging for a run, trouble was I was still suffering from the cold that wouldn't go away and I just wasn't sure that a drippy nose and raspy throat was going to make for the most memorable of runs. We'd had a long walk the day before along the coastal path and had a stroll through the dunes almost as a recce for a future run but it had left us both feeling peculiarly tired. Five miles of walking takes a bastard long time and we ended up needing a snooze afterwards like the two doddery geriatrics we actually are.

Still it seemed a shame to waste a good weather day so with the caveat that we would take it easy we donned our Oakleys and headed off towards the shore. The pair of us were more tired than we had bargained for and we ran sluggishly, both of us breathing heavily and unevenly. My tap of a nose had been turned on full blast and I was forced to hold a tissue to it permanently making it look to any bystander that I was having a particularly emotional run. I felt sweaty, tired and generally unwell. It reminded me of my post chemo runs when I fancied I could actually feel the chemicals rushing around my veins and into my system, today I could feel the Lurgy marching through my bloodstream adding lead to my legs and turning the heating in my face on full.

When we eventually reached the five mile turning point the pair of us looked destroyed, we clambered down a shaded pathway and melted onto a conveniently placed step. We needed to rethink or the run home would be torturous.

Marc suggested that we ditch the route and go off track for a little exploration, a look of twisted horror drifted over my face as I contemplated the lunacy of what he was saying, one does not simply 'go off track' as he so blithely put it. After calming me for several minutes and putting my nonsensical reaction to change into check we headed towards the path we had walked yesterday, it would slow us down and we could enjoy it more, stopping where we felt like along with benefiting from the water's edge breeze.

Much as it pains me to say it he was right.

There I've said it, in print, for all to see.

Now shut up about it.

After a little initial trepidation through the uneven track of the dunes we cornered into a small bay and my mouth gaped. Before us lay a tiny cove fringed with perfect dusty, yellow sand and a long thin jetty that stretched into the deep aqua water. The bay was freckled with numerous small seabirds who gathered and swooped from one side to the next and the shimmering water was bobbing with several graceful yachts. It was like we had stepped into some sort of tropical paradise. I'm not sure still if it were all the result of some elaborate hallucination (I did eat some chocolate hash cake at Glastonbury in 1994 and was yet to feel the effects so maybe it was an extremely delayed reaction) or some Brigadoon like phenomenon that caused this apparition but it was one of the most serenely beautiful places I've had the joy of finding.

Marc ran onto the shore and started cartwheeling across the sand (at school he was a junior gymnast and he still never misses an opportunity to terrify me with some random acrobatics) while I took an endless reel of photographs wanting to record every second of the unexpected gorgeousness. It was an incredibly beautiful moment as I looked at Marc doing handstands as carefree as a child, it was kind of moving. We ran along the sand, and for the second time recently I loved the feeling of it, the freedom and beauty of the sound of the water so close to my feet lapping at the shore.

As we headed off the beach our legs were filled with a renewed vigour and we trotted up pathways and down trails through the soft sandy dunes that would lead us back to the coastal path on our own beach.

I should tell you at this point that despite the mystic wonder of it all there was one very real irritation and that was sand in my trainers. Now I know that some people have romantic connotations with sandy soled feet but I'm telling you now that those people are psychopaths and not to be trusted - sand in your shoes is living hell.

As we came onto the tarmac path my feet felt oddly uncomfortable like I had put someone else's shoes on, I quickly realised that the open weave of the uppers of my trainers had allowed me to collect the best part of the surface of our idyllic hideaway and it was now gathering underneath my left big toe in a giant wedge. If that weren't discomfort enough I shall let you into another little known fact about sand, it fucking hurts. What starts out as soft, plushy heaven under your trotters as you paddle in the sea when it gets into your shoes turns into a billion shards of broken glass all vying to stab you at the same time.

Any other normal person would have stopped and emptied their shoes but as we've ascertained by now, I am a fool and so is Marc. We hobbled along in varying degrees of pain, the last mile pretty agonising as the heat of the day ramped up and the tiredness set in. Marc could hear me struggling and murmured words of support, I told him I felt lucky and he told me I was delirious. And it was true on both counts, I was delirious but I knew how lucky I was. Today I had gone out with the ass of all colds and seen a stunning, hidden beach on a beautiful day.

As much as I loved seeing how the other half live on their fancy yachts I realised I didn't need money or riches to experience something so beautiful or to take me to a tropical paradise. Just my own two feet and my goon of a boy.

**Saturday 23rd April 2016 Happy birthday Marc!**
CAKE, BEER, CAKE!

**Sunday 24th April 2016 London Marathon Day**
My alarm rang at 8.20 this morning which was insanely late for London Marathon day. But today we're not running it.

# Recovery Run
## Nicky Lopez

After three consecutive years of London Marathons we are absent from proceedings, missing in action.

That's not to say we haven't been present there in some form, at the Expo in the Excel Centre where every runner taking part has to go to pick up their bib there is a big screen and one of the slides is a photo of Marc and I hand in hand as we ran down the Mall last year. Many of our friends have messaged us to call us camera whores and we're inclined to agree.

Indeed when we heard that the athlete and coach Martin Yelling referred to us during his 'Meet The Experts' presentation at the Expo I tweeted him telling him I'd finished chemo, had just run ten miles and sent him a post run pic with my new shaggy pixie cropped hair. He stopped his presentation and told the audience who burst into applause; in his presentations after this he showed the tweet and my picture. I'm filled with the most intense pride that in the same way London left its indelible mark on us, we too have left some small imprint on it.

And it has become a part of me, much more than I had truly understood. All week I've been repressing little moments of panic. Why did we say we wouldn't do it? What have we done? Because of my jewellery business it's a prerequisite to be obsessed with big events so London Marathon has featured heavily in our home these last couple of weeks with thousands of trainer tags and bracelets being emblazoned with the event details. Each time I have imagined the journey they'll travel, each twist and bend of the route, each landmark, each step. I've felt a resigned sadness about our non-participation, it was the right thing to do but it hurts.

It's been a time of great change for me, some things I had bargained for like the end of chemo, the absence of hospital visits, the growth of hair, all of these things I knew were coming and whilst I'd underestimated their effect on me I accepted I would eventually adjust. What I hadn't bargained for was all the other crap a year can throw at you. The death of my beloved friend in July, my cancer pal, my girl Caroline. I knew it was coming, aggressive grade four brain tumours don't piss about, but it threw me off course in a way my cocky, over optimistic bollocks of an attitude wasn't prepared for. I don't think I'd ever fully accepted she would die and if I'm honest, I'm still not really there. Throw into the mix a major fallout with my closest friends, a year of traumatic issues with Cleo and leaving my job of eleven years and my life was beginning to look as unrecognisable as I did.

And we've sold the house. Our refuge, our retreat, our Geordie home is no longer ours. Next weekend over the bank holiday we will ship in and ship out, it will be our last time there and despite it marking a new stage in our lives it's also the end of an era. A very happy one at that. From next week our trips to Newcastle will be different, we will no longer be going home. It hurts my heart in a way that I don't know how to articulate; yes, change is good but change is also very hard.

London was yet another thing we'd changed this year and so it had started to feel like a loss, a death. Too much was different and I needed an anchor, a safe place, somewhere I knew who I was; London had hitherto been that for me and now it was gone. And so we found ourselves turning on the TV, feet under a blanket, holding hands while we held tears back.

The emotion of the event is tangible even through the screen and it was unexpectedly brilliant to watch the race itself. I was a little baffled when I saw the Grandstand at the start of the run so naturally assumed that the women's race must start from the Mall and be run in reverse. It was when I actually said this out loud that I realised how overwhelmingly stupid I really am. Marc said nothing, he just stared at me in worried disbelief.

It turned out to be an incredible day for athletics; the nail biting elite mens finish where Kipchoge missed the world record by just 7 seconds and the women's race where the warrior like Sumgong fell, hit her head then went on to win. The wheelchair race was equally exciting watching Hug take the lead and the title in the final few hundred yards. We'd never been able to see all this before and it added a new dimension to an event we thought we knew so well already.

The best part though was watching the superheroes, the non-elites, the not so average Joes each with their own journey, their mission, their challenge. As much as I scanned the faces for those of the numerous friends we had running I also stared with admiration into the eyes of strangers, each running their own story. I watched their joy, elation, pain, disappointment and ultimately triumph and I felt invisibly connected to every last one of them.

This is what London does, but more than that, this is what running does. It binds and connects us to each other whilst making us feel utterly and independently free. When the coverage came to an end there was only one thing we could do.
We ran.

### 1.30 pm London Marathon Day 2016, Leeds Liverpool Canal, Merseyside

After checking the Met Office for the nineteenth time we eventually opted for a cold weather outfit, despite the optimistic temperature there was a cool wind and a little rain forecast so we erred on the side of caution and layered up.
We never learn.

After about six minutes of running on the sheltered towpath we were puffing and sweating like it was our first ever run, we had gone a baselayer too far. We persevered for another minute then made the decision to ditch so we both embarked upon an urban striptease only with a little less glamour and a whole lot of swearing as the Lycra had essentially bonded itself to our sweaty torsos. I opted to tie my top around my waist while Marc went for the full on hide in a shady corner option, a little brave I thought considering the area we were in.

The minute we started running again the most Arctic of winds began blowing and so I quickly scrambled back into my top, feeling smug because I had the foresight to keep mine with me. We ran on until after about half a mile into the warm sun I realised I would need to again disrobe. I continued this on and off routine with my top for the following two miles until I absolutely believed that Marc was going to punch me in the face so I gritted my teeth and tied it in a permanent knot around my hips.

The run was unremarkable in itself but it was the conversation we had that made it significant. As we went along we started to talk about the possibility of doing another London Marathon or indeed another marathon at all. Marc's heart is set on New York and it's definitely up there on my bucket list but the colossal cost involved when we're in the process of buying a home and attempting to stabilise our sometimes chaotic lives has rendered it out of the question for the time being. And besides, there's a little unfinished business with London

. For the three times that we've done it we've been seriously hampered in both our training and our performance on the day, I've always done it on a wing and a prayer in the midst of heavy treatment and Marc has had to support me to the max, almost physically moving me at some points.

I've been daydreaming about how it would feel to do London Marathon when I'm not gravely ill, when I don't feel a sense of desperation. I'd like us to do it triumphantly for once. It was this thought that got us to talking about Good for Age places and the possibility of my getting one. If you're particularly fast for your age and gender category in another marathon then you can get automatic qualification to London on a GFA place. GFA qualifying times for women are (I believe) significantly more achievable than those for men and it's far more realistic that I could run the 3.49 finish time than Marc achieving the rather more unfair 3.15 finish his category demands.

We talked about what it would mean for me to train to achieve it and we decided that although ultimately I was probably capable of it with the right training it would be incredibly tough and not an experience I'd enjoy at all. And if that were the case then why in the hell would I put myself through it?

The thing is though that it's remarkable at all that we even had the conversation, two years ago I wasn't confident enough to make a plan for a few weeks ahead such was the dire state of my health, my future looked uncertain and my body was broken yet here I was now contemplating entering the fastest category in my range in the London Marathon. What a turnaround these past six years have been; what mountains we've climbed, what friends we've found, what roads we've run.

Sometimes when you're in the middle of a run or even at the end you can't fully appreciate the distance you've travelled, the miles you've covered, until you take a little time and look at the route that brought you to where you stand. And then when you stand at the finish line it is the most incredible thing to see a million more finish lines before you, only now they all seem within your reach and you know that you're going to get to cross them no matter how bumpy the road might be.

The last two miles of the run I imagined the pair of us in the final two miles of London. We went through the Tunnel of Piss and onto the Embankment only this time I wasn't walking I was running strong and getting faster.

In my head I smiled and waved at the crowds and I thanked them for being there, for believing in me, for willing me home. Onto Birdcage Walk we ran and I looked at Marc giving it his all, finally being able to stretch his legs and run free and fast instead of being tethered with worry and fear. And then onto the Mall we raced, faster than we had for the whole run, breathing loud and our hearts hammering in our chests. Racing towards the finish line feeling brave, joyful, victorious

And then we were done. It was just ten miles along the canal but in my heart it had been in the capital city with flags flying and crowds roaring. I felt different, hopeful, ready for anything; and the anchor, the safe place, the shelter in the storm I'd needed was at my side where he always had been and always will be.

So what was our decision? It's hard to say, there's so much we've been through and we're still standing in the wreckage at times, staring at the aftermath. But there's so much left for us to do, so much to rebuild. The last couple of years are only really the first chapter in what looks to be a pretty epic adventure.

I'll leave you with the post I wrote in Running the World on the day we received the result of last year's London Marathon Ballot.

## 2nd October 2015, Facebook

So the weirdest thing today.

I'd already agreed with Marc that we wouldn't do another London Marathon next year. The winter training has been gruelling for the last three years, it's eaten into our family time, our social lives and taken its toll on us physically. In fact at mile 20 this year I remember saying to Marc that I didn't want to do it again, I needed a break.

So why did my rejection email today bring me to disappointed tears? I went on a ten mile run after work and had a think about it. It was a good run, it was a great run. It reminded me of how far I have come as a runner, and as a person.

# Recovery Run
## Nicky Lopez

I guess London and I have become more than just friends. For the best part of three years I've spent most of my time either planning for it or recovering from it. And it's left its mark on us. It's taken us through some of the darkest and most difficult times of our lives. I'm thinking particularly of 2014 when Marc lost his Mum days before, of 2015 when I was emerging from the toughest treatment of my life. It's been a beacon to me, a light to guide me out of darkness and an anchor for me in the roughest storms. And to an extent it has defined me more than any other run. I ran a marathon through chemo, I ran two, I ran three. People cheered us and I felt special, heroic. And that feeling persuaded me to keep going, both along the Embankment and in my life. London has been proof that I am more than the sum of my parts, braver than I believed and stronger than I thought. But things are different now. I'm stronger. I'm faster. I'm tougher. I don't define myself as the runner with cancer, I'm a runner and not a bad one at all. I run long and far and I make good times. This girl can.

So despite the tears I'm handing London back. If you were lucky enough to get a place then treasure it. Allow London into your life and let it teach you, mould you, change you. Look after it and respect it, give it your best and give it your all.

I'll be in the background cheering you on, knowing you'll feel heroic, special, amazing.

And I'll tell you a secret, that feeling never goes away.

And maybe sometime in the future, I'll be back.

But this time I won't be crying, I'll be kicking ass.

In Running We Trust.

xxx